In the Ruins of
Neoliberalism

WELLEK LIBRARY LECTURES

The Wellek Library Lectures in Critical Theory are given annually at the University of California, Irvine, under the auspices of UCI Critical Theory. The following lectures were given in May 2018.

UCI Critical Theory

James A. Steintrager, Director

For a complete list of titles, see page 249.

In the Ruins of
Neoliberalism

THE RISE OF
ANTIDEMOCRATIC
POLITICS
IN THE WEST

WENDY BROWN

Columbia University Press

New York

Columbia University Press
Publishers Since 1893
New York   Chichester, West Sussex
cup.columbia.edu
Copyright © 2019 Columbia University Press
All rights reserved

Library of Congress Cataloging-in-Publication Data

Names: Brown, Wendy, 1955– author.
Title: In the ruins of neoliberalism : the rise of antidemocratic
politics in the West / Wendy Brown.
Description: New York : Columbia University Press, 2019. |
Series: The Wellek Library lectures | Includes
bibliographical references and index.
Identifiers: LCCN 2018060444 | ISBN 9780231193849
(cloth : alk. paper) | ISBN 9780231193856 (pbk. : alk. paper) |
ISBN 9780231550536 (ebook)
Subjects: LCSH: Democracy—Social aspects—Western countries. |
Neoliberalism—Political aspects—Western countries. | Right-wing
extremists—Western countries. | Populism—Western countries. |
Right and left (Political science)—Western countries. | Political
culture—Western countries.
Classification: LCC JC423 .B83 2019 | DDC 306.209182/1—dc23
LC record available at https://lccn.loc.gov/2018060444

Columbia University Press books are printed
on permanent and durable acid-free paper.

Printed in the United States of America

Cover image: © Reuters/Lucas Jackson

Contents

Acknowledgments

THIS BOOK emerged from reflections following the November 2016 election in the United States. It culminated in the 2018 René Wellek Library Lectures at Irvine, Gauss Seminars in Criticism at Princeton, and Robert S. Stevens Lecture at Cornell Law School. I had planned other research and writing for this period, for which I received a Simon Guggenheim Fellowship and UC President's Humanities Research Fellowship. I turned to the questions and analyses developed in these pages because it seemed irresponsible to do otherwise. I am deeply indebted to the two fellowship programs that supported the undertaking and to the institutions that hosted the lectures.

Class of 1936 First Chair funds permitted me to employ two superb research assistants at Berkeley, William Callison and Brian Judge. In addition to their extensive help with research and manuscript preparation, both influenced my thinking with their own. William Callison's deep knowledge of the ordoliberals and subtle thinking about political rationality was especially important in conceiving and revising chapter 2. He saved me from several gaffes and tutored me as we worked.

Acknowledgments

In addition to Brian and Will, Judith Butler, Michel Feher, Bonnie Honig, Steve Shiffrin, Quinn Slobodian, and Nelson Tebbe each offered excellent suggestions for improvement. The summer 2018 Lucerne Master Class permitted me to refine some of the ideas.

Wendy Lochner, at Columbia University Press, was encouraging, flexible and professional. Bud Bynack, copyeditor extraordinaire, and kind and funny as well, is a gift to writers and their readers.

Saba Mahmood's terminal illness accompanied much of the writing of this book. Helene Moglen died suddenly as I was completing it. Both were beloved friends. Both harbored irrepressible ardor for the beauty and possibilities of this world and clear-eyed fury at its cruelties, ruses, and wrongs. May their spirits animate our future.

The introduction and chapters 1, 2, and 5 draw on arguments first adumbrated in "Neoliberalism's Frankenstein: Authoritarian Freedom in Neoliberal 'Democracies,'" *Critical Times* 1, no. 1 (2018), https://ctjournal.org/index.php/criticaltimes/article/view/12. Chapter 1 also draws from "Defending Society," The Big Picture (series), *Public Books*, October 10, 2017, https://www.publicbooks.org/the-big-picture-defending-society/.

In the Ruins of
Neoliberalism

Introduction

*This tyrannical spirit, wanting to play bishop
and banker everywhere.*
> —George Eliot, *Middlemarch*

TAKING EVEN themselves by surprise, hard-right forces have surged to power in liberal democracies across the globe.[1] Every election brings a new shock: neo-Nazis in the German parliament, neofascists in the Italian one, Brexit ushered in by tabloid-fueled xenophobia, the rise of white nationalism in Scandinavia, authoritarian regimes taking shape in Turkey and Eastern Europe, and of course, Trumpism. Racist, anti-Islamic, and anti-Semitic hatefulness and bellicosity grow in the streets and across the internet, and newly coalesced far-right groups have burst boldly into the public light after years of lurking mostly in the shadows. Politicians and political victories embolden far-right movements, which in turn acquire sophistication as political handlers and social media experts craft the message. As recruits continue to grow, centrists, mainstream neoliberals, liberals, and leftists are reeling. Outrage, moralizing, satire, and vain hopes that internal factions or scandals on the right will yield self-destruction are far more prevalent than serious strategies for challenging these forces with compelling alternatives. We even have trouble with the naming—is this authoritarianism, fascism, populism, illiberal democracy, undemocratic liberalism, right-wing plutocracy? Or something else?

Failure to predict, understand, or effectively contest these developments is due partly to blinding assumptions about perduring Western values and institutions, especially progress and Enlightenment and liberal democracy, and partly to the unfamiliar agglomeration of elements in the rising Right—its curious combination of libertarianism, moralism, authoritarianism, nationalism, hatred of the state, Christian conservatism, and racism. These new forces conjoin familiar elements of neoliberalism (licensing capital, leashing labor, demonizing the social state and the political, attacking equality, promulgating freedom) with their seeming opposites (nationalism, enforcement of traditional morality, populist antielitism, and demands for state solutions to economic and social problems). They conjoin moral righteousness with nearly celebratory amoral and uncivil conduct. They endorse authority while featuring unprecedented public social disinhibition and aggression. They rage against relativism, but also against science and reason, and spurn evidence-based claims, rational argumentation, credibility, and accountability. They disdain politicians and politics while evincing a ferocious will to power and political ambition. Where are we?

Introduction

There has been no shortage of efforts by pundits and scholars alike to answer this question. A composite Left account, whose limits will soon become clear, goes roughly like this: in the Global North, neoliberal economic policy devastated rural and suburban regions, emptying them of decent jobs, pensions, schools, services, and infrastructure as social spending dried up and capital chased the cheap labor and tax havens of the Global South. Meanwhile, an unprecedented cultural and religious divide was opening. Hip, educated, slender, secular, multicultural, globetrotting urbanites were building a different moral and cultural universe from the midlanders, whose economic woes were salted with steadily growing estrangement from the mores of those who ignored, ridiculed, or disdained them. More than hard up and frustrated, the Christian white rural and suburban dwellers were alienated and humiliated, left out, and left behind. Then there was enduring racism, rising as new immigrants transformed suburban neighborhoods and as policies of "equity and inclusion" appeared to the uneducated white male to favor everyone over him. Thus, liberal political agendas, neoliberal economic agendas, and cosmopolitan cultural agendas generated a growing experience of abandonment, betrayal, and ultimately rage on the part of the new dispossessed, the white working-class and middle-class populations of the First and Second Worlds. If their dark-skinned counterparts were hurt as much or more by neoliberal decimations of union-protected jobs and public goods, by declining opportunities and educational access and quality, what blacks and Latinos did not suffer was lost pride of place in America or the West.

As this phenomenon first took shape, the story goes, conservative plutocrats manipulated it brilliantly: the dispossessed were thrown under the economic bus at every turn while being played a political symphony of Christian family values along with paeans to whiteness and to their young sacrificed in senseless and endless wars. That is "what's the matter with Kansas."[2] Combining patriotism as militarism, Christianity, family, racist dog whistles, and unbridled capitalism was the successful recipe of conservative neoliberals until the 2008 finance capital crisis devastated incomes, retirements, and home ownership for its working-class and middle-class white base.[3] With even the economists muttering that they had been wrong about unchecked deregulation, debt financing, and globalization, serious displacement was now required. This meant screaming about ISIS, undocumented immigrants, affirmative action myths, and above all, demonizing government and the social state for the economic catastrophe—slyly shifting the blame from Wall Street to Washington because the latter mopped up the mess by rescuing the banks while hanging little people out to dry. Thus was a second wave of reaction to neoliberalism born, this one more unruly, populist, and ugly. Already galled by an elegant black family in the White House, disgruntled whites were also fed a steady diet of right-wing commentary by Fox News, talk radio, and social media, inflected from the fringes as a potpourri of previously isolated movements—white nationalist, libertarian, antigovernment, and fascist—connected with each other via the internet.[4] Especially given widespread disillusionment with the interminable Middle East wars, militaristic patriotism and family values were no longer enough.

Introduction

Rather, the new hard-right populism was bled directly from the wound of dethroned privilege that whiteness, Christianity, and maleness granted to those who were otherwise nothing and no one.

The dethronement was easy enough to blame on job-stealing immigrants and minorities, along with other imagined undeserving beneficiaries of liberal inclusion (most outrageously, those of putatively terrorist religions and races) courted by elites and globalists. Thus were the causalities of neoliberal economic policies mobilized by the figure of their own losses, mirrored in a nation lost. This figure drew on a mythical past when families were happy, whole, and heterosexual, when women and racial minorities knew their place, when neighborhoods were orderly, secure, and homogenous, when heroin was a black problem and terrorism was not inside the homeland, and when a hegemonic Christianity and whiteness constituted the manifest identity, power, and pride of the nation and the West.[5] Against invasions by other peoples, ideas, laws, cultures, and religions, this was the fairy-tale world right-wing populist leaders promised to protect and restore. The campaign slogans tell it all: "Make America Great Again" (Trump), "France for the French" (Le Pen and the National Front), "Take Back Control" (Brexit), "Our Culture, Our Home, Our Germany" (Alternative for Germany), "Pure Poland, White Poland" (Poland's Law and Justice Party), "Keep Sweden Swedish" (Sweden Democrats). These slogans and the aggrieved spirit they express connected heretofore disparate racist fringe groups, right-wing Catholics and Christian evangelicals and merely frustrated white suburbanites falling out of the middle and working classes. Growing

5

siloization of media consumption, from cable TV to Facebook, strengthened these connections and widened the chasm between the midlanders and the educated, urban and urbane, mixed race, feminist, queer affirmative, and godless. At the same time, neo-liberalism's relentless diminution of nonmonetized existence, such as being knowledgeable and thoughtful about the world, converged with the privatization choking off access to higher education for the many. A generation turned away from liberal arts education was also turned against it.

The accent marks in this story vary. Sometimes they are on neoliberal policy, sometimes on putative Left-liberal absorption with multiculturalism and identity politics, sometimes on the increased political importance and power of evangelicals and Christian nationalists, sometimes on the growing vulnerability of an uneducated population to lies and conspiracies, sometimes on the existential need for horizons and inherent unattractiveness of a globalist worldview for all but elites, and sometimes on the enduring racism of an old white working class or the new racism cleaved to by younger uneducated whites. Some stress the role of powerful right-wing think tanks and political money. Others stress new/old "tribalisms" emerging from the breakdowns of nation-states or previously more (racially or religiously) homogenous regions. However, almost all agree that neoliberal intensification of inequality within the Global North was a tinderbox and that mass migration from South to North was a match to the fire.

With its various inflections, this has become the Left's common sense since the political earthquake of November 2016. The narrative is not wrong, but, I will argue, incomplete. It does not register the forces overdetermining the radically antidemo-cratic form of the rebellion and thus tends to align it with fas-cisms of old. It does not consider the demonized status of the social and the political in neoliberal governmentality nor the valorization of traditional morality and markets in their place. It does not recognize the disintegration of society and the dis-crediting of the public good by neoliberal reason as tilling the ground for the so-called "tribalisms" emerging as identities and political forces in recent years. It does not explain how the attack on equality, combined with mobilization of traditional values, could turn up the heat on and legitimate long-simmering rac-isms from colonial and slave legacies (what Nikhil Singh calls our "inner and outer wars") or the never-go-softly-into-the-night character of male superordination.[6] It does not register the intensifying nihilism that challenges truth and transforms tra-ditional morality into weapons of political battle. It does not identify how assaults on constitutional democracy, on racial, gender, and sexual equality, on public education, and on a civil, nonviolent public sphere have all been carried out in the name of both freedom and morality. It does not grasp how neoliberal rationality radically disoriented the Left as it fashioned an ordi-nary discourse in which social justice is at once trivialized and monsterized as "political correctness" or characterized as the Left's Gramscian Kulturkampf aimed at overthrowing liberty and morality and secured through a blasphemous statism.[7]

This book addresses these issues by theorizing how neolib-eral rationality prepared the ground for the mobilization and legitimacy of ferocious antidemocratic forces in the second decade of the twenty-first century. The argument is not that neoliberalism by itself *caused* the hard-right insurgency in the West today or that every dimension of the present, from the catastrophes generating great flows of refugees to Europe and North America to the political siloization and polarization generated by digital media can be *reduced* to neoliberalism.[8] Rather, the argument is that nothing is untouched by a neoliberal mode of reason and valuation and that neoliberalism's attack on democracy has everywhere inflected law, political culture, and political subjectivity. Understanding the roots and energies of the current situation requires appreciating neoliberal political culture and subject production, not only the economic conditions and enduring racisms that spawned it. It means appreciating the rise of white nationalist authoritarian political formations as animated by the mobilized anger of the economically abandoned and racially resentful, but as contoured by more than three decades of neoliberal assaults on democracy, equality, and society. White working-class and middle-class economic suffering and racialized rancor, far from distinct from these assaults, acquire voice and shape from them. These assaults also fuel (though they do not by themselves cause) the Christian nationalist ambition to (re)conquer the West. They also intermix with an intensifying nihilism manifesting as broken faith in truth, facticity, and foundational values.

To make these arguments, *In the Ruins* revisits selected aspects of the thinking of those who gathered as the Mont Pelerin Society in 1947, took the name "neoliberalism," and offered the founding schema for what Michel Foucault would call the dramatic "reprogramming of liberalism" that we know as neoliberalism today. Again, however, this does not mean that either the original neoliberal intellectuals—Friedrich Hayek, Milton Friedman, and their half-siblings, the German Ordoliberals— or even later neoliberal policy makers themselves aimed at the political and economic present. To the contrary, popular enthusiasm for autocratic, nationalist, and in some cases neo-fascist regimes, fueled by myth mongering and demagoguery, departs as radically from neoliberal ideals as repressive state communist regimes departed from those of Marx and other socialist intellectuals, even if, in each case, the deformed plant grew from soil fertilized by these ideas. Forged in the crucible of European fascism, neoliberalism aimed at permanent inoc-ulation of market liberal orders against the regrowth of fascistic sentiments and totalitarian powers.[9] Eager to separate poli-tics from markets, the original neoliberals would have loathed both the crony capitalism and international oligarchical power spawned by finance that yanks the chains of states today.[10] Seek-ing to get politics out of markets and concentrated economic interests out of policy making, they would have deplored the manipulation of public policy by major industries and capi-tal sectors and would have hated, too, the politicization of enterprise. Above all, they dreaded political mobilizations of an ignorant, aroused citizenry and looked to market and moral discipline and a severely leashed democracy to pacify and contain it. They would be horrified by the contemporary phenome-non of leaders at once authoritarian and reckless riding to power on this tide. In short, while the book will argue that the constellation of principles, policies, practices, and forms of gov-erning reason that may be gathered under the sign of neoliber-alism has importantly constituted the catastrophic present, this was not neoliberalism's intended spawn, but its Frankensteinian creation. Fathoming how that creation came to be requires examining the imminent failures and occlusions of neoliberal principles and policy, as well as their admixture with other powers and energies, including those of racism, nihilism, fatalism, and ressentiment.[11]

If this book does not argue that neoliberalism *aimed* at the current conjuncture of principles, policies, practices, and forms of rationality, neither does it argue that the fascisms of the 1930s are "returning," nor that Western civilization, otherwise on the path of progress, is in a bout of regression.[12] Rather, it theorizes the current formation as relatively novel, differing from authoritarianisms, fascisms, despotisms, or tyrannies of other times and places and differing as well from conventional or known conservatisms. It thus rejects the language that much of the Left uses to upbraid the Right, as well as much of the language that the Right uses to describe itself. It is especially focused on how neoliberal formulations of freedom animate and legitimate the hard Right and how the Right mobilizes a discourse of freedom for its sometimes violent exclusions and assaults, for resecuring white, male, and Christian hegemony, and not only for building the power of capital. It is also concerned with how this formulation of freedom paints the Left, including the moderate or liberal Left, as tyrannical or even "fascistic" in its care for social justice and at the same time as responsible for disintegrating moral fabrics, unsecured borders, and giveaways to the undeserving.

The project of *In the Ruins* requires thinking beyond and even revising the arguments of *Undoing the Demos: Neoliberalism's*

Stealth Revolution, my previous work on neoliberalism and democracy, where my characterization of neoliberalism's world-making rationality focused exclusively on its drive to economize all features of existence, from democratic institutions to subjectivity.[13] It also requires revising the arguments of an earlier essay, "American Nightmare," where I analyzed neoliberal and neoconservative rationalities as distinct in origins and characteristics.[14] Both arguments failed to grasp crucial features of the Thatcher-Reagan neoliberal revolution, features that took their bearings from what Phillip Mirowski named the Neoliberal Thought Collective and Daniel Stedman Jones described as "a kind of neoliberal international," a transatlantic network of academics, businessmen, journalists and activists.[15] This revolution aimed at releasing markets *and* morals to govern and discipline individuals while maximizing freedom, and it did so by demonizing the social and the democratic version of political life. Neoliberal reason, especially as Friedrich Hayek formulated it, casts markets and morals as singular forms of human need provision sharing ontological principles and dynamics. Rooted in liberty and generating spontaneous order and evolution, their radical opposites are *any kind* of deliberate and state-administered social policy, planning, and justice.

That markets have this role in neoliberalism is a commonplace—not so with traditional morality, although the latter features prominently in the founding statement of the Mont Pelerin Society.[16] The role of the family in the American neoliberal revolution is the subject of Melinda Cooper's rich 2016 book, *Family Values*, which reveals resecuring patriarchal family norms not as a sideshow, but rather as deeply embedded within neoliberal welfare and education reform. Cooper examines and links a series of policy domains in which the traditional family was explicitly adduced to substitute for multiple aspects of the social state. In her telling, market privatization of social security, health care, and higher education involved "responsibilizing" individual men, rather than the state, for teen pregnancies, parents, rather than the state, for the costs of higher education, and families, rather than the state, for the provision of every kind of care for dependents—children, disabled, the elderly.[17]

Cooper's book is brilliant. However, only through a return to founding neoliberal ideas and to Hayek in particular is it possible to bring into relief the architecture of reason binding traditional morality to neoliberalism and animating right-wing campaigns today. These campaigns cast as assaults on both freedom and morality all social policy that challenges the social reproduction of gender, racial, and sexual hierarchies or modestly redresses class extremes. For Hayek, markets and morals together are the foundation of freedom, order, and the development of civilization. Both are organized spontaneously and transmitted through tradition, rather than political power. Markets can do their work only if states are prevented from encroaching on or intervening in them. Traditional morals can do theirs only when states are likewise restrained from intervening in that domain and when expanding what Hayek calls the "personal, protected sphere" gives morality more power, latitude, and legitimacy than rational, secular social democracies otherwise permit. Thus, more than a project of enlarging the sphere of market competition and valuation ("economizing everything" as I argued in *Undoing the Demos*), Hayekian neo-liberalism is a moral-political project that aims to protect traditional hierarchies by negating the very idea of the social and radically restricting the reach of democratic political power in nation-states.

The contemporary attack on society and social justice in the name of market freedom and moral traditionalism is thus a direct emanation of neoliberal rationality, hardly limited to so-called "conservatives." If Clintonian welfare reform is the most obvious example of "progressive neoliberalism," it also contoured the marriage equality campaign, which built its case for same-sex marriage on the twin basis of the moral-religious singularity of marriage and the economic singularity of families to provide health, education, welfare, and an intergenerational transmission of wealth. Conservative forces, however, have made more direct appeals to traditional morality and homilies to the free market, wrapping the pair in patriotism, nativism, and Christianity. In the United States, a Supreme Court majority abetted these appeals with a stream of decisions overturning restrictions on production and commerce, pushing back antidiscrimination statutes, and expanding the meaning and reach of religious liberty.[18]

The founding texts rarely mentioned it, but white and male superordination are easily tucked into the neoliberal markets-and-morals project. On the one hand, deregulated markets tend to reproduce rather than ameliorate historically produced social powers and stratification. Racial and sexual divisions of labor are built into them: gendered household labor is unpaid, for example, and its woefully underpaid market version (child care, housecleaning, home health care, kitchen work) is disproportionately shouldered by nonwhites and immigrants. Deep inequalities in both public and private education (from kindergarten to the postgraduate level) compound this stratification, as do class, race, and gender cultures structuring hiring practices, promotions, and success. On the other hand, traditional morality serves to repel challenges to inequalities, for example, securing women's reproductive freedom or dismantling public iconography celebrating a slave-holding past. Traditional morality also links preservation of the past with patriotism by casting the latter not just as love of country, but as love of the way things *were*, which tars objections to racial and gender injustice as unpatriotic. Hence the rebuke of Colin Kaepernick's "take a knee" protests of racialized police brutality as disrespecting American troops. Kaepernick never mentioned the troops and never directed his protest at American military undertakings. However, more than metonymy links the national anthem, football, and the military, more even than racist remonstrance to black athletes that their job is to play and dance for whites, not claim a seat at the table with them. The logic casting his protest as unpatriotic is organized by a figure of the nation as comprising traditions indemnified from criticism, including traditions of policing and of racism. The military, identified with "defending our way of life," even or perhaps especially when fighting wars with limited support, is the brightest emblem of this figure.

The Rise of Antidemocratic Politics

Perhaps opponents of social democracy should welcome it for its conservative effects. Social democracy brings to society generally and to the political system contributions that serve to soften the potential radicalism of political democracy. All contribute, all benefit, and all have a stake. By promoting public education, social security, and expanded health care, social democracy helps to mitigate the divisiveness of wealth, race, ethnicity and other potentially explosive identities. It promotes a commonality of shared contributions and benefits that encourages a moderate, rather than an enraged form of majority rule.

—Sheldon Wolin, *Fugitive Democracy and Other Essays*

In the Ruins argues that the rise of antidemocratic politics was advanced through attacks on society understood as experienced and tended in common and on the legitimacy and practice of democratic political life. Chapter 1 begins this account of the markets-and-morals project of neoliberalism by examining neoliberalism's critique of society and aim to dismantle it. Chapter 2 explores the attack on democracy understood as popular sovereignty and shared political power. Chapter 3 delineates the neoliberal project of expanding the reach of traditional morality beyond the spheres of family and private worship to public and commercial life. In the United States, this expansion has been powerfully abetted by the Supreme Court, and chapter 4 reads two of the court's recent decisions in this light. Chapter 5 explores the imbrication of the neoliberal markets-and-morals project with nihilism, fatalism, and wounded white male supremacy.

The fifth chapter also develops a leitmotif running through the others: as I have already noted, neoliberalism yielded effects very different from those imagined and sought by its architects. The reasons for this are several. There is, first, a kind of return of the repressed in neoliberalism reason—a ferocious eruption of the social and political forces that the neoliberals at once opposed, underestimated, and deformed with their dedemocratizing project. What this means is that actually existing neoliberalism now features what Sheldon Wolin characterizes as an "enraged" form of majority rule (often termed "populism" by pundits) arising from the society that neoliberals aimed to disintegrate, but failed to vanquish, and thus left without common civil norms or commitments. There is, second, neoliberalism's accidental unleashing of the financial sector and the ways that financialization profoundly undermined neoliberal dreams of a competitive global order lightly tended by supranational institutions, on the one hand, and facilitated by states fully autonomous of economic interests and manipulation, on the other.[19] Third, there are the ways that markets and morals twisted as they were submitted to the grammars and spirit of one another—that is, as morality was marketized and markets were moralized. Through this process, both became politicized as fighting creeds, thus losing the "organic, spontaneous" character and mode of organizing conduct for which Hayek and his colleagues cherished them. Finally, neoliberalism intensified the nihilism, fatalism, and rancorous resentment already present in late modern culture. Together, these developments and effects generated something radically different from the neoliberal utopia of an inegalitarian liberal order in which individuals and families would be politically pacified by markets and morals and subtended by an autonomous authoritative, but depoliticized state. Instead, neoliberalism produced a monster its founders would abhor.

Neoliberalism, What?

I should conclude this introduction with a brief consideration of how the term "neoliberalism" is employed in this work. Neoliberalism carries no settled definition, and there now exists a substantial academic literature arguing about its constitutive characteristics. A few have gone so far as to suggest that its amorphous, protean, and contested character casts doubt on its very existence.[20] Yet as is the case with other world-altering formations, including capitalism, socialism, liberalism, feudalism, Christianity, Islam, and fascism, ongoing intellectual contestation about their underlying principles, elements, unity, logics, and dynamics does not vitiate their world-making power. Neoliberalism—the ideas, the institutions, the policies, the political rationality—has, along with its spawn, financialization, likely shaped recent world history as profoundly as any other nameable phenomenon in the same period, even if scholars continue to debate precisely what both are.

The term "neoliberalism" was coined at the 1938 Colloque Walter Lippmann, a gathering of scholars who laid the political-intellectual foundations for what would take shape as the Mont Pelerin Society a decade later. Neoliberalism is most commonly

associated with a bundle of policies privatizing public ownership and services, radically reducing the social state, leashing
labor, deregulating capital, and producing a tax-and-tariff-
friendly climate to direct foreign investors. These were precisely the policies imposed on Chile by Augusto Pinochet and
his advisors, the "Chicago Boys," in 1973 and soon after carried
elsewhere in the Global South, often imposed by the International Monetary Fund as "structural adjustment" mandates tied
to borrowing and debt restructuring.[21] What started in the
Southern Hemisphere soon flowed north, even if the executive
powers of the revolutions were rather different. By the end of
the 1970s, exploiting a crisis of profitability and stagflation, neoliberal programs were rolled out by Margaret Thatcher and
Ronald Reagan, again centering on deregulating capital, breaking organized labor, privatizing public goods and services,
reducing progressive taxation, and shrinking the social state.
The policies rapidly spread across Western Europe, and the
breakup of the Soviet Bloc at the end of the 1980s meant that
much of Eastern Europe transitioned from state communism
to neoliberal capitalism in less than half a decade.

The above account, hewing to a neo-Marxist approach, for-
mulates neoliberalism as an opportunistic attack by capitalists
and their political lackeys on Keynesian welfare states, social
democracies, and state socialism. In *Globalists: The End of Empire
and the Birth of Neoliberalism*, Quinn Slobodian adds sophistication to this picture by emphasizing the extent to which neoliberalism was both intellectually conceived and practically
unveiled as a *global* project in which nation-state economic sovereignty would be superseded by the rules and agreements set

by supranational institutions such as the World Trade Organization, World Bank, and International Monetary Fund.[22] In Slobodian's telling, neoliberalism aimed simultaneously at dismantling barriers to capital flows (and hence to capital accumulation) posed by nation-states and at neutralizing redistributive demands from the recently decolonized South, such as those embodied in the New International Economic Order. Slobodian's account also underscores the extent to which the neoliberal revolution was *designed* to quash working-class expectations in both the developed world and developing postcolonial regions as it produced a global race to the bottom. Put differently, releasing capital to chase cheap labor, resources, and tax havens around the world would inevitably generate lower standards of living for working-class and middle-class populations in the Global North and continued exploitation and limited sovereignty, accompanied by (uneven) development, in the Global South.[23]

In contrast with the neo-Marxist account, by conceptualizing neoliberalism as "reprogramming of liberalism," Michel Foucault offers a substantially different characterization of neoliberalism—its meaning, aim, and purpose. In his 1978–79 Collège de France lectures, Foucault emphasized neoliberalism's significance as a novel political rationality, the reach and implications of which go well beyond economic policy and the empowerment of capital.[24] Rather, in this rationality, market principles become governing principles applied by and to the state, but also circulating through institutions and entities across society—schools, workplaces, clinics, etc. These principles become saturating reality principles governing every sphere of existence and reorienting *homo oeconomicus* itself, transforming it from a subject of exchange and the satisfaction of needs (classical liberalism) to a subject of competition and human capital enhancement (neoliberalism). At the same time, according to Foucault, the neoliberals formulated competitive markets as necessitating political support and thus a novel form of what Foucault calls "governmentalizing" the state. In the new governmental rationality, on the one hand, all governing is *for* markets and oriented by market principles, and on the other hand, markets must be built, facilitated, propped up, and occasionally even rescued by political institutions. Competitive markets are good, but not exactly natural or self-sustaining. For Foucault, these two features of neoliberal rationality—the elaboration of market principles as ubiquitous governing principles and governing itself as reformatted to serve markets—are among those that divide neoliberal rationality from classical economic liberalism, and not only from Keynesian or social democracy. They constitute the "reprogramming of liberal governmentality" that could and would take hold everywhere, entrepreneurializing the subject, converting labor to human capital, and repositioning and reorganizing the state. For Foucauldians, then, more important than its rebooting of capitalism is neoliberalism's radical alteration of the values, coordinates, and reality principles that govern, or "conduct conduct," in liberal orders.[25]

This book draws on both the neo-Marxist and Foucauldian approaches to neoliberalism and also expands both to redress their mutual neglect of the moral side of the neoliberal project. It does not treat the two as opposites or as reducible to material versus ideational understandings of power and historical change, but employs them as featuring different dimensions of the neo-liberal transformations taking place around the world in the past four decades. The neo-Marxist approach tends to focus on institutions, policies, economic relations, and effects while neglecting the far-reaching effects of neoliberalism as a form of governing political reason and subject production. The Foucauldian approach focuses on the principles orienting, orchestrating, and relating state, society, and subjects and above all on neoliberalism's novel register of value and values, but it too little attends to the spectacular new powers of global capital that neoliberalism heralds and builds. The former casts neoliberalism as ushering in a new chapter of capitalism and generating new forces, contradictions, and crises. The latter reveals governments, subjects, and subjectivities as transformed by neoliberalism's refashioning of liberal reason; it regards neoliberalism as revealing the extent to which capitalism is not singular and does not run on its own logics, but is always organized by forms of political rationality. Both approaches contribute to understanding the characteristics of actually existing neoliberalism and of the current conjuncture. That said, this book is mainly concerned with rethinking the elements and effects of neoliberal rationality and with broadening our understanding of that rationality to include its multipronged attack on democracy and its activation of traditional morality in place of legislated social justice.

1

Society Must Be Dismantled

Democracy, Equality, and the Social

The English word "democracy" derives from ancient Greek terms, *demos* (the people) and *kratos* (power or rule). In contrast with oligarchy, monarchy, aristocracy, plutocracy, tyranny, and colonial rule, democracy signifies political arrangements through which a people rules itself.[1]

Political equality is democracy's foundation. Everything else is optional—from constitutions to personal liberty, from specific economic forms to specific political institutions. Political equality alone ensures that the composition and exercise of political power is authorized by the whole and accountable to the whole. When political equality is absent, whether from explicit political exclusions or privileges, from extreme social or economic disparities, from uneven or managed access to knowledge, or from manipulation of the electoral system, political power will inevitably be exercised by and for a part, rather than the whole. The demos ceases to rule.

The importance of political equality to democracy is why Rousseau insisted that differences in power among a democratic people must "not be so great that they can be wielded as violence" and also that none may "be so rich that he can buy another and none so poor that he is compelled to sell himself."[2] Rousseau's point was that more than a matter of injustice or suffering, systemization of group violence or destitution puts an end to democracy. The importance of political equality to democracy is why Alexis de Tocqueville identified democracy's modern emergence with "a revolution in the material of society"—a social transformation that destroyed rank, or what he called "inequality of conditions."[3] The importance of political equality to democracy is also why ancient Athenian democrats, savvier about power than most moderns, identified democracy's three pillars as *isēgoría*, the equal right of every citizen to speak and be heard by the assembly on matters of public policy; *isonomía*, equality under the law; and *isopoliteía*, equally weighted votes and equal opportunity to assume political office. Athenians may have cherished freedom, but they understood that democracy is moored by equality.

By the measure of political equality, what are variously called liberal, bourgeois, or capitalist democracies have never been complete, and what democratic provisions they contain have been weakening steadily in recent decades. How, indeed, is it even possible to secure political equality in large nation-states with capitalist economies? Sheldon Wolin contends that culturing democracy in such settings makes a specific demand on *the state*, namely, that it act deliberately to reduce inequalities in power among citizens. Only then can political equality be approximated; only then might political life serve the whole, rather than an elite.[4] To underscore his point about the paradoxical democratic requirement that states build political equality, Wolin quotes approvingly from Marx's critique of Hegel's *Philosophy of Right*: "It is evident that all forms" of the modern state "have democracy for their truth, and for that reason are false to the extent that they are not democracy."[5] Wolin takes Marx to mean that the legitimacy of the modern state rests in the claim to govern for the good of the entire society, to deliver the common good, rather than being the instrument of elites. He regards Marx as recognizing that democracy is "a distinct kind of association that aims at the good of all" that "depends on the contributions, sacrifices, and loyalties of all."[6] At the same time, Wolin characterizes the requirement that a state employ its own power to bring a democratic citizenry into being as moving against the natural course of political power.[7] That natural course, as Tocqueville made vivid in discussing this issue, is toward concentration and centralization; political and especially state power do not naturally dilute themselves through dissemination, even as effective governing may operate by that very means.

Democracy, then, is the weakest of warring triplets born in early European modernity, alongside nation-states and capitalism.[8] According to Wolin, there is no such thing as a democratic state, since states abduct, institutionalize, and wield "surplus power" generated by the people; democracy always lives elsewhere from the state, even in democracies.[9] Democratized capitalism is also an oxymoron, and radical democrats have good reason to promote alternative economic forms. This said, capitalism can be modulated in more or less democratic directions, and states can do more or less to nurture or quash the political equality on which democracy depends.

What, beyond general encomiums, advances and protects political equality in this context? Affirmative state actions to guarantee adequate conditions of existence (income, housing, health care) are crucial to preventing disenfranchisement through desperation. Vital, as well, is state support for access to quality civic education, to voting, and to officeholding for those otherwise effectively barred from sharing political power. Democracy also requires constant vigilance to prevent concentrated wealth from grasping the levers of political power. Wealth—corporate, consolidated, or individual—will never stop reaching for these levers, and once it has a significant hold, there is no limit to its self-serving practices, which may include efforts to prevent the ordinary, the poor, and the historically marginalized from staking political claims and even from voting.[10] In sum, an orientation toward democracy in the context of nation-states and capitalism requires state support for public goods ranging from health care to quality education, economic redistributions, and strong prophylaxes against corruption by wealth. Neither markets themselves nor winners within them can be permitted to rule if democracy is to prevail; both must be contained in the interest of political equality, democracy's foundation.

To be clear, the claim is not that democracies must deal with what, since the nineteenth century, has been called "the social question," which concerns whether and how to ameliorate capitalism's inherent impoverishment of the many as it generates unprecedented wealth for the few. "The social question" tends to be framed in terms of compassion for the poor, fairness, or concern about social upheaval. The point here is a different one, namely, that democracy requires explicit efforts to bring into being a people capable of engaging in modest self-rule, efforts that address ways that social and economic inequalities compromise political equality.

Democracy also requires a robust cultivation of society as the place where we experience a linked fate across our differences and separateness. Situated conceptually and practically between state and personal life, the social is where citizens of vastly unequal backgrounds and resources are potentially brought together and thought together. It is where we are politically enfranchised and gathered (not merely cared for) through provision of public goods and where historically produced inequalities are made manifest as differentiated political access, voice, and treatment, as well as where these inequalities may be partially redressed. Social justice is the essential antidote to otherwise depoliticized stratifications, exclusions, abjections, and inequalities attending liberal privatism in capitalist orders and is itself a modest rejoinder to the impossibility of direct democracy in large nation-states or their postnational successors, such as the European Union. More than an ideological persuasion, social justice—modulation of the powers of capitalism, colonialism, race, gender, and others—is all that stands between sustaining the (always unfulfilled) promise of democracy and wholesale abandonment of that promise. The social is where we are more than private individuals or families, more than economic producers, consumers, or investors, and more than mere members of the nation.

Tellingly, the existence of society and the idea of the social—its intelligibility, its harboring of stratifying powers, and above all, its appropriateness as a site of justice and the commonweal—is precisely what neoliberalism set out to destroy conceptually, normatively, and practically. Denounced as a nonsensical term by Hayek and famously declared nonexistent by Thatcher ("there is no such thing . . ."), "society" is a pejorative term for the Right today, who decry "social justice warriors" (SJWs) for undermining freedom with a tyrannical agenda of social equality, civil rights, affirmative action, and even public education. Neoliberalism forthrightly aimed to dismantle the social state, whether by privatizing it (the Reagan-Thatcher revolution), devolving its tasks (the UK's "Big Society" and Bush's "thousand points of light"), eliminating what remains of welfare altogether, or "deconstructing the administrative state" (Steve Bannon's aim for the Trump presidency). In each case, it is not only social regulation and redistribution that are rejected as inappropriate interference in markets or as assaults on freedom. Also jettisoned is democracy's dependence on political equality.[11]

The neoliberal attack on the social, which we are about to examine more closely, is key to generating an *antidemocratic culture from below* while building and legitimating *antidemocratic forms of state power from above*. The synergy between the two is profound: an increasingly undemocratic and antidemocratic citizenry is ever more willing to authorize an increasingly antidemocratic state. As the attack on the social vanquishes a democratic understanding of society tended by a diverse people equally entitled to share in self-rule, politics becomes a field of extreme and uncompromised positioning, and liberty becomes a right of appropriation, disruption, and even destruction of the social—its named enemy.

The assault on society and social justice over the neoliberal decades is most familiar in the project of dismantling and disparaging the social state in the name of free, responsibilized individuals. It reached an institutionalized crescendo in the Trump regime, where government agencies designed to steward social welfare in the domains of health, human services, education, housing, labor, urban development, and the environment are headed by those committed to marketizing or eliminating, rather than protecting or administering these goods.[12] Then there is the regime's newly minted Office of American Innovation, led by Trump's son-in-law, Jared Kushner. The White House introduction of the office as a "SWAT team aimed at fixing government with business ideas" captured in a phrase the displacement of democratic rule with policing and management, along with the disintegration of society into units of production and consumption.[13] Assuming the new position, Kushner said, "The government should be run like a great American company. Our hope is that we can achieve successes and efficiencies for our customers, who are the citizens."[14] Yet it is companies, not customers, that seek "successes and efficiencies"— customers are at the receiving end of their marketing and public relations strategies. Thus, more than simply revealing his lack of political knowledge and experience and failure to understand democracy, Kushner may have unconsciously confessed that when government is run like a business, especially the kinds owned by his father and father-in-law, citizen-customers would become its unprotected, exploitable, and manipulable objects of gain.

Society Must Be Dismantled

Of all the neoliberal intellectuals, Friedrich Hayek criticized most systematically the notion of the social and society and offered the most sustained critique of social democracy. Hayek's hostility toward the social is overdetermined, one might even say over the top, as it seeks epistemological, ontological, political, economic, and even moral grounds. He deems the very notion of the social false and dangerous, meaningless and hollow, destructive and dishonest, a "semantic fraud." Concern with the social is the signature of all misbegotten efforts at controlling collective existence, the token of tyranny. Hayek deems "society" a "makeshift phrase," the "new deity to which we complain . . . if it does not fulfil the expectations it has created."[15] At best, he says, the term carries nostalgia for ancient worlds of small and intimate associations and falsely presupposes "a common pursuit of shared purposes." At worst, it is a cover for the coercive power of government.[16] Social justice is a "mirage," and attraction to it is "the gravest threat to most other values of a free civilization."[17]

How can society and social justice be all of these things? And what is the taproot of Hayek's animus toward society and social justice? The first clue rests in Hayek's frustration with the ambiguity of the modern meaning of "society." The fact that it denotes so many different kinds of human connection "falsely suggests that all such systems are of the same kind," and Hayek sees more than mere sloppiness in society's semantic slide from small chosen groups to nation-states.[18] Noting that the Latin origin of the term (*societas*, from *soctus*) implies a personally known fellow or companion, Hayek detects a dangerous romance with a lost past in its contemporary usage, where "society" is inappropriately used to denote impersonal, unintentional, and undesigned human cooperation on a mass scale. Complex interdependence in modernity, Hayek says, does not arise from fellow feeling or organized common pursuit, but from individuals following rules of conduct that emanate from markets and moral traditions.[19] To call this "society" wrongly conflates "such completely different formations as the companionship of individuals in constant personal contact and the structure formed by millions who are connected only by signals resulting from long and infinitely ramified chains of trade."[20] More than merely being wrong, however, this conflation reveals the "concealed desire" by social justice or planning advocates to model modern orders on intentional, organized notions of the good—the stuff of totalitarianism.

Hayek spies a second dangerous illusion in the idea and idealization of society. The concept, Hayek says, is based on a false personification of a collection of individuals and a false animism in which "what has been brought about by the impersonal and spontaneous processes of the extended order" is imagined to be "the result of deliberate human creation."[21]

Both the personification and the animism generate the conceit that certain things are "of value to society" and ought to be supported by the state (legitimating its extended reach and coercive power), things that can be valued only by individuals or groups.[22] Personification and animism also lead to the belief that society is more than the effects of spontaneous processes and can therefore be manipulated or mobilized as a whole; this is the basis of totalitarianism.[23] And they lead to the belief that society is the product of design, improvable by a more rational design, one that would trammel the evolved traditions and freedoms that are the true basis of order, innovation, and progress.[24]

Above all, false personification and animism wrongly produce society as a tableau for justice. If society is imagined to exist apart from individuals, and if its order is thought to be the effect of deliberate construction, it follows that it ought to be designed by designers in a justice-minded way. This opens the door to unlimited state intervention in both markets and moral codes, which, Hayek argues, have "a peculiar self-accelerating tendency":

> The more dependent the position of the individuals or groups is seen to become on the actions of government, the more they will insist that the governments aim at some recognizable scheme of distributive justice; and the more governments try to realize some preconceived pattern of desirable distribution, the more they must subject the position of the different individuals and groups to their control. So long as the belief in "social justice" governs political action, this process must progressively approach nearer and nearer to a totalitarian system.[25]

Hayek's alternative to state-administered planning or justice is not, as is commonly said, free market capitalism. Rather, as chapter 3 will elaborate in more detail, morals and markets together generate the evolved and disciplined conduct to "create and sustain the extended order." Evolved conduct "stands between instinct and reason" and cannot be submitted to rational justification, even if it may be rationally reconstructed.[26] Although we can retrospectively articulate the function of both markets and morals, they are not the product of a functionalist design; indeed, their evolutionary emergence and inchoate operation are fundamental to Hayek: "If we stopped doing everything for which we do not know the reason, or for which we cannot provide a justification . . . we would probably very soon be dead."[27]

Markets and morals, then, are neither commensurate with nor opposed to reason, neither rational nor irrational. Rather, they endure and are valid because they arise "spontaneously," evolve and adapt "organically," knit human beings together independently of intentions, and establish rules of conduct without relying on state coercion or punishment. Both markets and moral tradition generate a dynamic, rather than static order and bring into being new human "powers that would otherwise not exist."[28] Both propagate felicitous conduct in large populations without relying on the overreach of human intention or the fallacies of human reason and without employing the powers of the state.

Markets and morals, for Hayek, also reveal the true nature of justice—its exclusive concern with conduct, rather than with effects or results. Justice is only about correct principles, universally applied, not conditions or states of affairs.[29] Justice also has nothing to do with rewarding effort or the deserving. Hayek even considers the Utilitarians erroneous in this regard, especially John Stuart Mill, whom he criticizes for writing that a just "society should treat all equally well who have deserved equally well of it."[30] Most significantly, he attacks Horatio Alger for popularizing the idea that capitalism's best defense is its rewards for the hard-working.[31] In fact, Hayek declares repeatedly, markets reward contributions, nothing more.[32] Such contributions, like wealth or innovation, may or may not be the fruit of great effort and, conversely, long and intense labors may come to little.[33] Hayek knows this may be disappointing, but claims it is not unjust—conflation of the one with the other is the great mistake of social democrats.

Traditional moral systems parallel markets in many ways, Hayek adds, especially in their provision of order without design and their location of justice in rules, rather than in outcomes. Moral traditions generate an "inherited system of value," which is "a device for coping with our constitutional ignorance," an ignorance comprising both the vast unknowability of the world and all the consequences of our actions.[34] If we knew everything, could anticipate all effects of action, and could agree "on the relative importance of . . . ends," Hayek says, "there would be no need for rules," including those of moral conduct.[35] Moral rules are ultimate values, then, not because they solve the problem of unknowable facts and unshared ends, but because they provide codes for action despite this problem—they are a peculiar kind of deference to unknowability. As such, however, they can only guide moral conduct; they cannot themselves generate a moral order. In the same way that effort may be incommensurate with reward in the economic domain, "moral conduct will not necessarily gratify moral desires" for particular outcomes.[36] This may seem woefully unfair and even unreasonable, just as repeatedly losing at a game of chance does.

"We understandably dislike morally blind results," Hayek writes of moral-economic arrangements generated by spontaneous order and protected from political interference, but they are the hard truth of free and progressive human history in a world where we are too ignorant to plot predictable collective outcomes or agree on common values. Moreover, "the fruitless attempt to render a situation just whose outcome, by its nature, cannot be determined by what anyone does or can know, only damages the functioning of the process itself."[37] And then, Hayek darts past the claim that the morally upright or the hard-working may not be rewarded for their virtue to declare that "inequality is essential to development" and "evolution cannot be just" in the popular sense of the word.[38] True justice requires that the rules of the game are universally known and applied, but every game has winners and losers, and civilization cannot evolve without leaving behind the effects of weakness and failure as well as chance. Thus, he describes the "game" that will advance civilization, satisfy wants, disperse information, feature liberty, and is wholly "undesigned' while still being capable of improvement:

> It proceeds, like all games, according to rules guiding the actions of individual participants whose aims, skills and knowledge are different, with the consequence that the outcome will be unpredictable and that there will regularly

be winners and losers. And while, as in a game, we are right in insisting that it be fair and that nobody cheat, it would be nonsensical to demand that the results for the different players be just. They will of necessity be determined partly by skill and partly by luck.[39]

Now we are in a position to understand what Hayek considers so dangerous about the "social justice warriors" who would remake the world according to a rational plan or grand moral calculus. They draw on the "fatal conceit" of society and wrongheaded principle of equality to attack the twin pillars of civilization, traditional morality and competitive markets. They are spirited by a form of social and intellectual primitivism that imagines a director behind "all self-ordering processes" and lacks the maturity to fathom historical evolution and social cooperation that exceed intentional design.[40] They are childlike as well in demanding equality of outcomes. They inappropriately submit morality to rational standards and conflate market and moral justice with outcomes, rather than rules. They intervene in markets in ways that damage innovation, development, and spontaneous order.[41] More than being merely misguided, social justice attacks the justice, freedom, and civilizational development secured by markets and morals. If belief in the social and political stewardship of society is what takes us down this path, then society must be dismantled.

In actually existing neoliberalism, this dismantling takes place on many fronts. Epistemologically, dismantling society involves denying its existence, as Thatcher did in the 1980s, or dismissing concern with inequality as "the politics of envy," a line presidential candidate Mitt Romney ran thirty years later and that is now a quotidian retort to proposals for taxing wealth.[42] Politically, it involves dismantling or privatizing the social state—welfare, education, parks, health, and services of all kinds. Legally, it involves wielding liberty claims to challenge equality and secularism along with environmental, health, safety, labor, and consumer protections. Ethically, it involves challenging social justice with the natural authority of traditional values. Culturally, it entails a version of what the ordoliberals termed "demassification," shoring up individuals and families against the forces of capitalism that threaten them.

This last turn, unfamiliar especially to Americans, requires brief elaboration. Ordoliberalism, known for its roots in the Freiburg School, featured a more overt constructivism—in the state, economy, and subject—than any other variety of neoliberalism. Demassification was among these constructivist projects: the aim was to challenge the process, believed by the ordoliberals to be inherent to capitalism, through which a population is generated that increasingly thinks and acts as a mass. Calling this process "proletarianization" (accepting much of Marx's historical account while opposing his political values and hopes), they viewed capitalism as generating a deindividualized and even deterritorialized social force likely to revolt against it with demands for a social state or socialist revolution. Ordoliberal demassification aimed at countering proletarianization by entrepreneurializing (hence reindividuating) workers, on the one hand, and regrounding workers in practices of familial self-provisioning on the other. Rerooting and self-provisioning, as Wilhelm Röpke referred to these practices and the policies that facilitated them, would develop a new "anthropological framework" to make workers "more resilient in the face of economic downturns."[43] "Anchored in community and family," they would be able to withstand what Röpke's colleague Alexander Rüstow termed the "cold society" of economic price and factor competitiveness.[44] This anchor also would prevent workers from "falling prey to the proletarian craze that asks for 'the rotten fruit of the welfare state.'"[45]

In the late twentieth century, "demassification" was replaced with neoliberal "entrepreneurialization" and "human capitalization" of subjects as political reforms aimed at transferring almost everything provided by the social state to individuals and families, strengthening them along the way.[46] Three important things happen by means of these strategies. First, entrepreneurialization, or what the French and British called "responsibilization," produces a subject that Foucault termed "a multitude of enterprises" or what, in its financialized form, Michel Feher calls a "portfolio of self-investments" designed to maintain or enhance human capital value.[47] (This portfolio includes child care, education, health, appearance, and old age provisions.) Second, substituting for Röpke's pastoral strategies for building resilience, in which urban households are meant to plant vegetable gardens and keep chickens, today's deproletarianized and deunionized workers enter the "sharing" and "contract" economy, where they transform their possessions, time, connections, and selves into sources of capitalization. By leasing out rooms on Airbnb, driving for Lyft or Uber, Task Rabbit freelancing, bike, tool, and car sharing, or simply managing a variety of part-time or short-term sources of income ("side hustles"), individuals and households aim to survive economic cutbacks and downturns. Third, as social investments in education, housing, health, child care, and social security are decreased, the family is retasked with providing for every kind of dependent—the young, the old, the infirm, the unemployed, the indebted student, or the depressed or addicted adult.[48]

In these three ways, not only did neoliberalism bring capitalism back from the brink when it was in crisis in the 1970s, neoliberalism rescued both the subject and the family from the disintegrating forces of late modernity. Indeed, the epistemological, political, economic, and cultural dismantling of mass society into human capital and moral-economic familial units, along with the resulting recuperation of both the individual and the family at the very moment of their seeming extinction, are among neoliberalism's most impressive achievements. Denaturalized to the core, the neoliberal versions of individual and family units may turn out to be stronger than any previous iterations.

Hayek Today: Freedom and the Social

If Hayek's critique of social justice was iconoclastic in the postwar decades, it has become the common sense of a robust neoliberal conservatism today. In April 2018, Housing and Urban Development Secretary Ben Carson refused to enforce the 1968 Fair Housing Act, decrying it as "social engineering." In its original design, the act indeed sought to remedy decades of redlining by lenders, as well as other forms of race discrimination and segregation in home sales, rentals, and public and private financing.[49] That same spring, Canadian Prime Minister Justin Trudeau was also rebuked for "social engineering," in this case for issuing a requirement that the police and military eliminate barriers to women in their ranks and that government offices use gender-neutral language in addressing clients.[50] The attacks on "social justice warriors"— that is, anyone who challenges exclusionary norms and stratifying distributions—that are ubiquitous on the Right today serve to buttress nativist, supremacist, and nationalist claims about "who built the West" and to whom it belongs.[51]

The neoliberal assault on the social, together with its exclusive identification of power with coercion, enacted a consequential reformatting of liberalism. As it saturated state and popular discourse, the neoliberal attack on social justice, social reform, and social provision challenged equality, reframed the culture wars, and produced massive disorientation for the Left. If there is no such thing as society, but only individuals and families oriented by markets and morals, then there is no such thing as social power generating hierarchies, exclusion, and violence, let alone subjectivity at the sites of class, gender, or race. Outside of a neoliberal frame, of course, the language of the social is what makes inequalities manifest; the domain of the social is where subjections, abjections, and exclusions are lived, identified, protested, and potentially rectified. Outside of a neoliberal frame, social power rests in what Marx identified as relations of exploitation and domination, what Foucault identified as forces of subjectification and social construction, or what critical race, feminist, and queer theorists identify as grammars of subordination and abjection. As every serious student of inequality knows, the social is a vital domain of justice because it is where the potted histories and hierarchies of a particular region, nation, or civilization are reproduced. Appreciation of social powers is the only way to understand "taking a knee" or the claim that black lives matter, the high suicide rates among queer teens or women working more for less. Moreover, the social is what binds us in ways that exceed personal ties, market exchange, or abstract citizenship. It is where we, as individuals or a nation, practice or fail to practice justice, decency, civility, and care beyond the codes of market instrumentalism and familialism. And it is where political equality, essential to democracy, is made or unmade.

When neoliberal rationality succeeds in disappearing social powers, critical claims rooted in them are nothing more than the baseless whining of "snowflakes." At the same time, neoliberalism's reduction of unfreedom to coercion casts principles (and laws based on them) of equality and inclusion as tyrannical political correctness. Thus, today we have a liberalism that disavows structural powers of domination—"if women want to be engineers and Latinos want to be philosophers, nothing and no one is stopping them!"—and spotlights as distortions of the spontaneous workings of markets and morals all efforts to generate equitable and inclusive environments. The logical consistency rests in the assumption that power is limited to coercion and that freedom is equivalent to the absence of law and its dictates.

In short, as neoliberal reason became ascendant, the attack on the social—on its very existence and its appropriateness as a province of justice—has been as consequential as more familiar facets of neoliberalism (e.g., antistatism) for building corporate power, legitimating inequality, and unleashing a novel, disinhibited attack on the most vulnerable members of society. On the one hand, delegitimizing concerns with equality apart from formal legal equality and concerns with power apart from explicit coercion provided this new meaning and practice of freedom with the exclusive mantle of right. This freedom doesn't simply trump other political principles; it is all there is. On the other hand, freedom dirempted from the social becomes not just unlimited, but legitimately exercised without concern for social context or consequences, without restraint, civility, or care for society as a whole or individuals within it. When the claim "society does not exist" becomes common sense, it renders invisible the social norms and inequalities generated by legacies of slavery, colonialism, and patriarchy. It permits the effective political disenfranchisement (and not only the suffering) produced by homelessness, lack of health care, and lack of education. And it permits assaults on whatever remains of the social fabric in the name of freedom.

This is the neoliberal reasoning that frames the contemporary right-wing attack on American universities concerning speakers, speech codes, curricula, hiring and admissions, codes of conduct, and more. As the Left struggles to articulate the various powers generating differentially constructed and positioned social subjects, the Right overwhelms this struggle with a discourse reducing freedom to censorship and coercion. As the Left seeks to make visible the complex histories and social forces reproducing white male superordination and hegemony, the Right mocks social engineering, groupthink, and the injection of social justice into a space properly organized by (the presumptively norm-free) selection for excellence, on the one hand, and "viewpoint diversity," on the other.[52]

The university is far from the only place where the Right gains a strategic edge through neoliberal reason's relentless delegitimation of the concepts of the social and society. Consider the controversy that broke out in fall 2017 after Google software engineer James Damore circulated a memo arguing that "personality differences" explain why so few women held engineering and leadership positions at the company.[53] Given immutable differences emanating from biological sex "everywhere in the world," Damore wrote, Google's efforts to recruit and promote more women in those fields were wrongheaded—"unfair, divisive and bad for business."[54] Immediately fired by Google for violating company rules about "advancing gender stereotypes," Damore sued and also became a cause célèbre on the Right—but not just for what he wrote or the price he paid for it. Rather, the claim of being first shamed and then terminated for his views made him an icon of freedom in a "culture built to suppress it."[55] The Right applauded his rejection of social explanations for inequality; it celebrated his insistence that the prevalence of men in tech and the upper echelons of business is rooted in nature and confirmed by the market; it promoted his belief that egalitarian policies trammel justice, social cohesion, and economic development; and it amplified his living testimony about an allegedly totalitarian Left pushing conformist, coercive, and censorious views and policies.

In short, the neoliberal critique of society and social justice in the name of freedom and traditional moral norms has become the common sense of a robust neoliberal culture today. At its extreme, it is the Alt-Right "red pill" ideology; in its more moderate form, it is the conviction that life is determined by genetics, personal responsibility, and market competition. Within this common sense, the social is the enemy of freedom, while "SJWs" are the enemies of a free people. However, as we have seen, the attack on the social—its existence and its appropriateness as a provenance of justice—also disinhibits the freedom identified with neoliberalism, converting it from mere moral libertarianism to an aggressive attack on democracy. It licenses freedom's exercise without concern for social context or consequences, without care for society, civility, or social bonds, and above all without concern for the political cultivation of a common good. Thus, the claim that "there is no such thing as society" does far more than challenge social democracy and welfare states as forms of market interference that create "dependency" and wrongful "entitlement." It does more than propagate the notion that taxes are theft, rather than the material by which common life and public things are sustained.[56] It does more than blame the poor for their condition or the "nature" of minorities and women of all races for their tiny numbers in elite professions and positions. Freedom without society destroys the lexicon by which freedom is made democratic, paired with social consciousness, and nested in political equality. Freedom without society is a pure instrument of power, shorn of concern for others, the world, or the future.

Reducing freedom to unregulated personal license in the context of disavowing the social and dismantling society does something else. It anoints as free expression every historically and politically generated sentiment of (lost) entitlement based in whiteness, maleness, or nativism while denying these to be socially produced, releasing them from any connection to social conscience, compromise, or consequence. Lost entitlement to the privileges of whiteness, maleness, and nativism is then easily converted into righteous rage against the social inclusion and political equality of the historically excluded. This rage in turn becomes the consummate expression of freedom and Americanness, or freedom and Europeanness, or freedom and the West. With equality and social solidarity discredited and the existence of powers reproducing historical inequalities, abjections, and exclusions denied, white male supremacism thus gains a novel voice and legitimacy in the twenty-first century.

Now we are in a position to grasp how Nazis, Klansmen, and other white nationalists gather publicly in "free speech rallies," why an authoritarian white male supremacist in the White House is identified with freedom by his supporters because of his "political incorrectness," and how decades of policies and principles of social inclusion, antidiscrimination, and racial, sexual, and gender equality come to be tarred as tyrannical norms and rules imposed by left-wing mobs. What happens when freedom is reduced to naked assertions of power and entitlement, while the very idea of society is disavowed, equality is disparaged, and democracy is thinned to liberal privatism? It is not simply that social justice becomes demeaned. Crude and provocative expressions of supremacism become expressions of liberty that the First Amendment was ostensibly written to protect—except it wasn't. The First Amendment was a promise to democratic citizens that they would be unmolested by the state in their individual conscience, faith, and political voice. It was not a promise to protect vicious attacks on other human beings or groups, any more than it was a promise to submit the nation to a corporacracy or Christian theocracy. But as chapters 4 and 5 will argue in more detail, a neoliberal culture of unsocial liberty paves the way for both.

Hannah Arendt Didn't Help

Critiques of the concept of society and the social have hailed from other quarters than Hayek and the neoliberals, none more notorious in political theory than Hannah Arendt's. We will only tarry briefly here, because our concern is not with this problem in political theory, but with the coordinates of contemporary political powers and discourse. We live in neo-Hayekian times and have never lived in Arendtian ones. Still, a note on Arendt is worthwhile both because of her peculiarly wide influence on Left political philosophers and because Arendt's antipathy to the social matches Hayek's in intensity, if not content. For Hayek, the social does not exist; for Arendt, its bloated modern development has destroyed the quintessential human capacities for freedom and action in the public sphere.

Arendt's tirade against the social in *The Human Condition* is well known: neither private nor public, she argues, the social's rise and valorization in modernity reduces politics to welfare concerns and generates polities on the model of giant households provisioning human needs. In social democracies and socialism, humans are reduced to workers and consumers, creatures of necessity rather than freedom. The casualty is not only a nobler form of political life and a protected sphere of privacy, but our very species distinctiveness as beings of action and intellection. In *The Human Condition*, there is almost nothing wrong with modernity that Arendt does not lay at the feet of the overtaking of everything by the social: inauthenticity as well as conformism; action replaced by behavior and epic narrative replaced by statistics;[57] the disappearance of a realm whose coordinates were risk and distinction in favor of one of equality and mediocrity;[58] political rule as a unique form of human achievement trammeled by the rise of "rule by nobody" in markets and bureaucracies; public life as a domain of *arête* and *virtu* replaced by society centered on work, "the one activity necessary to sustain life" that was formerly hidden away in the household as shameful;[59] and citizenship allocated only to the free and oriented entirely to self-rule disappearing into slavish crowds carrying "an irresistible instinct toward despotism."[60]

For all of her opprobrium directed toward the social in *The Human Condition*, however, Arendt's fiercest condemnation of the freedom-and-politics-destroying features of the social appears in *On Revolution*. Among the political revolutions ushering in modernity, she argues, only the American Revolution realized its emancipatory promise. Why? The American Revolution alone avoided "the social question in the form of the terrifying predicament of mass poverty."[61] The French Revolution, by contrast, was destroyed when the cry for freedom was replaced by the demands of the poor for bread, demands that flooded the political realm with bodies and their needs and brought about the Terror.

> When [the multitude] appeared on the scene of politics, necessity appeared with them, and the result was that the power of the old regime became impotent and the new republic was stillborn; freedom had to be surrendered to necessity, to the urgency of the life process itself. . . . It was necessity, the urgent needs of the people, that unleashed the terror and sent the Revolution to its doom . . . the revolution had changed its direction; it aimed no longer at freedom, the goal of the revolution had become the happiness of the people.[62]

Why is the struggle against want antipathetic to the revolutionary desire for emancipation? Why do needs cancel freedom? Arendt writes:

> Poverty is more than deprivation, it is a state of constant want and acute misery whose ignominy consists in its dehumanizing force; poverty is abject because it puts men under the absolute dictate of their bodies, that is, under the absolute dictate of necessity as all men know it from their most intimate experience outside all speculations. It was under the absolute dictate of necessity that the multitude rushed to the assistance of the French Revolution, inspired it, drove it onward, and eventually sent it to its doom, for this was the multitude of the poor. When they appeared on the scene of

politics, necessity appeared with them, and the result was that the power of the old regime became impotent and the new republic was stillborn; freedom had to be surrendered to necessity, to the urgency of the life process itself.[63]

Arendt's critique of the social differs significantly from Hayek's. Modernity's most damaging bequest to political life, society is the theater for production, welfare, needs, and satisfactions, rather than action, deeds, and immortality. For Hayek, society is the product of hubristic do-gooders, rationalists, and despots, those with ambitions to design and direct society, rather than honor the freedom and tradition that permit its spontaneous order and evolution. Arendt wants to save political life from the encroachment of bodies and needs, economics and behaviorism, which is worlds apart from Hayek's desire to save markets and morals from social justice schemes. Arendt idealizes deliberate action in the public sphere; Hayek idealizes morally disciplined individuals tending their own interests. Arendt worries that freedom has been lost to behavior; Hayek worries about its restriction by state power and dissolution in political cultures of dependence. For Hayek, the social is a toxic fiction animating the freedom-destroying monster of an invasive state. For Arendt, the social itself is the devouring force, one Hanna Pitkin compares to the figure of "an evil monster . . . intent on debilitating, absorbing, and ultimately destroying us, gobbling up our distinct individuality and turning us into robots that mechanically serve its purposes."[64]

Yet for all of their differences, something connects the hatred of the social shared by Arendt and Hayek, something beyond their alertness to the emergence of fascism from projects of national socialism and repressive state regimes from proletarian revolutions. Both Arendt and Hayek revile states dedicated to provisioning human needs and revile political life, including democracy, addressed to human welfare. Both dread the conquest or occupation of the political by the demands of the teeming masses, demands they view as imperiling freedom and even civilization. Above all, both reject the Left's critical understanding of the social as the essential modern site of emancipation, justice, and democracy. For both, freedom meets its death in the rise of the social. Social democracy and state communism are thus but points on a spectrum of what Tocqueville termed the "regulated, mild, and peaceful servitude" resulting from an administrative statism tending the needs and sculpting the aims of a people. Though Hayek affirms ontological individualism and liberal privatism and Arendt dreams of citizens "acting in concert" to make a world in common, they nonetheless share a conviction that the social question has overtaken modern political life and society has overtaken the individual. Freedom rests in demonizing and ultimately vanquishing the social. Society must be dismantled.

Losing the Political Imaginary of the Social

This chapter began by reflecting on the social as the foundation of democracy, the centrality of equality to any concept and practice of democratic politics, and why social justice is therefore important to generating and protecting democratic practices and institutions. It concludes by reflecting on why the social matters for generating and protecting a democratic imaginary.

In *Land and Sea*, Carl Schmitt writes, "every ordering of human affairs also materializes in an ordering of space. Consequently, revolutions of human societies always also involve alteration of our conceptions of space."[65] Schmitt develops this point differently in *Nomos of the Earth*, where he says, "every new age and every new epoch in the coexistence of peoples . . . and power formations of every sort, is founded on new spatial divisions, new enclosures, and new spatial orders of the earth."[66] In both texts, Schmitt is referring to physical, geopolitical space— annexations, subdivisions, the loss of coastlines, or even dissolutions of nations or inventions of new ones—the kinds of reorganization that often precipitate and follow wars. However, his point bears on nonliteral and even deterritorialized spatialization, such as the neoliberal dismantling and disintegration of the social.

Schmitt reminds us that space is not just an architecture for power, but the scene of political imagination and imaginaries. Human orderings of space and the meanings attributed to those orderings shape our conceptualizations of who and what we are, especially in life with others. These orderings may foreground hemispheric locations or topographical features: a nation loses its sea in postwar settlements, a dam changes a river to a lake, a neighborhood is cleaved by the building of a highway or a wall. But they also feature designations of public and private space, gendered space, racialized space, and more. We know this from protests in everything from Little Rock to Gezi Park, from the privatization of public lands to struggles over gentrification and gender-neutral bathrooms. We do not just live in marked territories, but also develop political imaginaries of the common (or lack of it) from spatial semiotics.

Alexander Somek draws a second insight from Schmitt's *Land and Sea*. This is the link Schmitt establishes between spatial orders and eschatological views. Somek writes, "Schmitt makes us realise . . . that alterations of the order of space also engage . . . the spatial dimension along which we imagine better worlds to arise in the future."[67] Simply put, we envision possible futures from and in terms of spatial orders of our present, especially in terms of their divisions and coordinates.[68] This insight is significant in considering the implications of dismantling society and producing in its stead an engorged sphere of traditional morality and an expanded operation of markets. As the social vanishes from our ideas, speech, and experience, it vanishes from our visions of the future, both utopian and dystopian. We imagine authoritarian nationalist futures, virtually networked futures, technocratic futures, anarchist futures, transnational cosmopolitan futures, and fascist futures. We speak in vague terms of the "multitude" or "the commons," absent the concrete democratization of the powers they harbor and by which they would be stewarded. None of these aim to invent twenty-first-century possibilities for democratic rule achieved and supported in part by democratizing social power. None work at the site of social power, even as such power continues to generate domination, stratification, exploitation, exclusion, and abjection. And none gather us as a society to deliberate about and rule society in common. The precise language is fungible—"the social" and "society" are hardly the only terms that can capture these powers and this gathering. However, something must approximate them to build the political equality required by democratic aspirations. It is a sign of the triumph of neoliberal reason that, in recent decades, the grammar of the social, including its importance to democracy, largely vanished from Left (and not only Right) visions for the future. In the United States, Occupy Wall Street may be credited with pushing it back into public discourse. More recently, new notions of socialism and projects such as the Green New Deal have been mobilized to call for political stewardship of social welfare, broadly conceived. Still broken, and absent from these important discourses of rebellion against neoliberalism's aim to vanquish society and the social, is the relation of the social to democratic rule.

2

Politics Must Be Dethroned

Today the only holders of power unbridled by any law which binds them and who are driven by the political necessities of a self-willed machine are the so-called legislators. But this prevailing form of democracy is ultimately self-destructive, because it imposes upon governments tasks on which an agreed opinion of the majority does not and cannot exist. It is therefore necessary to restrain these powers in order to protect democracy against itself.
—Friedrich Hayek, "The Dethronement of Politics"

"THE POLITICAL" is a twentieth-century coinage spurred by the work of Max Weber and differently inflected by Carl Schmitt, Hannah Arendt, Claude Lefort, Paul Ricoeur, Sheldon Wolin, and Ernesto Laclau and Chantal Mouffe.[1] These differences will not be examined here, nor will we dwell on the possibility that the extensive thematization of "the political" in the twentieth century is a case of the owl of Minerva flying at dusk, although that is what Arendt tacitly argued and Schmitt feared.[2] However, our focus is on the importance of the term for thinking about neoliberalism's production of the present.

Differentiated from politics, the political does not refer mainly to explicit institutions or practices, is not coterminous with states, and does not reduce to the particulars of political power or political order. Rather, the political identifies a theater of deliberations, powers, actions, and values where common existence is thought, shaped, and governed. The political is inescapably concerned with plotting coordinates of justice and order, but also with security, ecology, exigency, and emergency. Distinctive forms of power—whether legal or decisionist, shared or autocratic, rogue or legitimate and accountable—are the signatures of the political, but it is specific forms of reason that give it shape in any time and place. The powers of the political are generated by the (bare) community that it convenes, but not in the methodical, traceable fashion that labor is thought by Marxists to generate surplus value.[3] Nor are we talking about superstructure; the political is not a mere reflection of social powers, a stage on which "the real struggles" of civil society are played out.[4] Rather, political power always materializes and is given shape by a distinct rationality, a form of reason and its occlusions, a set of norms and its generative effects. As Michel Foucault reminds us, power is neither independent of the construction of truth nor assimilable to truth, and political power is no exception.[5]

Pace Schmitt and Arendt, the political neither bears ontological fundamentals nor historically unchanging characteristics and coordinates. It is not autonomous of other domains or powers; rather, porous, impure, and unbounded, it is suffused with economic, social, cultural, and religious forces and values. Still, the political is singular in directing the fate, even the life and death, of large-scale human and nonhuman worlds. It is also a distinctive domicile of meaning for a people, generating individual and collective identity vis-à-vis others. Above all, the political alone holds the possibility of democracy, understood as rule by the people.[6] Democracy without the political is an oxymoron; the sharing of power that democracy entails is a uniquely political project requiring cultivation, renewal, and institutional support. Democracy's legitimacy is drawn from exclusively political vocabularies and ordinances.

Neoliberal thinkers regarded the political with wariness, and as we will consider in depth shortly, were openly hostile to both its sovereign and democratic variant. Neoliberalism thus aims at limiting and containing the political, detaching it from sovereignty, eliminating its democratic form, and starving its democratic energies. From its "postideological" aspirations and affirmation of technocracy to its economization and privatization of government activities, from its unbridled opposition to egalitarian "statism" to its attempted delegitimation and containment of democratic claims, from its aim to restrict the franchise to its aim to limit sharply certain kinds of statism, neoliberalism seeks to both constrict and dedemocratize the political.[7] To this end, neoliberals forwarded depoliticized states and supranational institutions, laws that would "encase and protect the space of the world economy," governance modeled on business principles, and subjects oriented by interest and disciplined by markets and morals.[8]

Management, law, and technocracy in place of democratic deliberation, contestation, and power sharing: several decades of this multifaceted hostility to democratic political life has generated in neoliberalized populations, at best, widespread disorientation about the value of democracy and at worst opprobrium toward it. Yet because the political has been disparaged and attacked, but not extinguished while democracy itself has been thinned and devalued, undemocratic and antidemocratic political powers and energies in neoliberalized orders have swollen in magnitude and intensity. Thus have neoliberal effects such as growing inequality and insecurity generated angry right-wing populisms and political demagogues in power that do not comport with neoliberal dreams of pacified, orderly citizenries, denationalized economies, lean, strong states, and international institutions focused on facilitating capital accumulation and stabilizing competition.[9]

There is, on the one hand, an obviousness to the claim that the neoliberal attack on political life contributed to today's antidemocratic rebellions. Neoliberal policy aims to loosen political control over economic actors and markets, replacing regulation and redistribution with market freedom and uncompromised ownership rights. The Reagan-Thatcher years were shaped by the refrain that "government is the problem, not the solution" to economic as well as social problems, a refrain that became the pretext for tax cuts, dismantling the welfare state, and unchaining capital from every kind of restriction, including that imposed by union bargaining power. The challenge to political control went further, however, to dedemocratize the political culture and the subjects within it. In the 2000 U.S. presidential election, George W. Bush became an icon of this process as the first MBA ever to assume presidential office.[10] Another icon emerged during the 2016 campaign of a real estate developer who parlayed his *lack* of political knowledge and experience into a reason to make him president. Donald Trump's declared war on the "Washington swamp" and promise to bring business principles and "the art of the deal" into the Oval Office were complemented by the ambition of his chief henchman, Steve Bannon, to "deconstruct the administrative state" and by the privatizing agendas of his cabinet appointees, many of whom also had little or no political experience before assuming leaderships of government agencies.[11] Neoliberal demonization of "statism" also provided grounds for otherwise unlikely alliances between economic libertarians, plutocrats, armed right-wing anarchists, Klan vigilantes, zealous pro-lifers, and homeschoolers.[12] In short, as the principle of "getting government off our backs" morphed into a generalized animosity toward the political, it animated a movement affirming authoritarian liberalism in some domains and authoritarian moralism in others. This would be the quick account of how we get from neoliberalism to the present.

On the other hand, there is much that does not line up in the argument that neoliberal antipolitics spawned the swell of antidemocratic authoritarianism across the Euro-Atlantic. How, precisely, are popular attraction to political strongmen and the clamor for law-and-order states born of a rationality that figures concentrated political power as the supreme danger to markets and liberty? Doesn't growing ultranationalism signal a radical break with neoliberalism? Isn't that why so many pundits heard neoliberalism's death knell in Brexit, Trump's election, and the rise of the nationalist Right in Europe?[13] And how to square the intense political polarization of our times with an antipolitical and antidemocratic governing rationality?

To appreciate how neoliberal political reason contributed to the rise of the antidemocratic right, we have to examine more closely its assault on the democratic form of the political. What are the precise contents of neoliberalism's wariness about the political and hostility to democracy? Is its core objection to political power as such, to expansive statism, to sovereignty, to democracy, or all of the above?[14] Is neoliberalism mainly concerned with containing the powers of nation-states in order to build those of supranational federations and institutions organizing global capitalism, as Quinn Slobodian argues?[15] Or is its opposition to the political deeper, rooted in concerns with elevating other domains and powers—tradition, markets, morality, but also perhaps science and technique?[16] How does it enact its opposition to political power and especially democratic political power? What blindnesses and unintentional effects might its aversion to political power and dynamics introduce into its own project? How does it end up yielding plutocratic and fascistic forces that it aimed to fence out and the politicized mass affect that it aimed to still? What does it politicize or depoliticize, intentionally or inadvertently, such that rancorous populist rage becomes one of its spawn? What other forces intersect neoliberal rationality—gendered and racial orders within the West, the imperial-colonial imaginary constitutive of the West, nihilism, deracination, desublimation—that yield formations actively dreaded by the founding neoliberal intellectuals and that they aimed to prevent with their novel reformatting of liberalism and capitalism?

Neoliberal Antipolitics

The neoliberal intellectuals differed in their antagonism to the political, especially in their efforts to reset the state-economy relation and limit democracy. Milton Friedman and Friedrich Hayek cast the political as a dangerously self-expanding domain that had to be tightly bound and conformed to neoliberal purposes. The ordoliberals drew closer to Carl Schmitt, seeking to build the strong state required for economic order and stability while giving it a technocratic form and insulating it from democratic demands. We will explore some of these specifics shortly. What makes it possible to draw them together is that each and all regarded individual liberties and markets, along with traditional morality, as endangered by the coercive, unruly, and arbitrary interests and powers harbored by the political. They also all objected to the platform that the political provides for market-distorting interests, whether those of big capital, democratic majorities, the poor, or those advancing notions of the common good. They objected to politically designed societies, hence to most public policy and public goods.[17] Thus, they all sought to radically contain political powers by submitting politics to economic coordinates and metrics, on the one hand, and by yoking it to the requirements of markets, on the other. Economization of its fabric and subordination of its powers to the economy would together still its dangers.

Above all, the neoliberals united in opposing robust democracy—social movements, direct political participation, or democratic demands on the state—which they identified with totalitarianism, fascism, or rule by mobs. To this end, Hayek challenged popular sovereignty as incoherent and the very notion of political sovereignty as inappropriate to free societies. James Buchanan of the Virginia Public Choice School of neoliberalism decried public goods, and especially public higher education, for generating "too much democracy." Buchanan aimed to strengthen (Southern) "states' rights" against federal equality and antidiscrimination mandates and proposed writing "balanced budgets" into the American Constitution to rebuff permanently democratic demands for a social state.[18] He argued forthrightly for curtailing "democratic excesses," understood the importance of gerrymandering and voter suppression, and alloyed his brand of free enterprise with the project of white supremacism. The ordoliberals sought essentially to replace democracy with technocracy and a strong, autonomous state. Several schools of neoliberalism affirmed "liberal dictatorship" as a legitimate transitional regime from "totalitarian democracy" (social democracy) to freedom. However, neoliberalism's attack on democracy is often less bold. It involves altering democracy's meanings, reducing it to a "method" of setting rules, rather than a form of rule, curtailing its purview, or detaching it from governing.

Throttling democracy was fundamental, not incidental, to the broader neoliberal program. Democratic energies, the neoliberals believed, inherently engorge the political, which threatens freedom, spontaneous order, and development and at the extreme yields state despotism or totalitarianism. Even ordinary rule by democratic majorities yields a redistributive, administrative, overreaching state, and robust democratic activism both challenges moral authority and disrupts order from below. The exceptionally thin version of democracy that neoliberalism tolerates is thus detached from political freedom, political equality, and power sharing by citizens, from legislation aimed at the common good, from any notion of a public interest exceeding protection of individual liberties and security, and from cultures of participation.[19]

Of course, no neoliberal intellectual sought a weak state. Rather, the twin aim was to limit the purview and sharply focus the work of the state.[20] While the classical liberal state drew on the economic model of laissez-faire and the political model of the "night watchman," the neoliberals sought to build, consolidate *and* bound a unified, strong state, one they understood political sovereignty to unbind, democracy to disorient and divide, and bureaucracy to deplete. The neoliberal state had to be lean, nonsovereign, and laser focused, insulated from vested interests, pluralist compromise, and the demands of the masses.[21] The incompatibilities of representative democracy with such a state are many. Logrolling, rent seeking, and other self-serving conduct by powerful interests are obvious. The most serious problem, however, is posed by the laboring and the poor, given their inevitable demand that the social question be addressed with a social state.[22] Notwithstanding their differences, the neoliberals converged in recognizing that representative democracy based on universal suffrage in large capitalist nation-states would inevitably be controlled by the numerically largest class, making social democracy, with its tendentially totalitarian trajectory, inevitable. Unless they are tricked, trained, or effectively disenfranchised, the workers and poor will always fight markets as unfair in their distribution of opportunities and rewards.

This class can be tricked, however, with appeals to other lines of privilege and power, such as whiteness or masculinity, especially since liberty, rather than equality reproduces and secures those powers. It can be trained to accept TINA ("there is no alternative") as a reality principle, such that the policies through which neoliberal rationality guides the conduct of the subject become unchallengeable. It can be disenfranchised through voter suppression, gerrymandering, bought elections and legislation, and other ways of insulating legislative power from democratic will or accountability. That each of these has been an important part of the American political landscape during the neoliberal decades helps explain why and how neoliberal reason gained its grip so easily without an overt assault on representative democracy.

In both neoliberal thought and practice, the critique of democracy and of the political is masked as a brief for individual liberty, especially by Friedman and Hayek. Curtailing the reach of political power in the name of freedom justifies repealing the regulatory state (while making the state itself the subject of regulation) and limiting the political voice of the people. Friedman offers this program in the most familiar libertarian frame, Hayek is most attuned to the complexities of checking political power, and the ordoliberals are most forthright in divesting democracy from a state bound by the device they name an "economic constitution." Each is content with voting and personal freedoms constituting the extent of democracy and, whether in the breach or as a norm, each endorses authoritarian liberalism—undemocratic political power subtending private freedoms. Let us now consider the thought of each more closely.

Milton Friedman

Of the founding neoliberal intellectuals, Milton Friedman alone advances the cause of neoliberal economics through "democracy," loosely defined as "political freedom" or "individual freedom."[23] *Capitalism and Freedom* is dedicated to establishing the incoherence of democratic socialism and social democracy: "there is an intimate connection between economics and politics . . . only certain combinations of political and economic arrangements are possible, and . . . a society which is socialist cannot also be democratic, in the sense of guaranteeing individual freedom."[24] Friedman's argument about the codependence of economic and political freedom depends on both synergy and similarity. Historically, he insists, true political freedom was born only with capitalism, and the two kinds of freedom are almost always conjoined.[25] Moreover, if a society features only one of the two, that one will incite or secure the other in time.[26] Logically, his claim rests on the fact that free markets ("competitive capitalism") require limited government and the sharp separation of economic from political power, which "in this way enables the one" form of power "to offset the other."[27] Capitalism, in this account, inadvertently promotes freedom by limiting and restraining government.

However, much more than the size and reach of government is at stake here. For Friedman, any kind of exercise of political power, including that of popular majorities, threatens freedom in both economic and political life. For this reason, he opposes almost all democratically enacted legislation. Why? For Friedman, the twin danger posed by the exercise of political power pertains to its inherent concentration (markets, by contrast, naturally disperse power) and fundamental reliance on coercion (which markets eschew for choice). In addition, political power requires or enforces conformity, while the market "permits wide diversity"—rather than submitting to the majority, "each man can vote, as it were, for the color of tie he wants and get it."[28]

Acknowledging that some measure of political power is required to secure societies and establish both "rules of the game" and umpirage for markets (property and contract law, monetary policy, etc.), for Friedman, all political mandates are simple subtractions from freedom. "The fundamental threat to freedom is power to coerce, be it in the hands of a monarch, a dictator, an oligarchy, or a momentary majority."[29] Even democratic legislation compromises freedom as it imposes the will of the majority on minorities. Markets, by contrast, always allow individual preferences to prevail, the equivalent of getting whatever one votes for. At the same time, markets "remove the organization of economic activity from the control of political authority," enabling "economic strength to be a check to political power rather than a reinforcement."[30]

Friedman comes closer to pure libertarianism than the other original neoliberals do. That said, he articulates clearly their shared ideal of separating economic and political power, even while affirming the importance of the state in facilitating the conditions for markets. He also joins them in identifying political life exclusively with coercion and in reducing the meaning of freedom to coercion's absence. This discredits any form of robust democracy, and not just social democracy. On the other hand, Friedman joins his compatriots in legitimizing political authoritarianism to forge liberalized markets, such as the regimes installed in post-Allende Chile and post-Saddam Iraq.[31] As we will see, by tarnishing "democracy" with an image of majoritarian coercion, on the one hand, and by distinguishing the importance of state power for stabilizing markets from the question of personal freedom, on the other, Friedman, like Hayek, eliminates altogether the worth of democratized political power.

Friedrich Hayek

The effective limitation of power is the most important problem of social order. Government is indispensable for the formation of such an order only to protect all against coercion and violence from others. But as soon as, to achieve this, government successfully claims the monopoly of coercion and violence, it becomes also the chief threat to individual freedom. To limit this power was the great aim of the founders of constitutional government in the seventeenth and eighteenth centuries. But the endeavor to contain the powers of government was almost inadvertently abandoned when it came to be mistakenly believed that democratic control of the exercise of power provided a sufficient safeguard against its excessive growth.

—Friedrich Hayek, *Law, Legislation, and Liberty, Volume 3*

Hayek's critique of Jean-Jacques Rousseau is even more scathing than his critique of Keynes and Marx. For Hayek, *The Social Contract* contains every principle responsible for deluding moderns about the nature of freedom and government—it wrenches democracy away from liberalism, embeds it in popular sovereignty, and glorifies the state. With the device of the general will, Rousseau also unbounds legislative power, regardless of how dangerous or discordant with justice legislative actions might be.

Hayek favors what he terms the "empirical and unsystematic British tradition" of modern political thought (comprising Burke as well as Locke and the Scottish Enlightenment) and loathes the Continental tradition. He describes the former as based on "an interpretation of traditions and institutions which had spontaneously grown up" and the latter as scurrilously speculative, rationalist, romantic, and utopian.[32] In his time, he says, this opposition appears as the opposition between "liberal democracy" and "social or totalitarian democracy."[33] Hayek then quotes approvingly from Jacob Talmon's *Origins of Totalitarian Democracy*: one tradition "finds the essence of freedom in spontaneity and the absence of coercion, the other believes it to be realized only in the pursuit and attainment of an absolute collective purpose. . . . One stands for organic, slow, half-conscious growth, the other for doctrinaire deliberateness; one for trial and error procedure, the other for an enforced solely valid pattern."[34] For Hayek, everything wrong with republican democracy and social democracy, not to mention socialism and communism, is compressed into Talmon's indictment. The sins of the Continental tradition include doctrinalism, rationalism, and deliberate imposition of a plan and collective purpose, which together stifle organicism, spontaneous development, tradition, and individual liberty. The cardinal sin of the Continental tradition, however, is its worship of popular sovereignty, a concept, like society, that Hayek calls a dangerous "nonsense notion."

Popular sovereignty threatens individual freedom, licenses unbounded government, and confers supremacy on precisely the domain that needs to be leashed, the political.[35] It permits legislative power to run amok, exceeding its task of formulating universal rules of justice, inevitably expanding the powers of the administrative state as it does so.[36] Given the mantle of popular sovereignty, legislatures take promoting "the public interest" as their mandate. This dedication to the public interest (yet another "nonsense notion," according to Hayek) both engorges the state and makes bribes and deal making a quotidian part of legislative culture. Thus does the supposed icon of democracy, an elected law-making body, invert into its opposite, governing by special interests and corruption.[37] Finally, as legislative practice that exceeds universal rule making expands state power and curtails freedom, justice itself becomes confused. We mistakenly call "just," Hayek says, whatever lawmakers do, or whatever we think they should do, rather than reserving the term for what the ancient Greeks called *isonomía*, "equal law for all."[38]

Such is the avalanche that results from popular sovereignty: it unbinds the legislature from limits and justice, ceaselessly expands state power, and sets loose corrupting interests and practices in government. To prevent this disaster, Hayek would place radical limits on the political, above all by divesting liberal democracy of sovereignty *en toto*. The error of popular sovereignty, he writes, "lies not in the belief that whatever power there is should be in the hands of the people, and that their wishes will have to be expressed by majority decisions, but in the belief that this ultimate source of power must be unlimited, that is, *the idea of sovereignty itself*."[39] Sovereignty, by nature unlimited, is flatly incompatible with limited government and "the dethronement of politics," both of which are necessary for a flourishing economic and moral order. Moreover, the very notion of sovereignty rests on a "false constructivist interpretation of the formation of human institutions which attempts to trace them all to an original designer or some other deliberate act of will."[40] Thus, Hayek concurs with Schmitt that sovereignty is a secularized theological concept, but, unlike Schmitt, regards sovereignty as false and dangerous *because* it is theological. For Hayek, political institutions do not emerge from acts of will, but from "the existence among the people of certain opinions of what is right and wrong."[41] He adds, "since all power rests on pre-existing opinions, and will last only so long as those opinions prevail, there is no real personal source of this power and no deliberate will which has created it. The conception of sovereignty rests on a misleading logical construction."[42]

Put another way, for Hayek, creative capacity and creative power always emerge from below and do so organically, spontaneously, and authentically. Containment and repression of this capacity and power—a containment and repression that he considers the essence of the political—come from above and are artificial, but dangerously worshipped as generative. (Hayek is in a war with Hobbes here.) Sovereignty is theological because it posits *creation* from above, whether by God, the king, or the state. Hayek therefore holds the concept responsible for the delusion that societies ought to be shaped by the political, for the ever-expanding state resulting from this delusion, and above all for the demented democratic ideal of the power of the people. Sovereignty identified with the people and deposited in the democratic state will aim to make itself true.[43]

Hayek builds his claim about the fatal place of sovereignty in modern democratic states through a critical revision of Whiggish history. The notion of political sovereignty, he writes, did not exist in the West "until the arrival of absolutism in the sixteenth century."[44] When they overthrew the monarchs, democrats adopted this absolutism for government ostensibly representing the people. In this way, popular consent, which was supposed to be a check on political power, instead "came to be regarded as the sole source of power."[45] The result was unlimited political power "for the first time invested with the aura of legitimacy," a legitimacy perversely provided by democracy.[46]

To be clear, Hayek is not saying that absolutism or sovereignty are inherent in democracy. Rather, his point is that historically in the West, democracy uncritically inherited these principles from its predecessor, abetted by the fairy tale that popular sovereignty means "the people are acting together . . . and that this is morally preferable to the separate actions by individuals."[47] Hayek debunks both parts of this fairy tale with his claim that the fiction of popular sovereignty serves only to anoint absolutism with democratic legitimacy. In other words, democracy attached to popular sovereignty "has yet to cut off the king's head" in political theory or practice and consequently fails to realize the freedom it promises.[48]

The move to divest democracy of popular sovereignty might suggest that Hayek would follow Friedman in straightforwardly reducing democracy to liberalism. However, in *The Constitution of Liberty*, he does something else. Hayek sharply distinguishes liberalism from democracy, claiming that the only principle they share is equality before the law.[49] Beyond this, "liberalism is a doctrine about what the law ought to be, democracy a doctrine about the manner of determining what will be the law."[50] Democracy is a "method of government—namely, majority rule," while liberalism "concerns the scope and purpose of government."[51] He quotes Ortega y Gasset in a footnote: "Democracy answers this question—'Who ought to exercise the public power?' Liberalism asks, 'regardless of who exercises the public power, what should its limits be?'"[52]

More than simply distinguishing them, however, Hayek identifies strong tensions between liberalism and democracy. Liberalism, he says, is concerned with "limiting the coercive powers of all government," while democracy limits government only according to majority opinion.[53] Liberalism is committed to a particular form of government, while democracy is committed to the people. Liberalism "accepts majority rule as a method of deciding but not as an authority for what the decision ought to be." For the democrat, "the fact that the majority wants something is sufficient ground for regarding it as good."[54] Not so for the liberal.

Above all, Hayek argues, democracy and liberalism have radically different opposites. Democracy's opposite is authoritarianism, concentrated but not necessarily unlimited political power. Liberalism's opposite is totalitarianism, complete control of every aspect of life. This makes authoritarianism compatible with a liberal society—freedom, traditional morals, a protected private sphere. And totalitarianism can be brought into being and administered by democratic majorities. If both totalitarian democracy and authoritarian liberalism are logical and indeed historical possibilities, it becomes reasonable for Hayek to join his fellow neoliberals in accepting authoritarianism's legitimacy in the transition to liberalism, thus justifying a Pinochet or Bremer and the coups or wars that installed them.[55]

In addition to authorizing authoritarian liberalism, these two sets of opposites—democracy versus authoritarianism and liberalism versus totalitarianism—are what generate the otherwise paradoxical notion of "excesses of democracy." All of the neoliberals used this phrase to reproach 1960s social movements and an enlarged "scope of state action guided by democratic decision."[56] Repeatedly, Hayek declares that democracy is a method for making decisions, "not a good in itself" or a principle with general application. "While the dogmatic democrat regards it as desirable that as many issues as possible be decided by majority vote, the liberal believes that there are definite limits to the range of questions which should thus be decided."[57] The "crucial conception" of the dogmatic democrat? Popular sovereignty."[58] However, it was the infamous 1975 Trilateral Commission Report that would popularize the "excess of democracy" charge. The report's claim that democracy was in crisis *because* of its unbounded reach and energies was straight out of the neoliberal playbook, linking as it did increased demands on the social state with decreased respect for autonomous state functions and authority and treating both as simultaneously symptoms and damages of this excess.[59] The authors compress this point: "The vitality of democracy in the United States in the 1960s produced a substantial increase in governmental activity and a substantial decrease in governmental authority."[60]

If too much democracy means too much social state, combined with too little respect for political authority, the latter problem abetted by the social state's replacement of family functions and replacement of moral law with social justice, it is clear that Hayek's aim for placing limits on government vastly exceeds respecting and protecting markets. Organically evolved rules of conduct, based on inherited shared principles, are not only to be left untouched, but also made supervenient. Respect for private property, gender norms, and other traditional beliefs—these are the true foundations of a free, moral and orderly society. Here is how Hayek converts them into limits on government, especially democracy:

> It is the acceptance of common principles that makes a collection of people a community. And this common acceptance is the indispensable condition for a free society. A group of men normally become a society not by giving themselves laws but by obeying the same rules of conduct. *This means that the power of the majority is limited by those commonly held principles and that there is no legitimate power beyond them.*[61]

"There is no legitimate power beyond them"—with this phrase, Hayek rallies all "commonly held principles," and not only those securing markets to limit political power. These principles are what will cut off the head of the king, that is, eliminate both political sovereignty and the sovereignty of the political.

It should be clear at this point that Hayek goes well beyond criticizing social democracy and popular sovereignty or protecting the market in his dethronement of politics. He radically rejects, indeed inverts, Aristotle's formulation of political life as making humans free. He rejects Rousseau's formula for gaining moral and political freedom through the social contract and even rejects the classical liberal contractarian tradition of legitimation. For Hayek, our freedom is founded neither in law nor in politics, but in the evolved, often inarticulate principles of conduct and opinion forming a cohesive people, principles that we "freely" accept and abide. Political power—concentrated, wielded from above—negates this freedom with coercion and disturbs, suppresses, or replaces these evolved and tested principles of community with artifice and rationalism. Democracy compounds these damages with rule by majorities and private interests masquerading as public ones. Thus, the political in general and democracy in particular meet their limits in the commonly held principles that make and bind communities.

Hayek's concern with the threat posed by democracy to organically evolved community norms, and not only to freedom, reveals the logic underpinning what the Left often regards as inconsistency or hypocrisy on the Right today, namely, its aim simultaneously to shore up individual liberties and to expand the reach of traditional values. Yet these nest quite compatibly in the doctrine Hayek offers. By dedemocratizing the state and removing it from the equality business, not only markets but commonly held principles of a people, from racial norms to religious ones, may be legitimately protected from state interference and legitimately govern conduct. End-running school desegregation mandates through strategies of local control or privatization (vouchers, "school choice"), refusing to provide services related to contraception, abortion, or same-sex weddings through such things as a "Religious Freedom Restoration Act," maintaining Christian iconography in or around public buildings—all of these are enabled by the limit placed on the political where it meets community norms or individual freedoms (or as chapter 4 will argue, where community norms are juridically codified and upheld *as* individual freedoms).[62] In her history of the public choice school of neoliberalism, Nancy MacLean tracks the strategies of the Cato Institute to resist or repeal federal racial equality legislation in the South.[63] The strategies drew on expanded states' rights (community norms), First Amendment freedoms (individual liberty), and privatization of schools, parks, swimming pools, and more (market freedom). These strategies exemplify neoliberalism's antidemocratic resistance to social and economic equality. They also reveal the extent to which neoliberalized democracy, divested of sovereignty and legislating for the common good, detached from pursuit of the public interest or social justice, restricted from touching individual liberties, markets, and evolved community norms, has little left to do and little power to do it.[64]

The Ordoliberals

The ordoliberal formulation of the political is complex and internally diverse. We will focus only on their concern to build a strong and technocratic state, their anxiety about democracy, and their brief for authoritarian liberalism.[65] In making this examination, it is most important to keep in mind that the ordos share Friedman's and Hayek's wariness of the political, but not their rejection of state sovereignty. They seek to dedemocratize the state and replace it with one supported by technical expertise, directed by competent authorities and bound to the principles of a liberalized, competitive economy.[66]

The idea of an "economic constitution" is the unique ordoliberal contribution to the neoliberal theory of the state-economy relation. As we will see, this is not a literal document, but a way of orienting the state to support the framework, essential elements, and dynamics of markets, especially competition and the price mechanism.[67] The aim of the economic constitution is to commit the state to economic liberalism; the confession it makes is that this commitment is neither natural nor guaranteed, but must be secured politically—capitalism, the ordos understood, has no single form. Thus, the state bound by an economic constitution securing economic liberalism is the opposite of what the ordos term the "economic state" (and what we call the "social state"), which they regard as having the double vice of being a weak state and weakening capitalism. The ideal ordo state is autonomous of the economy, but dedicated to it; by contrast, the economic state / social state is integrated with the economy, undermining political autonomy and capacity and distorting markets.[68]

This much already makes clear that the ordos are as concerned about the damage that democracy inflicts on states as on markets.[69] The "economic state" suffers from lack of independent will formation and will execution; it submits to powerful interest groups (including the workers or the poor) on the one hand and is buffeted by economic vicissitudes on the other. "Every serious economic depression rocks the state itself," Walter Eucken writes, "demonstrating the shackling of state to economy."[70] Such a state cannot "make its own decisions" or "realize purely state interests" and such states also "restrict the initiative of the entrepreneur," constrict forces of development, and cripple the "regulator of the economy, the price system." Damages to the economy in turn deplete the capacities of the state bound up with it.[71]

If the ordos are unique among the neoliberals in arguing that social states are weak, compromised, and lack independent power for the economy, they share with the others the conviction that democracy is the root of the problem. Eucken openly decries the "democratization of the world and consequent unleashing of the demonic powers of peoples."[72] The "destruction of liberal states," he argues, was "forcibly brought about . . . by the masses," who demanded "interventionism and the economic state," which led "to the reverse of what they had sought: weakening of the state and disorganization of the economy."[73]

The ordo solution to this problem involves insulating the state from both democracy and the economy. This is achieved by rendering the political constitution more of an animating ethos than a sovereign document and supplementing this political constitution with an economic one. The political constitution, Franz Böhm writes, "lays down the enduring *telos* of the nation, such that the organizational bases are considered not so much for their technical utility, as for their accordance with the spirit

and genius of the nation."[74] Far from setting out legal principles, the political constitution codifies the spirit of "a people that
comes into being over a long period of time through blood and
historical-emotional experience."[75] This codification of "the particular moral outlook of the people, or the better spirit of the
people," which Böhm sometimes calls "the power of the people," is precisely not a formulation of individual or collective
rights and powers. There is, then, already a sharp turn away
from democracy in the Burkean formulation that Böhm offers:
the political constitution commits the state to protect the con-
tinuity of a nation's spirit, history, and experience. (Enacting
this commitment is exactly what contemporary European white
nationalist parties take themselves to be demanding from the
state, even if their variation on it is not what Böhm had in mind.)

The supplement to the political constitution provided by the
economic constitution, which Böhm terms "practical-technical,"
is required in part because "the good will and social moral
standing of the economic community cannot master the national
economic challenge on its own."[76] Capitalist economies are not
self-sustaining or self-righting, and capitalists themselves cannot provide the steering the economy requires. The economic
constitution is also necessary because the moral-political community faces "a specific choice among a variety of possible economic orders."[77] This choice, Böhm adds, must be practical,
functional, and insulated from the demands of the moment. Its
application and management in turn require a technical blue-
print for a technical order managed by technical experts.[78] Con-
stitutionally enshrined commitment to a market economy must
bind state actors consistently and over time, just as the political

constitution binds state actors to the spirit of the nation. Both limit and direct the state. Neither empowers the people or promulgates democracy.

In their insistence on technical expertise to guide disinterested state action on behalf of markets, the ordos do not share Hayek's suspicion of science in this domain.[79] To the contrary, the complexity of steering capitalism requires specialized, expert knowledge, likened by the ordos to the knowledge required for maintaining any complex machine.[80] In contrast with the ideologues administering a planned economy, Eucken argues, technocrats administering a capitalist one will be steeped in economic theory and its applications.[81] However, these experts (appropriately) lack political authority and the capacity to disseminate their knowledge as power. Hence the importance of building into the ordoliberal state what Böhm calls "a clear, unassailable expression of political will." He writes:

> The only orders equal to this task are those *generated by a conscious and intelligent political will*, and *by an authoritative leadership decision founded in expert knowledge*: there is no room here for silent growth, for an ordered fashioning of doings within the bosom of the economy itself, or from the bottom-up. Such social towers of Babel . . . can only result in a hopeless babble of tongues should the ordering ideal— the sole element seeking to represent unity and to give meaning to the whole in all of its parts—not be grounded in the phrase: everything obeys my command![82]

Böhm is describing a kind of neoliberalized Hobbism: a state comprising authority and decisionism grounded in technical economic knowledge to condition and correct markets. The European Union's remarkably close accordance with this vision in managing its post-2008 fiscal crisis has led several scholars to argue that the EU has become an ordoliberal polity.[83] If this is correct, its "democratic deficit" is now an intrinsic, rather than inadvertent and easily solvable part of the project.[84]

What should be clear at this point is that in contrast with Hayek and Friedman, authoritarian-technocratic liberalism is not a transitional phase for the ordos, but rather the governmental form appropriate to modern capitalism. Ordoliberal states cannot embrace citizen participation or democratic power sharing; rather, they are shaped by "a clear and unassailable expression of political will" grounded in technical expertise.[85] Steering capitalism requires nonpolitical, nondemocratic management by expertly informed authorities that intervene "not on the market but for the market . . . on the conditions of the market."[86] This economic "Third Way" (neither laissez-faire nor state regulation or ownership) is possible only if the state is insulated from both political interests and democratic decision making. Yet this nondemocratic state need not be antiliberal, even in a crisis, even when its authoritarian features show forth clearly. The imposition of austerity measures and other policies that buffet, uproot, or destitute certain populations can avoid touching personal freedoms. Moreover, the market itself is liberally ordered by the microeconomic principles of competition and the efficient price mechanism.[87]

While ordoliberal prescriptions for a neoliberal state differ from those of Hayek and Friedman, the three schools of neoliberalism share a rejection of robust democracy and of the expansive notion of the political on which democracy rests.[88]

They share, as well, the aim of binding political power to support for economic liberalism and moral order. Even the strong statism of ordoliberalism is limited in this way. Thus, Christian Joerges parses the difference between Schmittianism (and its implicit endorsement of Nazism) and ordoliberalism: Schmitt sought "to establish the priority of politics over the economy without consideration for the law, while the ordoliberals wanted to prescribe a stable legal framework for the economy which politics would have to respect."[89]

What Went Wrong?

The neoliberal dream was a global order of freely flowing and accumulating capital, nations organized by traditional morality and markets, and states oriented almost exclusively to this project. Nailed to the requirements of markets that are neither self-stabilizing nor enduringly competitive, the neoliberal state, with its commitment to freedom and legislating only universal rules, would also protect the traditional moral order against incursions by rationalists, planners, redistributionists, and other egalitarians. To this end, democracy would be divorced from popular sovereignty and demoted from an end to a means of facilitating the peaceful transfer of power.[90] Citizenship would be limited to voting, legislation to generating universal rules, courts to umpirage.[91] In this vision, within nation-states, the demos would not rule, but neither, crucially, would capital or its most powerful segments. For the neoliberals, plutocracy is no friendlier than democracy to the project of a rationally organized state aimed at securing the domains of markets and morals. Both democracies and plutocracies will instrumentalize states in their interests, simultaneously weakening their steering capacity while expanding their reach and penetration into society, thus compromising the health of the economy, competition, and freedom.[92]

As the properly constituted neoliberal state is dedemocratized and divested of sovereignty, its authority would be strengthened and the citizenry politically pacified. The state's task of securing conditions for markets grows more complex as the economy does, making technocracy essential and further demoting the value or even the possibility of democratic participation. Technocracy also serves as a buffer against inevitable efforts by powerful market actors to distort competition. Hence the ordo dream of an authoritarian liberal order, bound to an economic constitution and guided by technocrats. Hence Hayek's goal of a strict separation of powers, severe restrictions on legislative reach, and displacement of state sovereignty by the principles of markets and morality. Hence the effort of the public choice school to direct and contain legislative power through a balanced budget amendment and use "locks and bolts" to secure capitalism from democratic contestation or interference.[93]

The aim of dismantling society, choking democracy, and leashing and reprogramming the state was to neutralize a panoply of corrupting forces—powerful market actors, egalitarians and social engineers, and ignorant, myth-mongering masses. However, things went awry in actually existing neoliberalism, as they did in the Marxist revolutions of the last century, which is one reason there is such confusion about what neoliberalism is and whose fault its economic and political disasters are. Democracy has been throttled and demeaned, yes. However, the effect has been the opposite of neoliberal aims. Instead of being insulated from and thus capable of steering the economy, the state is increasingly instrumentalized by big capital—all the big industries, from agriculture and oil to pharmaceuticals and finance, have their hands on the legislative wheels. Instead of being politically pacified, citizenries have become vulnerable to demagogic nationalistic mobilization decrying limited state sovereignty and supranational facilitation of global competition and capital accumulation. And instead of spontaneously ordering and disciplining populations, traditional morality has become a battle screech, often emptied of substance as it is instrumentalized for other ends. As antidemocratic political powers and energies in constitutional democracies have swollen in magnitude and intensity, they have yielded a monstrous form of political life—one yanked by powerful economic interests and popular zeal, one without democratic or even constitutional coordinates, spirit, or accountability, and hence, perversely, one without the limits or limitability sought by the neoliberals. Thus do parties of "limited government" morph into parties of exorbitant state power and spending.

Why did the neoliberal "dethronement of politics" run off the rails so badly? What did it fail to reckon with or consider, or what poisoned it from outside?[94] William Callison argues that occlusion of the domain, dynamics, and powers of the political results in a "deficit" in both neoliberal theory and practice.[95] Opprobrium toward the political and the democratic

84

kept the neoliberals from theorizing both domains with care, which made their project intrinsically vulnerable (for example, to continued domination by large capital interests, especially, but not only those of finance) and also made them unable to anticipate neoliberalism's transmogrification by rogue political powers, including antidemocratic rebellions against its effects. It was not only the founding neoliberal intellectuals who bore this "political deficit." The economists, policy makers, politicians, and technocrats who rolled out neoliberalism as a global project in the 1990s were deeply wedded to its antipolitical "postideological" features, which is one reason they were so dismissive of political critics and disdainful of political protests.[96]

In its failure to reckon deeply with the political, neoliberalism perversely shares a crucial weakness with Marxism. Not only do both inadequately theorize political life, both reject the siting of freedom (which they cherish, if differently) in the political domain, and both fetishize the independence of "the economy" from political discourse.[97] Above all, both conflate their deconstructive and normative critique of political powers (in excess of the administrative ones they want to make use of) with the practical withering away of these powers "after the revolution."

One result of neoliberalism's repetition of the Marxist failure to address political life and power is its deformation by what it ignores.[98] Actually existing neoliberalism features states dominated by every kind of major economic interest and compelled to address a populace seething with rancor, rage, and resentment, not to mention material needs. Hayek imagined an order of strictly limited and separated governmental powers, while today, courts make law, legislatures make political policy, and the executive branch issues "orders" to work around both. The ordos imagined an order that would subordinate democracy to technocracy in policy formulation. Instead, legislating in the United States is dominated by the need to satisfy both a donor class and an angry electorate, with a resulting political culture of logrolling and pork for the plutocrats and meat thrown to the base. In American politics today, because political parties must woo voters, but are beholden to donors, they pull the state in two directions. Only a few large donors are invested in traditional moral values, and not many "values voters" are excited by corporate tax cuts.[99] Deals can be made, of course, and contractual relations among these forces are now so normalized that nothing shocks—the most vulgar plutocrats bow their heads as needed, and the most ardent religionists bracket their beliefs when political predicaments require it. Groups opposing abortion and same-sex marriage or seeking to re-Christianize public schools through voucher systems, prayer, and textbook wars often use this contractual language explicitly.[100] As chapter 5 will suggest, however, it emanates from and intensifies a nihilism that further compromises both the moral program and the economic program of neoliberalism.

Four decades of neoliberal rationality has resulted in a profoundly antidemocratic political culture. More than submitted to an economizing semiotics, as I argued in *Undoing the Demos*, democracy is explicitly demonized and at the same time stripped of protections against its worst tendencies.[101] It is opposed from above and below, from the Left and the Right—Silicon Valley and finance elites at times disparaging it as fiercely as authoritarians and white nationalists, if for different reasons.[102] With democracy thus demeaned and diminished, the exercise of political power, while not disappearing, is increasingly deprived of modulation by informed deliberation, compromise, accountability, and legitimation by the will of the people. Realpolitik rules, with the result that raw maneuvering, deal making, branding, spinning, and indifference to facts, argument, and truth all further discredit the political and further disorient populations about the meaning or value of democracy. "Russian interference in elections," in this context, lacks the scandalous quality it would have had in another era of liberal democracy. So also do voter suppression, court stripping, and legislative power stripping become normalized and become the vehicles through which plutocratic authoritarian liberalism is secured.[103] The more democracy is loosened from standards of truthfulness, reasonableness, accountability, and problem solving through comprehending and negotiating differences, in turn, the more discredited it becomes. Combined with the declining living standards in the Global North that were a predictable feature of neoliberal globalization, and with existentially threatened futurity, populist rage attacking democracy is inevitable, but perhaps, also, the least of the dangers on the horizon. We will consider some of those other dangers in chapter 5.

3

The Personal, Protected Sphere
Must Be Extended

There is . . . a moral inheritance, which is an explanation of the
dominance of the western world, a moral inheritance which con-
sists essentially in the belief in property, honesty and the family,
all things which we could not and have never been able ade-
quately to justify intellectually. . . . We must return to a world
in which not only reason, but reason and morals, as equal part-
ners, must govern our lives, where the truth of morals is simply
one *moral tradition, that of the Christian west, which has created*
morals in modern civilization.
—Friedrich Hayek, 1984 Address to the Mont Pelerin Society

Theorizing Moral Traditionalism as
an Element of Neoliberalism

"God, family, nation, and free enterprise" is a familiar conservative mantra. These commitments, however, do not cohabit easily
outside of a Cold War binary in which socialism is presumed
opposed to each and thus binds them together. Enthusiasm for
the market is typically animated by its promise of innovation,

freedom, novelty, and wealth, while a politics centered in family, religion, and patriotism is authorized by tradition, authority, and restraint. The former innovates and disrupts; the latter secures and sustains.[1] Moreover, even before globalization, capital generally has disregarded creed and political borders, while nationalism has fetishized them. Consequently, most scholars have treated the Right's commitments to neoliberal policy and to its other values as running on separate tracks.[2] Their relationship has been variously theorized as one of supplement, genealogical hybrid, resonance, contingent convergence, or mutual exploitation. Each approach is reprised briefly below.

Supplement: Irving Kristol, often called the godfather of neoconservatism, treated the political project of shoring up moral values as an essential supplement to free markets. In the late 1970s, he famously offered capitalism "two cheers" for the freedom and wealth it promised, but withheld the third cheer because "consumer societies are empty of moral meaning if not forthrightly nihilistic."[3] An explicitly conservative moral-political program is required, he argued, to counter these effects, as well as to counter capitalism's contribution to the "steady decline in our democratic culture . . . sinking to new levels of vulgarity."[4] This nihilism and degradation render moral issues "proper candidates for the government's attention."[5] Concretely, this entails promoting traditional values in families, schools, and civic spaces, affirming religious influence in political life, and cultivating patriotism. Beyond these, neoconservative politics addresses the need for a strong state to promote the national interest.[6] Again, in this view, none of these state and cultural projects are naturally secured or supported by capitalism. Rather, they are its essential supplements.

Hybrid: Taking Kristol at his word, in previous work, I treated neoliberalism and neoconservatism in the United States as two distinct political rationalities.[7] While bearing few overlapping formal characteristics, I argued, they have convergent effects in generating an antidemocratic citizenry that "loves and wants neither political freedom nor social equality . . . expects neither truth nor accountability in governance and state actions," and "is not distressed by exorbitant concentrations of political economic power . . . or undemocratic formulations of national purpose at home or abroad."[8] Though emanating from different sources and addressing different purposes, the two rationalities mingled to produce dark forces of dedemocratization.

Resonance: William Connolly theorizes the "resonance" between contemporary evangelical Christianity and capitalist culture. Unlike logics of entailment, dialectics, conspiracy, or even genealogy, Connolly argues, resonance consists in "energized complexities of mutual imbrication, and interinvolvement, in which heretofore unconnected or loosely associated elements *fold, bend, blend, emulsify and resolve incompletely into each other*, forging a qualitative assemblage resistant to classical modes of explanation."[9] Connolly is especially interested in the "spiritual disposition to existence"—vehemence and ruthlessness, ideological extremism, and the "readiness to create or condone scandals against any party who opposes their vision of the world"—shared by aggressive religious evangelicals and champions of neoliberalism.[10]

Writing in *Politico* a decade later, Tim Alberta offered a different version of resonance between Bible-thumping working-class whites and the rich, vainglorious, nonreligious, thrice-divorced, "pussy grabbing" former casino owner they supported for president. Evangelicals, Alberta insists, identify deeply with Trump because of their shared experience of being disdained by cultural elites and attacked by worldly forces. "Both he and they have been systematically targeted in the public square— oftentimes by the same adversaries," especially those hailing from academia, entertainment, and the media.[11] Trump often refers to this shared experience of defamation when speaking to crowds of white evangelicals, and evangelical activists make frequent mention of their opponents' mocking and derisive characterizations of their beliefs.[12]

Convergence: Melinda Cooper studies the convergence between neoliberalism and social conservatism at the site of the traditional family: "Despite their differences on virtually all other issues, neoliberals and social conservatives were in agreement that the bonds of family need to be encouraged—and at the limit enforced."[13] Cooper sees both as hewing to the principles of the Elizabethan poor laws, in which, among other things, "the family, not the state, would bear primary responsibility for investing in the education, health, and welfare of children."[14] While neoconservatives promoted family values for moral reasons and neoliberals for economic ones, their agendas came together in policies through which the "natural obligations" and "altruism" of families would substitute for the welfare state and operate as both "a primitive mutual insurance contract and . . . a necessary counterweight to market freedoms."[15]

Moreover, for neoliberal intellectuals and policy makers, the family was not just a safety net, but a disciplinary container and authority structure. They looked to it to thwart the democratic excesses and the breakdown of authority they believed to be incited by the provisions of the social state, especially those of welfare and public higher education. If individuals could be returned to dependence on the family for everything from out-of-wedlock children to college costs, they would also be resubmitted to its authority, morality, and economic discipline.[16]

Mutual exploitation: Over the past several decades, scholars Nancy MacLean, Michael Lienesch, Susan Harding, Linda Kintz, and Bethany Moreton all anticipated what the 2016 Trump campaign put brilliantly into practice.[17] Each contributes to understanding how Christian traditionalists could be bought off by neoliberals concerned with other agendas, from deregulating industries and winning corporate tax cuts to challenging laws and policies aimed at racial equality.[18] Nancy MacLean argues that the Virginia public choice school of neoliberalism, heavily funded by the Koch Brothers, understood well the importance of recruiting Christian evangelicals to the project of contesting democracy with a white male plutocracy. MacLean writes:

Cynicism ruled Koch's decision to make peace . . . with the religious right despite the fact that so many libertarian thinkers . . . were atheists who looked down on those who believed in God. But the organizers who mobilized white evangelicals for political action—men such as Reverend Jerry Falwell and Ralph Reed and Tim Phillips—were entrepreneurs in their own right, so common cause could be made. The religious entrepreneurs were happy to sell libertarian economics to their flocks—above all, opposition to public schooling and calls for reliance on family provision or charity in place of government assistance.[19]

The Trump campaign, particularly Steve Bannon, grasped early on the importance of the white evangelical vote. And after assuming office, Trump never stopped throwing this constituency meat—on abortion, same-sex marriage, transgender acceptance, Jerusalem, and expanded power for churches in civic, educational, and political life. Only 17 percent of Americans are white evangelicals today, but this population constitutes a full one-half of Trump's base.[20] Tim Alberta writes, "Evangelicals do not believe that Trump is one of them, as former presidents Carter and the younger Bush were, but never has a president catered to them so directly." Ralph Reed, chairman of the Faith and Freedom Coalition, who led the evangelicals' battle to rescue the Supreme Court nomination of Justice Kavanaugh from sexual assault allegations and argued against sanctioning Saudi Arabia following its assassination of journalist Jamal Khashoggi, is forthright about the difference between religious beliefs and the character of the political fights required to advance them.[21] Jerry Falwell Jr., head of Liberty University and crucial to delivering the evangelical vote for Trump, is equally blunt: "Conservatives & Christians need to stop electing 'nice guys'. They might make great Christian leaders but the US needs street fighters like @realDonaldTrump at every level of government b/c the liberal fascists Dems are playing for keeps & many Repub leaders are a bunch of wimps!"[22]

Mutual exploitation between religious zealots (and their followers) and irreligious ambitious politics is hardly unprecedented—Machiavelli was one of its most brilliant and early cartographers.[23] However, the explicit transactionalism and politicization of religious values themselves are striking expressions of a nihilism that will be more carefully considered in chapter 5. Open tolerance of the alien values of others in exchange for advancing one's own intolerant moral agenda is possible only when moral values have paradoxically lost their moral weight, when "values themselves have been devalued," as Nietzsche put it. This was certainly on display in the December 2017 special election for U.S. Senator in Alabama: in an effort to defeat a "godless democrat" who fought the Klan as a young lawyer, evangelicals voted overwhelmingly for an accused pedophile seeking to criminalize abortion and homosexuality and equating the Koran with *Mein Kampf.*[24] Contemporary Christian nationalism has this contractualism at its core: "The view is that God can use anybody as long as they're promoting Christian nationalist ideals or values," argues one sociologist of religion; "it's all about a quest for power and what serves the purpose in the political moment."[25] The belief that God has explicitly chosen Donald Trump as his instrument for bringing about a more Christian world or the End of Days is common among white evangelicals.[26]

Each of the above accounts illuminates important aspects of the political present. None of them, however, apprehends the place of traditional morality—both securing and emanating from the family—*within* neoliberal reason. While some ordo-liberals formulated this place in their concern to "re-embed" the proletarianized subject in the authority and provisioning of the family, it acquires its strongest theoretical articulation in Friedrich Hayek's work. For Hayek, the relation of markets and morals in the neoliberal project has nothing to do with supplements, hybridity, resonance, convergence, or mutual exploitation. Rather, markets and morals, equally important to a thriving civilization, are rooted in a common ontology of spontaneously evolved orders borne by tradition. This ontology features perfect compatibility between and among discipline and freedom, inheritance and innovation, evolution and stability, authority and independence. Moreover, far from constituting a compensatory program to counter the ravages of capitalism, Hayek seeks to cultivate and extend "conventions and customs of human intercourse" in order to constitute a crucial bulwark against the wrong-headed designs of social justice warriors and the despotism of an overreaching state that those designs inevitably yield.

Friedrich Hayek on Tradition

For Hayek, freedom requires the absence of explicit coercion by other humans, whether that coercion is direct or comes through political institutions.[27] Freedom for Hayek is not emancipation, it is not power to enact one's will, and it is not license. Indeed, it is not even choice.[28] Importantly, it is also not independence of the traditions generating rules of conduct and the habits of following them.[29] Hayek writes in one of his notebooks, "Restraint is a condition, not the opposite of freedom."[30] But what kind of restraint can be noncoercive? Not those set by political decisions or imposed by one person on another, but rather, those "commonly accepted by the members of the group in which the rules of morals prevail." Lest this seem a minor point, Hayek concludes this note to himself: "the demand for 'liberation' from these restraints is an attack on all liberty possible among human beings."[31] Hayekian freedom, then, has nothing to do with emancipation from accepted social norms or powers. Rather, it is the uncoerced capacity for endeavor and experimentation within codes of conduct generated by tradition and enshrined in just law, markets, and morality.[32] Schooled by Edmund Burke, whom he modernizes via Darwin, Hayek marvels at the capacity of tradition to produce social harmony and integration along with a means of change, all without recourse to the coercive agency of institutions or groups.

Liberty, more than limited by moral tradition, is partly constituted by it. Conversely, moral freedom, more than challenged by politically imposed justice schemes, is destroyed by them. This framework sets the stage for dismantling robust democracy in the name of freedom and moral values. Tradition parallels the ontology of markets. At times, Hayek even identifies markets as a form of tradition: both "spontaneously" yield order and development without relying on comprehensive knowledge or reason and without a master will to develop, maintain, or steer them. Both are antirationalist (neither designed by reason nor fully apprehended by it) without being irrational.[33] "We stand," Hayek writes, "in a great framework of institutions and traditions—economic, legal and moral—into which we fit ourselves by obeying certain rules of conduct that we never made, and which we have never understood."[34] These qualities of spontaneous, nonintentional development both prevent tradition from impinging on our freedom and supply its capacity for development and orderly adaptation to changing conditions. They do not compromise, but comport with a non-Kantian liberalism in which we are moral agents, even if we are not morally autonomous.[35] They insulate norms emanating from tradition from requiring defense by reason or reasons for their legitimacy.

Sharing Burke's insistence that what preserves society is organic to it, Hayek also recognizes variety in cultural traditions and warns against trying to import elements from one tradition into another. That said, the Darwinian in Hayek believes that traditions not only evolve internally, but also compete externally with one another. Only those that center family and property, he insists, will survive this competition.[36] So, too, with personal freedom: traditions that fail to feature it prominently are doomed. This is not just because humans desire freedom, but because freedom strengthens tradition (through promoting adaptive innovations), while tradition moors freedom (through promoting conventions and order). This symbiosis is also revealed in the negative. Those seeking to replace traditional practices and institutions with deliberately contrived ones are the "enemies of freedom" insofar as they seek to impose rules of conduct designed by the few on the many and to replace intelligent design spontaneously generated by tradition with inevitably flawed rational design.[37] For Hayek, then, tradition promotes a free way of life in contrast to that organized by political power: it promotes individual freedom through voluntary compliance with its norms, as well as through innovation, and it is sustained by protecting freedom against politics. "Paradoxical as it may appear," he concludes, "a successful free society will always in a large measure be a tradition-bound society."[38]

We need to dwell with this seeming paradox. While insisting on tradition as the proper basis for social order and norms of conduct, Hayek does not treat the past as possessing intrinsic wisdom or authority. Rather, "the evolutionary view is based on the insight that the result of the experimentation of many generations may embody more experience than any one man possesses."[39] Traditions that develop the best possible ways of living together emerge not from the sheer authority of the past, but from the experimentation and evolution that freedom permits. At the same time, tradition promotes freedom and avoids coercion only because with tradition "a high degree of voluntary conformity exists."[40] *Voluntary conformity*—both terms really matter in Hayek's formulation. On the one hand, tradition produces conformity through habitual conduct, rather than "conscious adherence to known rules." On the other hand, the voluntary nature of the conduct is what makes tradition dynamic, as well as a space of freedom. "It is this flexibility of voluntary rules which in the field of morals makes gradual evolution and spontaneous growth possible," and "such an evolution is possible only with rules which are neither coercive nor deliberately imposed. . . . Rules of this kind allow for gradual and experimental change."[41]

Hayek's emphasis on competition, development, freedom, innovation, and change as fundamental elements of tradition suggest that his account of tradition is itself drawn from the model of the market, not only from Burkean organicism and authority. Equally important, however, markets are themselves a *form* of tradition for Hayek, which adds another layer to their legitimate insulation from political intervention. Indeed, the order generated by markets embodies the evolved, free, incomprehensible, unintentional, voluntary, yet socially integrated order of tradition at its finest. We are disciplined and oriented by market rules; they evolve, change, and develop; yet no one designed them, no one is in charge, and no one coerces us within them.

No mastermind, design, or enforcer imposes or secures tradition, and yet, Hayek acknowledges, it is religion that almost always codifies and transmits it. "How could traditions which people do not like or understand, whose effects they usually do not appreciate and can neither see nor foresee, and which they are still ardently combating, continue to have been passed on from generation to generation?"[42] Religious mystifications supply the conduit: "We owe the persistence of certain practices, and the civilization that resulted from them, in part to support from beliefs which are not true . . . in the same sense as are scientific statements."[43] Feeling the slipperiness of the ground he is on, Hayek quickly moves to call religious beliefs "symbolic truths" that promote survival and flourishing. God, he speculates, may be a kind of shorthand required for a cosmology otherwise too complex to apprehend, describe, or even imagine. "Perhaps what many people mean in speaking of God is just a personification of that tradition of morals or values that keeps their community alive."[44] Besides, the fiction of religion is vastly superior to the "rationalist delusion" that we can use our reason to design moral orders.[45] If religious mystifications and reifications are shortcuts to preserving traditions on which civilization depends, he implies, so be it.

Yet Hayek cannot be so sanguine about the role of religion and religious beliefs in reproducing tradition. Religious conceits of personification and animism are precisely what he seeks to dismantle in popular conceptions of social and political life, especially the dangerous conceit of sovereign intentionality, design, and will. As we saw in chapter 2, Hayek shares Schmitt's appreciation of the theological underpinnings of political sovereignty; contra Schmitt, however, Hayek also locates the profound error and danger of sovereignty in its theological formulation of power. Hayek writes: "The pretended logical necessity of such an unlimited source of power simply does not exist." Instead,

the belief in such a necessity is a product of the false constructivistic interpretation of the formation of human institution which attempts to trace them all to an original designer or some other deliberate act of will. The basic source of social order, however, is not a deliberate decision to adopt certain common rules, but the existence among the people of certain opinions of what is right and wrong. What made the Great Society possible was not a deliberate imposition of rules of conduct but the growth of such rules among men who had little idea of what would be the consequence of their general observance.[46]

If political sovereignty is rooted in the mistaken belief that societies are ordered by will and design, this belief must be undone. Hayek thus seeks to challenge, conceptually and practically, the anthropomorphized version of a divine will inscribed in political sovereignty.

Folding tradition into liberalism, as Hayek does, then, sets liberalism on a dangerous course by Hayek's own lights. His refashioning of liberalism withdraws authority from political life and confers it to religiously embedded norms and practices. The political, divested of sovereignty and the public interest, is confined to generating universally applied rules (themselves best when they are codifications of norms emanating from tradition) and techniques that have the status of being practical, rather than true. Tradition secured by religion, on the other hand, acquires the mantle of incontestability and symbolic truth at the same time that it serves as a limit on the political. This formulation explains a strand of the rationality organizing our current predicament: truth withdrawn from political life is rolled over to moral and religious claims rooted in the authority of tradition.[47] The effect is to sever truth from accountability (a recipe for authoritarianism), to contest equality and justice with tradition, and to eliminate the legitimacy of popular sovereignty.

Still, Hayek's quandary has not been solved. If the dangerous and fictive belief in sovereignty attributes to a power above what is spontaneously generated from below, that religion secures tradition remains a serious problem. His critique of sovereignty deconstructs a religious-political worldview featuring omniscience, omnipotence, master design, and master will. With his insistence that each is a dangerous ontological error, he aims to affirm freedom against political mandate, individuals against the collective, and spontaneous development against rational social design. He seeks to dereify society as nothing more than individuals and seeks the dethronement of politics so that markets and morals may resume their pure and rightful place. However, the state is neither the source nor the enforcer of morality—that Hobbesian path would wrongly inflate state power and convert moral law into unfree mandates and restrictions in place of voluntary conformity with conventions. State-dictated morality of any kind, whether religious dicta or secular social justice principles, is the signature of totalitarianism. Thus, the state can secure only the *prerequisites* of moral life—freedom, property, universal rules of justice, and political deference to tradition. It cannot legislate moral conduct or belief.[48]

How, then, to recover traditional moral principles from the corrosive effects of capitalism (and the decades of corruption by the social state, from which Hayek's order would have to arise), when the neoliberal state cannot legislate morality or be a moralist? How to employ law and the state to shore up the authority of tradition without violating its organic nature and its voluntarism? How to minimize political coercion while securing "rule" by tradition? There are three techniques in the Hayekian arsenal: limit legislative power to generating universal rules and exclude it from making policy in the public interest; discredit all social justice talk as nonsense and totalitarian; and expand what Hayek calls the "personal protected sphere" to extend the purview of traditional morality beyond the confines of church and family. Together, these three techniques grant claims from tradition and its peculiar freedoms social place and power while restricting reforms rooted in rationalism, planning, or other nonorganic formulations of the good. Together, they promote traditional morality and markets while containing the reach of the political and restricting democratic reforms of society.

The first two techniques, discussed in previous chapters, are direct limits on the state. The third, both a limit and a kind of state action, is the only one that can actually restore traditional mores to a society where the social state has damaged or displaced them. It is precisely the technique that, in recent decades, has been used in executive orders, legislation, and adjudication empowering market and traditional morality claims against those of equality, secularism, and the common good. "Expanding the personal protected sphere" is Hayek's novel contribution to neoliberalism and to reformatting traditionalism as freedom.

Coercive state power, Hayek writes in the *Constitution of Liberty*, is most effectively blocked by designating spheres and activities that it is prohibited to touch.[49] Beyond this concern to secure a "protected sphere of a person or persons," a familiar idea in all forms of liberalism, it is Hayek's aim to enlarge this sphere's contents and domain. He is specifically designating ever more activity within it as private, hence appropriately shielded from state impingement and democratic norms.[50] "The recognition of property," Hayek writes, is "the first step in delimiting the private sphere protecting us against coercion" but, he adds, "we must not think of this sphere consisting exclusively, or even chiefly, of material things."[51] Rather, through its unique formation by acceptance of "general rules governing the conditions under which objects or circumstances become part of the protected sphere of a person or persons," this sphere gives us "protection against interference with our actions" from a range of sources.[52] It walls out that monster coercive power, the state, but also coercion by democratic norms such as equality, inclusion, access, and social justice. This is how Hayek links freedom with diffusing traditional mores beyond the family and private sphere of worship. Personal freedom so expanded is the means by which "the traditional moral values alone can flourish."[53] Protection of the "personal protected sphere," so expanded, is the means by which tradition and liberty repel their enemies— the political and the social, the rational and the planned, the egalitarian and the statist.[54] Enlarging the domain in which personal freedom is rightly unrestricted allows traditional beliefs and mores, or what Hayek calls "conventions and customs of human intercourse," to legitimately reclaim and indeed recolonize, the civic and social where democracy once ruled.[55] It is a way of reclaiming the order from what Hayek depicts as the symptomatic and dangerous substitution of the "word 'social' for the word 'moral' or simply 'good.'" He reads in this substitution the "growing influence of the rationalist conception" of human nature and human order in place of inherited moral traditions and rules that do not emerge from reason, cannot be fully fathomed by it, and do not depend on individual judgment.[56] The "appeal to the 'social,'" Hayek says wryly, "really involves a demand that individual intelligence, rather than rules evolved by society, should guide individual action."[57] It is an argument to "dispense with what could truly be called 'social' (in the sense of being a product of the impersonal process of society)" and to cast out moral tradition and its spontaneous effects in ordering society and our conduct.[58]

Here, we must remind ourselves what is at issue in seeking to reclaim democratically organized society with norms and codes of conduct derived from market and moral traditions. Of the "conventions and customs of human intercourse" harbored by tradition, Hayek writes, "the moral rules are the most important but by no means the only significant ones."[59] Rather, at stake are such things as heteropatriarchal norms and family forms; racial norms and enclaves; property ownership and wealth accumulation, retention, and transmission—in short, all that reproduces and legitimates historical powers and ordinances of class, kinship, race, and gender.[60]

Consider once more the importance of the ontological symmetry Hayek establishes between moral codes and market rules. Both are evolved practices, not simply natural, but are "good" because they are evolved, adaptive, and have stood the test of time. Both "conduct conduct" (in Foucault's formulation) or produce "a high degree of voluntary conformity" (in Hayek's) without coercion.[61] And both require the state to secure and protect them with laws of property, marriage, contracts, and inheritance while also constituting limits on state action.

This symmetry in markets and morals sets Hayekian liberalism apart from libertarian or even classical liberal formulations. So also does Hayek's affirmation of the conformist pressures of traditional morality; he does not share, for example, J. S. Mill's worries about the effect of that kind of conformism on freedom or individuality.[62] For Hayek, as long as these pressures are not coercive (which in this discussion he defines, tellingly, as "being in someone else's interest rather than our own"), they are legitimate and valuable. They are especially important in contesting moral claims that emanate from sources other than tradition and that challenge family, property, and freedom.

It should now be clear that Hayek's antipathy to social democracy and socialism does not derive solely from his appreciation of markets, an appreciation that is ubiquitous in the history of liberalism. Nor does it derive solely from his fear of expansive state power, also ubiquitous in classical liberalism and intensified by the twentieth-century experience of totalitarianism. Rather, for Hayek, the great error of social democracy rests in its attempt to replace historically evolved spontaneous order, borne by tradition, settled into custom, with rational master designs for society. This is the error that misunderstands the nature of human beings, history, change, and social cooperation, not to mention justice and freedom.[63] Neoliberalism fights this misapprehension by affirming order rooted in tradition and freedom; it wages this fight through a far-reaching deregulatory ethos and practice by demonizing state justice schemes, by empowering tradition against such schemes, and by opposing the very idea of popular sovereignty.

Actually Existing Neoliberalism

Installing markets and morality where society and democracy once were, through the principle of freedom from state regulation—this is the Hayekian dream. This vision was also central to actually existing neoliberalism, especially its rollout in the United States and Britain. It took a different form than that imagined by Hayek and his brethren, and the moral half of the project tended to be ignored or rejected by some ardent advocates of market deregulation and globalization. This may be why economic privatization remains the familiar face of neoliberalism and keeps more veiled the equally important force of privatization constituted by extending the reach of the "personal, protected sphere." In fact they work together conceptually and practically: dismantling public provision is routinely coupled with extended private sphere norms to delegitimize the concept of social welfare provision and the project of democratizing the social powers of class, race, gender, and sexuality. As everyday life is marketized from one direction and "familialized" from the other by neoliberal rationality, these twin processes challenge principles of equality, secularism, pluralism, and inclusion, along with democratic determination of a common good.

In her study of neoliberalism's rollout in the United States, Melinda Cooper provides examples of this process in welfare reform, education financing, "fatherhood initiatives," and "faith-based" welfare.[64] Other examples include:

- School voucher systems and charter schools, in place of public control over primary and secondary education, permit parents to choose "value-aligned" schools for their children and to avoid student bodies and curriculums they abhor.[65] As vouchers indemnify family "choice" against a secular, pluralistic public, they simultaneously challenge the promise of equal opportunity embedded in public education, its limited, but important counterweight to the otherwise straightforward reproduction of (racialized) class. They thus embody both the antidemocratic familialization and economic privatization of one of the most crucial domains of modern public life.

- Court decisions and proliferating state versions of the Religious Freedom Restoration Act enable religious claims to displace democratically enacted principles of equality, inclusion, and nondiscrimination. More than "losers' revenge" on issues such as abortion and marriage equality, these instruments empower Christian family values to trump legally secured reproductive autonomy for women, along with marriage equality and protections for persons of nonnormative gender.[66] The expanded reach of religious liberty permits the rebuff of equality and restoration of supremacies and abjections iterated by traditional morality.

- Repealing the 1954 Johnson Amendment, which prohibits churches and nonprofits from direct or indirect participation in political campaigns is one of Trump's biggest promises to his evangelical base.[67] The repeal would amplify the already considerable political power of the largest and wealthiest churches, giving them political voice both from the pulpit and in the statehouse.[68] The repeal would be to Christianity in politics what the *Citizens United* Supreme Court decision was to corporations in politics, with the additional boon of allowing megachurch pastors to incorporate voting directives into their sermons.

The most powerful tool for replacing democratic rule with deregulated markets and traditional morality is liberty disembedded from society and from democracy, traced in chapters 1 and 2. Liberty claims have been core to the religious right-wing strategy to re-Christianize the public sphere since the early 1990s, but have been ramped up and popularized in the past decade. The kinds of things now framed as protections of individual liberty include: the right of adoption agencies and T-shirt print makers to discriminate against LGBT people, the right of "pregnancy crisis centers" to lie about abortion and contraception, the right of legislatures to hold Christian prayer sessions, the right of Christian teachers and students to evangelize in classrooms, and the right of a college professor to refer to students by the pronoun of *his* choice, rather than theirs.

Challenging equality and antidiscrimination law as protections of individual liberty is the strategy brilliantly honed by the Alliance Defending Freedom, the most powerful arm of evangelical Christianity in the United States. (ADF International takes the cause to other lands and other courts, national and transnational).[69] The alliance is dedicated to challenging limitations faced by Christians to exercise their faith expansively and publicly. This work includes contesting prohibitions on displays of crucifixes or required sex education in public schools; fighting legal abortion; and above all, pushing back against protections for what conservatives call "SOGI laws"—protections against discrimination on the basis of sexual orientation and gender identity.[70] Described by its founder as the "Christian legal army" and supported by private contributions of more than $50 million annually, the ADF has trained thousands of lawyers and legislators, judges, prosecutors, professors, and attorneys general. It is the fount of most recent state and federal religious freedom legislation, and its attorneys appear frequently in front of the Supreme Court and the European Court for Human Rights.[71]

Both the legal and popular rhetoric of the ADF decries an overreaching state whose mandates threaten the liberties of Christians in public and commercial life. Thus, while domestic ADF cases invoke religious liberty or free speech in generic fashion, the ADF is no ACLU: freedom is but the mantle under which it strives to empower Christianity socially and politically. While insisting that Christian beliefs and voices are oppressed by LGBT and reproductive rights agendas, the ADF also filed a brief on behalf of Trump's second Muslim ban, whose judicial critics they accuse of "inappropriately combing through a government actor's tweets."[72] Moreover, ADF efforts to dismantle abortion law and transgender protections, battle same-sex marriage, and permit Christian prayer and iconography in schools and town halls make clear that more is at stake than allowing Christian bakers, pharmacists, teachers, and anti-abortion activists to follow their conscience.[73] The ADF's long game is to (re)Christianize the culture through challenges to political and legal apparatuses bound to secularism, egalitarianism, and inclusion. As one ADF webpage declares: "Your faith isn't private, and it's more than where you worship on Sundays. It's who you are, and it influences the way you live every day of the week. But today, efforts are being made to remove religion's moral influence on society by censoring it from the public square. People of faith are increasingly threatened, punished, and silenced for simply living according to their beliefs."[74]

Another page on the website depicts an aggressive secular war on the Christian fundamentals underpinning the United States legal system:

> The Founding Fathers recognized that all people have inalienable rights that flow from the Creator. These rights are grounded in the unique, Judeo-Christian concept of man's inherent dignity as a creature made in God's image, endowed with reason, free will, and an eternal soul. . . . As secular forces chip away at our nation's Judeo-Christian roots, religious freedom is increasingly threatened. Alliance Defending Freedom . . . opposes all attempts to compel people to compromise their beliefs or retreat from civil and political life as the price for following their faith.[75]

The ADF's Blackstone Legal Fellowship Program, through which it develops new cadres of attorneys from law schools, also describes inculcating fellows in a jurisprudence aimed at

Christianizing the culture, not simply protecting the rights of individuals. The ADF describes the program as offering "the highest level training in Christian worldview and constitutional law to help break the stranglehold the ACLU and its allies have on our nation's law schools and judicial system."[76] Blackstone Fellows must hew to the ADF's "Statement of Faith and Guiding Principles," which includes affirmation of the Christian God as the only god and rejection of transgender, same-sex marriage and abortion rights.[77] According to one testimonial from a fellow, the program employs "Christ's Truth" to "recover the rule of law in America."[78]

The commitments and strategies of the Alliance Defending Freedom have been warmly embraced by the Trump administration. The president himself appears frequently with ADF leaders, and Vice President Pence and several past and present cabinet members enjoy close ties with the organization. Education Secretary Betsy DeVos is a major donor. ADF influence is everywhere in the administration's judicial appointees and is the strongest hand in developing its Christian-friendly legislation. In July 2018, then-attorney general Jeff Sessions announced his launch of a "religious liberty task force" with these words:

> A dangerous movement, undetected by many, is now challenging and eroding our great tradition of religious freedom. . . . This is no little matter. It must be confronted and defeated. . . . We have gotten to the point where courts have held that morality cannot be a basis for law; where ministers are fearful to affirm, as they understand it, holy writ from the pulpit;

and where one group can actively target religious groups by labeling them a "hate group" on the basis of their sincerely held religious beliefs.[79]

The Supreme Court majority also frequently affirms ADF legal formulations, especially its use of the First Amendment as a means of expanding the power of traditional morality to repel democratic law. Above all, as we will see in chapter 4, it has affirmed the ADF's strategic conversion of religious liberty from a private right to a public liberty, shaping it as a public force and also permitting its extension to businesses (large and small) and municipalities.

Rights are the flying wedge with which democratic commitments to equality, civility, and inclusion are challenged in neoliberal legal battles. But the forces behind them, staging incursions against society and democracy, are the values and claims of the market, combined with those of heteropatriarchal Christian familialism.

This use of civil liberties consecrates a specific mode of twinning individual freedom with traditional morality, and it is not exactly what Hayek or the ordoliberals had in mind. Indeed, it is noteworthy that the Mont Pelerin Society "Statement of Aims" decries a society in which "private rights are . . . allowed to become a basis of predatory power." Criticism of the way rights and "rights talk" is displacing democratic deliberation styled from "household table talk . . . born of shared family and, often ethnic history" was also the subject of an important 1993 book by Mary Ann Glendon, today a prominent ADF board member who appears to have abandoned her earlier critique, aimed as it once was, mainly at the Left.[80]

As rights become a crucial vehicle for expanding conservative Christian morality into the public sphere, this morality is disembedded from tradition and therefore detached from both the organic roots and the spontaneous effects that Hayek ascribed to tradition. Instead of evolved and adapted codes of conduct with which an entire people "voluntarily conforms," morality—and not only rights themselves—becomes politicized and weaponized. Such politicization alters the meaning of "morality" and the mode of governing conduct and at the same time increases their vulnerability to the contractualism that at once signifies and abets their nihilistic deterioration. We will pursue this further in chapter 5.

Refiguring the Nation as Family and Private Firm

Neoliberal *economic* privatization is deeply subversive of democracy. It generates and legitimates inequality, exclusion, private ownership of the commons, plutocracy, and a profoundly dimmed democratic imaginary.[81] The other order of privatization we have been considering, privatization by familialization and Christianization achieved by extending the "personal, protected sphere," subverts democracy with antidemocratic moral values, rather than antidemocratic capital values.[82] Thatcher's infamous dictum that "there is no such thing as society" concludes, after all: "only individuals and their families."

Enacting this aspect of the proclamation wages familial, rather than market warfare on democratic principles and institutions. It generates exclusion, patriarchalism, tradition, nepotism, and Christianity as legitimate challenges to inclusion, autonomy, equal rights, limits on conflicts of interest, and secularism. While both kinds of privatization occur under the neoliberal rubric of expanding freedom against state dictates of social justice or market distributions, the second is especially important in generating the psychic and political formation of a liberal authoritarian political culture today. The ordinates of religion and family—hierarchy, exclusion, homogeneity, faith, loyalty, and authority—acquire legitimacy as public values and shape public culture as they join markets in displacing democracy. When this twin model of privatization extends to the nation itself, the nation is alternately rendered as a competitive business needing to make better deals and as an inadequately secured home, besieged by ill-willed or nonbelonging outsiders. Right-wing nationalism oscillates between the two. Consider Trump's campaign speeches about America's history of bad international deals on everything from trade to NATO, Iran to climate accords, and his depiction of the United States as savaged by its unsecured borders and his promise to build a southern border wall featuring a "great big beautiful door" through which legal entrants may visit or join "our family."[83] He would later analogize his proposed border wall to the "walls, fences, and gates" that wealthy politicians build around their homes, "not because they hate the people on the outside, but because they love the people on the inside."[84] Far from public and democratic, the nation is figured as privately owned and familial, and the president is the paterfamilias. Or consider Marine Le Pen's 2017 "France for the French" campaign, in which she also perfectly combined economic and familial languages to depict the nation: "We are the owners of our country," she declared at rallies in eastern France, and "we must have the keys to open the house of France, to open it halfway," or "to close the door." "It is our house," the crowds chanted back.[85] Or as one of her supporters explained, "She's not against immigrants, only securing justice. . . . It's like when the refrigerator is full we give to our neighbors, but when the refrigerator is empty we give to our children. The refrigerator of France is empty." And another self-professed "moderate" Le Pen supporter, a mayor of a small town, asked of "the well-dressed young immigrant men" in his town: "what are they doing *chez moi* [in my house]?"[86]

When the nation is privatized and familialized in this way, it becomes legitimately illiberal toward aversive insiders and invading outsiders; thus does neoliberalism plant seeds of a nationalism that it formally abjures. Statism, policing, and authoritarianism also ramify, since walling and securitization of every kind is authorized and required by this privatization. Walls and gates of homes, of course, are the strongest visual signifiers demarcating the private from the public, the protected from the open, the familiar from the strange, the owned from the common. At the same time, as the domain of the private expands, it requires ever more state protection through law, public and private security forces, border patrols, police, and the military. In this way, the securitarian state grows along with privatization and is legitimated by it. Similarly, nationalist calls to wall out refugees and expel immigrants draw upon the

figure of the nation as an endangered household where principles of democratic justice and human rights have no bearing.
Expanding the "personal protected sphere" in the name of freedom, then, not only secures inegalitarian powers of class, gender, sexuality, and race; it generates an imago and ethos of the
nation that rejects a public, pluralistic, secular democratic order
for a private, homogenous, familial one.[87] The former features
commitments to modest openness, diversity, social and political
equality, and the rule of law. The latter, especially in its traditional form, is walled, homogenous, unified, hierarchical, and
authoritarian.

As we have seen, however, the play of markets and morality
in actually existing neoliberalism is quite different from what
Hayek imagined. States dominated by finance and other powerful industries seeking legislation and state action in their interests depart radically from the neoliberal aim of political institutions insulated from interests while promoting competition and
stabilizing (or in the case of the ordoliberals, steering) capitalism.
Traditional values, rather than spontaneously integrating social
life and ordering conduct, are politicized, tacticalized, and commercialized. Morality in this form short-circuits tradition and
is further unmoored from the natural authority Hayek imagined for it by its advancement through libertarian instruments
and discourses.[88] Instead of organically reproducing civilization,
securing social bonds, and governing conduct, traditional values
become battle cries against godless elites, egalitarians, secular-
ists, and Muslims. As badges worn by political, religious, and
corporate leaders routinely caught in behaviors violating them,
traditional values are reduced to a corporate and political brand,
at which point their nihilistic ablation is nearly complete.

Deracinated from tradition, traditional values are depleted of their integrative function. Politicized as "freedoms," they lose what Hayek affirmed as their noncoercive constraint on freedom, apart from limiting practices they oppose. Weaponized as individual and corporate prerogatives against equality and antidiscrimination laws, they become a means to attack and disrupt rather than foster social bonds and integration. The spontaneous order and common acceptance of rules of conduct through which Hayek affirmed tradition as free has no bearing on the *fight* for traditional values against democratic ones. Rather, winning strategies to repel policies of egalitarianism, diversity, and pluralism make recourse to individual and corporate freedoms secured through statism, rather than spontaneous order or commonly accepted norms. With their aggrieved melancholy for a phantasmatic past and aggressive supremacism, they rebel against rather than reproduce the order.

One twist away from Hayekian governmentality today, then, comes from (de)formation by battle and its framing by rights discourse and value pluralism. Hayek's thought was intrinsically vulnerable in this regard. His formula for transitioning from social democracy to a neoliberal order featured political authoritarianism, which could hardly rebuild the bedrock of tradition—organicism, evolution, spontaneity, freedom—even if it touted traditional principles. Indeed, from Weber we know that instrumental rationality cannot mix with traditional rationality without destroying the latter—that is the meaning of the process Weber calls "rationalization."[89] From Dostoyevsky, we know faith cannot become politicized without inverting into its opposite—dictate and violence.[90] Put another way, bringing tradition "back" is oxymoronic. Even in Hayek's understanding, what remains of "tradition" after social democracy has had its way with it for half a century? How can an intensely politicized evangelical church, rife with contractualist, capitalist, and vengeful ambitions, recoup what Hayek valued for its organic, evolved, tacitly accepted mode of binding communities and conduct? In an important way, then, Hayek's utopia crashes on the shoals of the political and the social it seeks to vanquish both theoretically and practically. It could not "govern" without deformation by the powers it sought to fight and was also required to wield. William Callison calls this a "political deficit" in neoliberal rationality.[91]

A second twist away from Hayek in contemporary mobilizations of traditional morality pertains to its uptake today by those for whom freedom is not a central principle or desire, those who would be sanguine about state and church authority used to compel obedience and secure order. Hayek sought to reconcile freedom with political and familial authority, not to sacrifice the former to the latter. His own distance-taking from conservatism is relevant here. Conservatives, he argues in "Why I Am Not a Conservative," care for freedom only selectively and are willing investors in state power when it is deployed for things they favor: "The conservative does not object to coercion or arbitrary power so long as it is used for what he regards as the right purposes."[92] Conservatives thus share with the Left two things Hayek regards as consummately dangerous: confidence that they know the good for society and willingness to employ political power to impose it. This kind of conservatism, especially fierce on the religious Right today, builds not just the authority of the state endorsed by neoliberals, but its expansion and extended reach, which they dreaded.

There is a third twist away from Hayek's formulation of traditional morality in actually existing neoliberalism. This pertains to morality's imbrication with the reactive energies of white male woundedness and displacements, its function as a retort to those it holds responsible for its wounds. As cosmopolitan urbanites champion feminism, nonnormative sexualities, nontraditional families, secularism, the arts, and education, aggrieved white midlanders reflexively roar against abortion, same-sex marriage, Islam, "attacks on whites," godlessness, and intellectualism. This is not "tradition" or even morality speaking, but hatred of a world perceived to be wishing and washing theirs away.

Hayek says that tradition provides "order without commands" in the form of authority, hierarchy, and rules of conduct.[93] This abstraction, made concrete, is a reminder that tradition carries the ordinances and stratifications generated by relations of property, kinship, caste, race, gender, sexuality, and age. Whatever else it provides and promulgates, the "traditional" family secures secure male supremacy, heteronormativity, and ethnic-racial loyalties. In the United States, Southern "tradition" carries the legacies of slavery and Jim Crow, even as it may also carry modes of decorum and hospitality. Small-town "traditions" are generally built around ethnic, racial, and religious homogeneity, if not explicit exclusions.[94] When traditional values campaigns are fueled by rancor about endangerment or loss, these features tend to become boldfaced and politicized, linking with fealty to nation and civilization.[95] This is most evident at the extremes: Alt-Right white nationalist groups such as the Proud Boys and Identity Evropa explicitly mobilize Christian family values and the subordination of women for the war against "white genocide" (race mixing that dilutes the white race). They also express pride in what they identify as the white supremacism of America's slave-holding Founding Fathers.

And yet, the cocktail of disinhibited because disembedded freedom and politicized tradition abets a nihilism that tradition is supposed to inoculate against. Hayek's formulation, after all, was freedom *restrained* by tradition, not unleashed as an attack dog on order. Perhaps no one better exemplified the deformation of the neoliberal architecture of tradition, markets, and morals than right-wing provocateur Milo Yiannopolous. Soaring briefly to commercial success by subjecting every subordinate social group and progressive cause to vicious supremacist taunts, he also fashioned a flamboyant queer persona of bacchanalian public disruptiveness and unqualified freedom to say anything about anyone anywhere. Claiming that such freedom is all he cares about, if he cares about anything, and inviting his followers to be equally irreverent and irresponsible, this composite perfectly expressed the raw will to power revealed in traditional values unbound from tradition and dropped in the acid wash of a nihilism that dissolves social bonds and meanings.

This brings us squarely to the problem of nihilism, fatalism and ressentiment, the subject of chapter 5. First, however, we need to examine more closely how the language of markets and morals has been fashioned into an antidemocratic jurisprudence by the U.S. Supreme Court.

4

Speaking Wedding Cakes and Praying Pregnancy Centers

Religious Liberty and Free Speech in Neoliberal Jurisprudence

*Private rights [must] not [be] allowed to become a basis
of predatory power.*
—"Statement of Aims," Mont Pelerin Society

IT IS a commonplace that for much of the twentieth century, the
First Amendment of the United States Constitution was a shield
against state, social, and corporate censorship or repression. It
was especially important in protecting expressions by vulnerable minorities and political dissenters, but also by labor, the
press, entertainers, atheists, and others opposing hegemonic
norms and concentrated power. Then came the neoliberal revolution, and with it, neoliberal jurisprudence—a framework for
interpreting the First Amendment on behalf of broad deregulation, especially for corporate and religious interests. In recent
decades, the First Amendment has been wielded to enhance the
economic, social, and political powers of capital, ownership,
Christianity, and traditional morality. Corporations and Christian conservatives and their allies on the Supreme Court have

employed it to release businesses from all manner of regulation and to empower traditional gender and sexual norms against constraints by equality or antidiscrimination law. Free speech is the lead instrument here, but freedom of conscience ("free exercise") is a frequent, close, and sometimes necessary companion. Their explicit or implicit intertwining and their embedding in a discourse of deregulated markets constitutes a novel political-legal force, the focus of this chapter.

The new First Amendment jurisprudence pushes back against equality and antidiscrimination law in education, employment, welfare, and commerce; against secularism in the commercial and public sphere; against campaign finance limits and transparency in politics; against truth in advertising; against public health and safety regulation; and against informed consumer choices and rights. Protection of speech or religious conscience for individuals, groups, nonprofits, small businesses, and large corporations has rendered every kind of democratically enacted equality provision vulnerable to being overturned or undermined through individual exemptions. Supreme Court decisions affirming this trend grow increasingly expansive and bold. As Justice Stephen Breyer wrote in the dissent for the 2018 decision, *National Institute of Family and Life Advocates v. Becerra*, "the majority's approach" to protecting free speech in this case "threatens . . . the constitutional validity of much, perhaps most, government regulation."[1]

Many constitutional scholars have written about the mobilization of the First Amendment by business and the religious Right in recent decades.[2] Most have focused on the deregulatory effects of the new First Amendment jurisprudence and its applications. More than deregulation, however, is at stake in the expanded meaning and reach of First Amendment freedoms today, which is why it is important to focus on how free exercise and free speech work together. Twinned, they have been mobilized to challenge the significance of social powers in democracies and to empower traditional morality against equality mandates—the themes of the previous three chapters. Far from securing and protecting political dissent, conscience, and diverse private beliefs and neutral state, public, and commercial spheres, the new jurisprudence mobilizes religious liberty and free speech to permit the (re)Christianization of the public sphere.[3]

Free speech, expansively interpreted and applied to many kinds of entities and varieties of "expression," pushes back against democratic mandates legitimately organizing commercial, public, and social life. Free exercise, expansively interpreted and applied to many kinds of entities and their relationships, opens the way to religiously based practices legitimately organizing commercial, public, and social life. Linked, as they are in the cases I am about to discuss, a novel power is born to challenge democracy. Thus, as it upholds a stream of First Amendment challenges to laws of equality, regulated markets, and secularism, the Supreme Court is helping to enact a twisted version of the Hayekian dream—replacing democratically governed society with one organized by markets and traditional morality, under the sign of freedom.

The techniques of this replacement involve three important designations: the designation of everything from money, to cakes, to advertising, to posted legal notices and much else as "speech"; the designation of corporations, small businesses, and nonprofits as entities that "speak"; and the designation of specific acts, practices, and laws as "controversial" among those with "deeply held beliefs." Together, these designations permit escapes from laws claimed to endanger free exercise or compel speech. Combined with the court's inclination to expand privileges of ownership and grant civil rights to associations and corporations, the effect is to empower capital and restrict labor, empower religionists and restrict secularism, and threaten half a century of legislation and adjudication designed to rectify the historical subordination or marginalization of women and racial and sexual minorities. Moreover, taking the place of these groups in the spotlight for legal protection or redress is a different pool of the ostensibly ostracized or victimized: businesses and moral-religious traditionalists.[4]

In this developing jurisprudence, First Amendment liberties are expanded beyond their classical civic meaning and even beyond a market meaning. Rather, they are freighted with a comprehensive neoliberal charge, pushing back against the overweening regulatory and social state that imposes schemes of justice where the spontaneous orders generated by markets and morals ought to prevail. The named enemy is the state, easy enough to vilify in any iteration of liberalism. But behind this charge is the real enemy—an engorged democratic project that valorizes equality, expands political power, and contrasts with the spontaneous orders and outcomes, and hence the freedom, of a world of markets and morals.

We turn now to two recent Supreme Court decisions illustrating the work of this jurisprudence.

Speaking Cakes: *Masterpiece Cakeshop v. Colorado Civil Rights Commission*

Notwithstanding the victory cries of the Christian right and the laments of LGBT activists about the outcome of *Masterpiece Cakeshop v. Colorado Civil Rights Commission*, pundits and legal scholars largely concur that the case came in with a bang and went out with a whimper.[5] Evidently determining that the case was not a "clean vehicle" for adjudicating the larger issues, the court delivered a narrow ruling focused on the failure of the Colorado Civil Rights Commission to be religiously neutral in its hearings on the case.[6] However, the case and the court and concurring opinions reveal the opening of a new front and a new jurisprudential arsenal in the battle between traditional morality and social justice. It is far more than a rearguard action from the Right in the aftermath of the court's legalization of same-sex marriage in 2014. The concurring opinion by Neil Gorsuch and Clarence Thomas, in which almost all antidiscrimination law in commerce is treated as potentially abridging free speech, is particularly foreboding.

In the encounter that led to the case, Jack Phillips, the Colorado baker who owned Masterpiece Cakeshop, refused a request by two Colorado men to make a cake for their wedding celebration. The incident occurred in 2012, before *Obergefell v. Hodges* legalized same-sex marriage across the land. However, the men had married in Massachusetts, where same-sex weddings were legal, and wanted to celebrate with friends and family in Colorado. After Phillips's refusal to provide one of his custom cakes for the occasion, the couple filed a complaint with the Colorado Civil Rights Commission (CCRC) accusing Phillips of violating the Colorado Anti-Discrimination Act. That act, among other things, protects against discrimination based on sexual orientation by "a place of business engaged in any sales to the public and any place offering services to the public." Phillips, however, cited his religious liberty and free speech rights as the basis of his refusal: his religious faith deemed that same-sex marriage was wrong, and being compelled to create a cake to celebrate a same-sex marriage would force him to use his artistry to "speak" against his beliefs.

A CCRC investigation took place, its findings were submitted to an administrative law judge, and the commission concluded that the couple's civil rights had indeed been violated by Phillips's refusal. It rejected Phillips's argument that the First Amendment allowed him to refuse to "exercise his artistic talents to express a message with which he disagreed" and rejected as well his claim that being forced to make a cake for a same-sex wedding celebration violated his free exercise of religion. Phillips appealed, and the Colorado Court of Appeals upheld the CCRC position. The Colorado Supreme Court declined to hear the case, but the U.S. Supreme Court took it up in 2017.

In its ruling, the court declined to rule on the free speech argument and did not even rule substantively on the free exercise claim. Instead, it found that the Civil Rights Commission had violated Phillips's free exercise because a transcript revealed that the commission had failed to be religiously neutral in its hearings and deliberations. One commissioner decried ways that "freedom of religion has been used to justify discrimination throughout history," citing slavery and the Holocaust, and referred to this practice as "one of the most despicable pieces of rhetoric that people can use" in order to "use their religion to hurt others." The Supreme Court majority seized on these sentences and the fact that they went unremarked by the other commissioners to rule that the commission failed to treat Phillips's religious beliefs neutrally and respectfully. It found that the commission disparaged Phillips's religion "in at least two distinct ways: by describing it as despicable, and also by characterizing it as merely rhetorical—something insubstantial and even insincere."[7]

When it reversed the Colorado Court of Appeals judgment, the Supreme Court did not settle any of the complex or controversial issues in the case: whether Phillips's cake baking is artistic expression, hence expressive conduct, hence free speech; whether a wedding cake itself is a kind of speech, and thus whether being compelled to bake one for an event that one considers sinful constitutes forced speech or a violation of religious freedom; whether an owner is equivalent to a business or whether or how an owner or a business are bound to the meaning or message of the product they make or sell; whether refusing to provide a cake for a gay marriage constitutes refusal to create and sell to gay people or only to their marriage, that is, whether it discriminates against persons or only—as Phillips sought to establish with his offer to make cakes for other occasions for the couple—acts. As Justices Thomas and Gorsuch lament in their concurring opinions, in ruling only on the commission's failure to perform state neutrality toward religion, the court did not decide the case.

Still, both the case and the opinions are rich sources for understanding how the First Amendment is being used to privilege traditional morality and undermine democratic determinations of equality and justice in commercial, public, and social life. The argument that Jack Phillips's First Amendment rights would be violated by requiring Masterpiece Cakeshop to bake and sell a cake for a same-sex wedding is built on a constellation of claims, none of which could stand on their own. This constellation links free speech and free exercise to make a new space and power for traditional morality in the public realm. Moreover, the constellation itself is built on a set of oscillations and substitutions—between ownership and artistry, creation and provision, expression and semiotics.

Owner or Artist?

Jack Phillips is described by the court not merely as a baker or business owner, but as an expert baker, a business owner, and an artist; each of these different identities comes into play at different moments in the majority opinion, and the case could rest on none of them alone. Phillips is also depicted not merely as religious, but as a "devout Christian whose main goal in life is to be obedient to Jesus Christ and Christ's teachings in all aspects of his life." He is a man, the court reports, who "seeks to honor God through his work at Masterpiece Cakeshop."[8]

From the beginning, then, Phillips's religious belief and devotion is unconfined, extending to his (co)ownership of the bakery, his work within it, and his artistic craft. This characterization prepares Masterpiece Cakeshop as a miniature of Hobby Lobby, the corporation that sued for and won the legal right to withhold insurance coverage for certain kinds of birth control for its employees. As with the Green family, which owned Hobby Lobby, Phillips's Christianity is formulated as saturating his ownership and controlling every aspect of his business.[9]

However, the case does not turn on Phillips's ownership, even as it presumes and mobilizes it in identifying his bakeshop with his faith.[10] Rather, the petitioners rest Phillips's violated free speech rights on his status as an artist. Were the case to depend on ownership, this would weaken the free speech claim and raise the flag of discrimination—violation of public accommodations law—in Phillips's refusal of custom. As Kennedy writes for the court, "The baker, in his capacity as the owner of a business serving the public, might have his right to the free exercise of religion limited by generally applicable laws."[11] So it is Phillips's artistic work that must carry his religious liberty, even though nowhere in the case are Phillips's artistic talents explicitly linked to his religious beliefs. Nor do any of the wedding cakes on his website feature Christian themes, iconography, or messages; rather, they range from hyperbolically romantic to playful to baroque.[12]

Phillips's status as a Christian owner of an enterprise, on the other hand, is discussed at length in Justice Thomas's concurring opinion, where it is offered as evidence for the extent to which his religious beliefs permeate the shop—its Sunday closure and its refusal to make Halloween goods, cakes with alcohol, or cakes with certain kinds of messages, including those criticizing God. For Thomas, all of this establishes that Phillips's Christian faith exceeds his concern with profit, hence that the bakery is an extension of his religious beliefs, which in turn makes the baked goods "expressive" of these beliefs.[13]

A conundrum then: If it is only Phillips's artistry that carries his potential free speech rights, why discuss all the ways in which Phillips's religious beliefs suffuse his management of Masterpiece Cakeshop (e.g. Sunday closure, refusal to bake Halloween goods, etc.)? Why not focus exclusively on artistry as speech? Only through ownership does religious liberty permit the bakeshop, and not just Phillips, to refuse to make a cake. This is what makes the silence about Phillips's employees—noted by Lawrence Glickman in a comment on the case in the *Boston Review*—so loud and significant. As with the Hobby Lobby decision, ownership is being empowered as Christian ownership, capital is obtaining civil rights as Christian capital. In *Hobby Lobby*, this ownership expands control over the lives of employees; in *Masterpiece Cakeshop*, it expands control over the lives of consumers. The petitioners' crafting of the case, reiterated without contest in the majority and concurring opinions, implicitly ties religious liberty to commercial ownership, not just to persons. This crafting, however, also makes it difficult to determine which is the Trojan horse for moving traditional morality into the public sphere—religion or speech, ownership or artistry. Is it the artist or the owner who is wrongly compelled? Or is the artist the front for the owner?

Artist or Purveyor?

The case also oscillates between Phillips's artistry as a baker and Phillips's provision of baked goods for (sinful or sacrilegious) events as the scene of his potentially violated rights.[14] Although it is a simple fact that Phillips's business is a bakery, not an art studio or gallery, the petitioners and the court draw on Phillips's artistry to formulate his wedding cakes as "speech." Clearly, Phillips puts inordinate care into the preparation of his custom cakes, takes pride in the work, and wants the cakes to be beautiful and admired. The court underlines these things in describing Phillips's close consultation with bridal couples and occasional appearances at wedding receptions for the cake ceremony. Regardless of one's views about same-sex marriage, all of this generates inevitable sympathy for Phillips. Who should be required to create for what they regard as abominations?

Ultimately, however it is not the art that petitioners cast as the site of the rights violation. Phillips believes that "God's intention for marriage is that it is and should be the union of one man and one woman," and the court affirms that creating a wedding cake for a same-sex wedding "would be equivalent to participating in a celebration that is contrary to his own most deeply held beliefs."[15] Artistry makes no appearance in that sentence, just as it makes no appearance in an episode discovered by the Colorado Civil Rights Division investigator in which Phillips refused to sell cupcakes to a lesbian couple for their commitment ceremony because the shop "had a policy of not selling baked goods to same sex couples for this type of event."[16] There are no artists here, no wedding cakes, or even any marriages—only shops, policies, baked goods, and events celebrating particular kinds of couples. Phillips seeks to refuse custom at his bakery—not just his artistry—for the celebration of same-sex unions because of his religious objection to the union. Both Phillips and the court use the fact of his artistry to expand speech rights for businesses and to circumvent public accommodations law.

So why the ruse? The focus on refusing to make art for same-sex unions makes the refusal act or event-based, rather than person-based, allowing escape from concern with discriminating against a protected class. Phillips says he will "bake cakes for the birthdays and showers" (!), but not the weddings of clients he refuses. The petitioners in *Hobby Lobby* made the same distinction, targeting certain types of contraception, rather than the women who would use them. Of course, if certain acts, such as marrying your partner or having access to an IUD or Plan B, are fundamental to your equality, the act-person distinction liquefies, which is why laws securing rights to these things were matters of equality law in the first place. That said, the focus on same-sex unions makes the refusal act-based or event-based, rather than person-based, allowing escape from concern with discrimination. Yet the act-person distinction is what permits the religious objection from appearing discriminatory as it perpetuates inequality. The distinction protects freedom while rebuffing state-mandated egalitarianism. It permits objectors to avoid complicity with a sinful act while also avoiding being tarnished with bigotry. It frames the objector as hating the sin, but not the sinner, and seeking only the personal right to follow their own God. By contrast, the state that would compel their conduct appears invasive, dogmatic, one-sided, and illiberal. Freedom and Christianity are thus allied and preserved, together opposing statism, social justice, and social engineering: Hayekianism realized.

Artistic Expression or the Semiotics of Cake?

The petitioners rest Phillips's right to refuse to make a wedding cake for a same-sex couple on the argument that his artistry as a baker is a form of "expressive conduct," i.e., speech. This is the argument that Justices Alito, Gorsuch, and Thomas forthrightly accept in their concurring opinions and that the majority opinion presents in a favorable light. Yet Phillips's artistry is a red herring in the legal argument, a rhetorical device that produces great sympathy for Phillips while not being the actual basis of his free speech claim. Phillips acknowledges as much, and Justice Thomas makes it even clearer in his concurring opinion: the case rests not on Phillips's speech, but on the meaning, hence the speech, of a *wedding cake*.

A wedding cake, the petitioners declare, "inherently communicates that a wedding has occurred, a marriage has begun, and the couple should be celebrated."[17] More than merely communicating these things, Justices Alito and Gorsuch declare in their concurring opinion, "like an emblem or a flag," the cake "is a symbol that serves as a short cut from mind to mind signifying approval of a specific system, idea or institution."[18] And Justice Thomas writes, "forcing Phillips to make custom wedding cakes for same-sex marriages requires him to, at the very least, acknowledge that same-sex weddings are 'weddings' and suggest that they should be celebrated—the precise message he believes his faith forbids."[19] For Phillips, "to create a wedding cake for an event that celebrates something that goes against the teachings of the Bible would have been a personal endorsement and participation in the ceremony and relationship that they were entering into."[20]

It is not Phillips who speaks with his art, then, but the cake that speaks, by virtue of being a wedding cake. As Justice Thomas is at pains to establish in his remarkable disquisition on the singular nature of wedding cakes, while rarely valued for its taste, the cake is an indispensable element of weddings: "No wedding, no matter how Spartan, is missing the cake," and "if an average person walked into a room and saw a white, multi-tiered cake, he would immediately know that he had stumbled upon a wedding."[21] The potential for compelled speech therefore rests neither on Phillips's artistry nor on religious dictates about wedding cakes—there is no mention of cake in the Bible. Rather, the potential for compelled speech hails from Phillips's *belief* that weddings, for which the cake is a synecdoche, are the hallmark of unions dictated by God and of investiture of this belief, by Phillips, in the wedding cakes that he makes. The cake speaks wedding; according to Phillip's faith, only certain people are eligible for weddings; celebrating weddings of the ineligible goes against God.

Crucially, absent Phillips's religious beliefs about weddings and marriage and his folding of these beliefs into his wedding cakes along with the flour and sugar, it does not matter if the cake is art or if Phillips is an artist. According to Justice Thomas (and Jacques Derrida), Phillips does not control the significa-tion of wedding cake or even the meaning of "wedding" or "marriage," although of course he longs to do so. Rather, the cake bears *for Phillips* the meaning he attributes to marriage, that it is a sacred and exclusively heterosexual event, which is why Phillips will not sell any "baked goods" to homosexuals trying to participate in it. Put the other way around, the argument that Phillips's wedding cakes are his speech rests not on his artistry, but on his conviction about the divine sacrament of heterosexual marriage and corresponding belief that homosexual marriage goes against God, and his investment of that religious conviction in his cakes. His cakes carry that religious meaning for him, though not necessarily for others and thus not necessarily when they "speak" wedding at the events they adorn. Phillips himself speaks, then, not through his art, but through his willingness or refusal to provision for events he believes to be divinely ordained or condemned. Indeed, the instability and ultimate lack of force in the claim that Phillips "speaks" with his artistry is evident in the inability of petitioners and the court's opinion to settle whether what Phillips aims to withhold with his refusal is his "speech," his "participation," his "endorsement," or his "recognition" of the same-sex wedding.

At this point, an obvious question emerges: If it is the wedding cake, rather than Phillips's art that speaks, and if the cake, in speaking "wedding," does not speak *as* Phillips, why pursue the free speech argument at all? Why not concentrate exclusively on Phillips's free exercise of religion? In effect, this is what the court's narrow ruling did. However, to understand why the petitioners and the court give the speech argument so much airtime, despite its rickety footing, we need grasp the political strategy that depends on binding conscience to speech such that religion can exercise more power in the commercial and public sphere. The court and much commentary tend to treat the two claims separately and sequentially. In fact, they are crucially bound together in a new antidemocratic constellation.

Free Exercise *as* Free Speech

Free speech is the *means* by which free exercise is extended into the commercial and public sphere, where, the Colorado Civil Rights Commission argued, "religious beliefs cannot legitimately be carried."[22] The court interpreted the CCRC's position as religious nonneutrality, with its implication that "religious beliefs and persons are less than fully welcome in Colorado's business community." This statement, however, cloaks, rather than opens up the argument about secularism contained in this dispute.

A secular liberal democracy authorizes the protection of one's religious values as a private right, generally limiting enactment of these values to comportment with secular law protecting the public interest. Even after the 1993 passage of the federal Religious Freedom Restoration Act, which strengthened the test for this comportment, when exemptions from federal mandates are sought on the basis of religious requirements or beliefs, the public interest remains the threshold criterion. Religious liberty to believe and worship as one chooses is not expected to burden third parties, which is why Douglas NeJaime and Riva Siegel regard the recent turn to "complicity-based conscience claims" as so troubling.[23] Exercise of one's religious liberty is not supposed to bear upon those outside the faith and is not generally concerned with public or commercial exercise of religious values, but with protection from discrimination or, at the extreme, persecution. Thus, individuals whose faith designates Saturday as the Sabbath have sought exemption from rules about qualifying for unemployment benefits; those whose faith requires head coverings sought loosened requirements for photographs for federal documents, where coverings are normally prohibited; the Amish famously obtained exemptions from mandates for educating youngsters through the age of sixteen. Each of these exemptions were based on the conclusion that the public interest was not sacrificed for the protection of religious worship.[24] When free exercise brushes against widely accepted norms or generally applicable law, it has been due to a fundamental belief about personally appropriate practices of dress, food, family, or worship that those norms and laws constrain or violate. Historically, then, the exercise of religious liberty is not centered on the public exercise of religious values, but authorizes and protects one's personal relationship to conscience or the divine.[25]

Freedom of speech is the obverse. Meaningless in the private realm or personal relationships, free speech signifies the right *to say in public* what one wants to say and only what one wants to say. It is a right to speak in an unrestricted and unforced public fashion even if some are disturbed or wounded by one's speaking. The right of free speech at once acknowledges and subordinates concerns of third parties and public culture to that right. It is a right exercised in public and may well shape the public realm and how it is experienced by others. Importantly, it also carries a great deal of our individual public power in democracies, which is why it is fundamental to democratic citizenship and why extending it to corporations is so consequential.[26]

What is developing today as a right-wing political and legal strategy is this: free speech takes free exercise by the hand, pulls it into the public and commercial world, and uniquely empowers it there. Only by treating Phillips's cake making as speech can actions based on his religious beliefs circumvent public accommodations law. By itself, as the CCRC argues and the court acknowledges in its decision, Phillips's right to free exercise cannot permit discrimination. Only the conjoining of free speech and free exercise, achieved by insisting that Phillips's cake making is art and that art is speech, permits exercise of his religious convictions *as speech* in the public and commercial realm and, conversely, makes the case for his commercial speech as the vehicle of his private religious convictions. Indeed, only through the artful conjoining of free speech and free exercise can one make sense of this otherwise bewildering summary of Phillips's claim by the court: "requiring him to create a cake for a same-sex wedding would violate his right to free speech by compelling him to exercise his artistic talents to express a message with which he disagreed and would violate his right to the free exercise of religion."[27]

In this sentence, the sheer number of prepositions and verbs and lack of subordinate clauses makes it nearly impossible to specify the source or site of the violation. Where, precisely, is the action? Requiring the creation of a cake does not violate a right to free speech. Compelling exercise of artistic talents to express a message with which one disagrees does not violate one's First Amendment rights. (Commercial artists presumably do this all the time at the behest of their bosses or managers.) And creating a cake for a wedding does not violate one's free exercise of religion any more than being required, commercially, to exercise one's artistic talents to express a message with which one disagrees. However, all of these phenomena pressed together— required creation of art expressing a message contrary to one's religious beliefs—bolstered by the unmentioned right of commercial ownership, sets free exercise loose in the public and commercial sphere and generates the scene of its entitlement to discriminate, indeed, to abridge laws of equality. This is more than constitutional constructivism. This is the U.S. Supreme Court empowering a revolutionary antidemocratic force through a novel joining together of ownership, religion, and speech.

There are some cracks in this new configuration, produced in part by the fact that it is a political strategy and thus politicizes the religious claim it seeks to bolster. Free speech secures, among other things, the right to political dissent. Free exercise secures one's right to personal beliefs and faith. As the case slides toward protecting political dissent, it slides away from protecting religious practice. Because there is nothing about cake making or artistry in scripture or any other religious code, the grip that free speech has on free exercise requires the supplement of claims about artistry and ownership. It is thus unclear that a nonproprietor at a bakery could claim that her free exercise rights were violated by having to make wedding cakes for all comers—presumably, she would simply have to look for a different job. It is also unclear how many, if any, claims apart from objection to same-sex marriage could carry the religious investiture of Phillips's refusal. His free exercise of religion, then, is not really at stake. Rather, it is his combined status as property owner, baker, and Christian that enables him to mount a resistance to what is now the law of the land. This reveals the strategy as carrying a nihilistic spirit, discussed in chapter 5, in which religion is less the basis than the *instrument* of political dissent.[28]

No sooner was the *Masterpiece Cakeshop* decision announced than the Alliance Defending Freedom, the anti-LGBT organization representing Phillips, upped the ante. It is suing the state of Arizona for prohibiting a pair of (beautiful, young, white, female) commercial artists from posting a sign in their business declaring their refusal to serve couples celebrating same-sex unions.[29] To my knowledge, the artists at Brush & Nib have *not* been approached by any same-sex couples to create wedding announcements or other wedding art. Rather, the alliance is suing for the artists' right to post a sign in their establishment or on their website that would be the equivalent of a "whites only" placard at a segregated soda fountain in the 1950s. The ADF writes: "While the case proceeds for Joanna, Breanna, and Brush & Nib, they continue to create art reflecting God's beauty. And they hope to soon have the freedom to only create that art and to fully explain their artistic and religious beliefs to others. Alliance Defending Freedom is here to protect the right of creative professionals to use their God-given talents in ways that are consistent with their beliefs."[30] This is the next turn in the campaign for God and freedom in the public sphere—businesses not merely exempt from public accommodations law, but promoting themselves on the basis of their objections.[31] There is no reason to expect this bid to be limited to small businesses, to arts or crafts . . . or to concern with same-sex marriage.

Praying Pregnancy Centers: *National Institute of Family Life Advocates, DBA NIFLA, et al. v. Becerra, Attorney General of California*

We turn now to a second case concerned with compelled speech decided by the Supreme Court in 2018. In this one, petitioners use the First Amendment as a deregulatory power to perpetuate simultaneous concealment and expansion of their religiously motivated policy aims into public space.

National Institute of Family Life Advocates, DBA NIFLA, et al. v. Becerra, Attorney General of California (hereafter identified as *NIFLA*) tested the constitutionality of California's 2015 Reproductive FACT Act. That act required unlicensed crisis pregnancy centers (hereafter identified as CPCs) to post a statement that they are not medical facilities and required all CPCs to post or distribute a statement identifying the availability of free or low-cost comprehensive reproductive health care, including prenatal care and abortions, provided by the state of California.

Petitioners alleged that both notices abridged their freedom of speech. The majority opinion, delivered by Justice Thomas, upheld this claim, arguing, "the FACT Act unduly burdens protected speech. It imposes a government-scripted, speaker-based disclosure requirement" while leaving "unburdened those speakers whose messages are in accord with" the government's "own views."[32] In addition, the opinion argued that the FACT Act perpetrated "viewpoint discrimination" against the CPCs and that the speech it aimed to impose was "content based," rather than essential, uncontroversial, factual information.

None of the opinions in the case—majority, concurring, or dissenting—explains the context and motivation for the FACT Act, an absence that gives the decision a technical, rather than political ring and downplays its significance for women's reproductive freedom. Without appreciation of what crisis pregnancy centers are and how they operate, it is impossible to understand what the FACT Act aims to redress and why CPCs resisted it so fiercely.

There are now approximately four thousand crisis pregnancy centers in the United States.[33] Most obtain organizational, financial, legal, and personnel support from large umbrella organizations such as NIFLA, CareNet, and Heartbeat International.[34] By all accounts, CPCs have one goal, which is to convince women carrying unwanted pregnancies not to abort them. However, their self-representation and techniques for attracting clients intentionally obscure this goal and often their religious backing, as well. That is because their target clientele is women whom they call "abortion vulnerable"—women carrying unwanted pregnancies and seeking or considering an abortion.[35] As antiabortion activist Abby Johnson said of CPCs at the annual Heartbeat International conference in 2012, "We want to appear neutral on the outside. The best call, the best client you ever get is one that thinks they're walking into an abortion clinic."[36]

To this end, most CPCs indicate on their websites and other materials that they offer "abortion counseling," even if the fine print may reveal that they do not provide or refer for abortions. Reception staff are trained to dodge the question when potential clients ask on the phone if they provide abortions. CPCs advertise a "supportive and non-judgmental" environment, "no matter what you decide to do." All claim to offer "unbiased, confidential and free medical, educational and support services" for women facing an unplanned pregnancy.[37] Many CPCs present themselves as providing a panoply of services related to pregnancy although the unlicensed ones offer only a drugstore pregnancy test (which the client must self-administer) and "counseling" aimed at convincing women to carry their babies to term. In many CPCs, even where there are no licensed medical personnel, staff wear white lab coats or scrubs, request health information on intake forms, and replicate the look and feel of a medical office. Others appropriate the spirit and tone of feminist groups. Claris Health, for example, (whose motto is "Choices you can live with"), on its softly sleek website featuring pictures of radiant young women of many hues, proclaims: "Claris Health's story began over 40 years ago, when a small group of women were inspired to start an organization that offered life-changing services to women, men, and families. Our mission from the start has been to empower individuals to make fully informed pregnancy and sexual health choices."[38]

CPCs, which draw federal funding and are often subsidized by state funds, as well, frequently locate near Planned Parenthood and other pro-choice clinics, at times even in the same building, with the explicit aim of drawing off or confusing clients attempting to access those agencies. In a few cases, CPCs have moved into the space of shuttered abortion clinics or Planned Parenthood offices.[39] Some use Planned Parenthood's initials in their signage (PP for "Problem Pregnancy") or take the name of a local comprehensive reproductive health clinic with just one word altered, e.g. Oakland Women's Center instead of Oakland Women's Clinic. CPC billboards, too, are often intentionally designed to be mistaken for those of Planned Parenthood. The national umbrella organizations sponsoring the clinics dedicate substantial funds to pay-per-click methods for advertising their clinics in response to search engine keywords such as "abortion" or "morning after pill."[40] The San Francisco Women's Clinic, for example, appears at the top of a Google search for "abortion clinic near me."[41] CPCs are also developing tools to reach clients via chat, text, and online video appointments.[42]

CPC "abortion counseling" may involve berating clients considering it, showing them pictures of mutilated fetuses or dead women on gurneys, and of course, showing them pictures and videos of fetuses in utero where the actual stage of development may be fictionalized. Abortions are depicted as carrying greater health risks than childbirth (perforated uterus, sepsis, death) and as increasing the possibility of future miscarriage, suicide, depression, drug addiction, infertility, breast cancer, and other health problems.[43] Abortion providers may be described as dangerous, unscrupulous, greedy, and dirty. Some CPCs offer misinformation about abortion availability, telling women that they can delay their decision for many months or telling them that miscarriage is likely and there is therefore no need to seek a medical abortion. The developmental stage of the fetus the client is carrying may be mischaracterized, the fetus is invariably called a "baby" or "preborn baby," and the client is referred to as a "mom." Staff occasionally pray with their clients over the "baby" at the first visit.

Many CPCs are located near high schools or colleges to attract the young and frightened. Others are located in neighborhoods where other vulnerable constituencies are targeted—poor and nonwhite women who may not have regular doctors, health insurance, or other resources. Here the (often false) offer of free health care, housing, and financial support is as important as the medical misinformation in convincing women to carry their pregnancies to term. Some CPCs also offer factually false information about the dangers of contraception—pills, IUDs, even condoms—in an effort to get unmarried girls and women to practice sexual abstinence.[44]

Not every crisis pregnancy center in the United States does all of these things, but all do many of them. All obscure their raison d'être by attempting to appear as neutral, all-purpose resources for women with unplanned or "crisis" pregnancies, hiding their Christian sponsorship and funding. None has a commitment to science, facticity, transparency, or women's informed understanding of their legal and practical choices in dealing with an accidental pregnancy.[45]

Crisis pregnancy centers may therefore be fairly characterized as engaging in deceptive self-representation and misinformation to exploit the needs, fears, and anxieties of women facing unplanned pregnancies. This is what the California FACT

Act aimed to address with its two simple requirements. First, all licensed healthcare facilities must either post or distribute to clients the following statement: "California has public programs that provide immediate free or low-cost access to comprehensive family planning services (including all FDA-approved methods of contraception), prenatal care, and abortion for eligible women. To determine whether you qualify, contact the county social services office at [phone number]." Second, all unlicensed CPCs must also post a notice indicating that they are not licensed medical facilities.[46] Neither requirement would be controversial if abortion (and promotion of sexual abstinence) were not in the mix. Neither requirement would be needed if CPCs were not engaged in so much dissimulation and misinformation to advance their aims. The FACT Act was imposed on a structurally duplicitous and exploitative industry to correct for this duplicity.

In rejecting the constitutionality of the act, unlike the arguments in *Masterpiece Cakeshop*, neither the *NIFLA* petitioners nor the court invoke free exercise, even though the court describes the petitioners as "a group of covered medical facilities that object to abortion for religious reasons" and Justice Kennedy's concurring opinion refers to CPCs as "pro-life pregnancy centers."[47] The petitioners and the court thus throw the same cloak over religion as CPCs do in order to attract unwitting clients to their premises.[48]

And yet, free exercise is everywhere in this case. Protective of the mission of CPCs and offering zero discussion of their tactics, the court argues that the act forces CPCs to post or provide information that compels speech in violation of "deeply held beliefs." The court also argues that the California law does not impose factual disclosures, but a "viewpoint" in a controversy. The treatment of CPCs as having free speech rights is possible only by thoroughly identifying the "views" of each center with its personnel—making shared belief constitutive of their existence and purpose. Claiming that there is no special meaning or class of "professional speech," even while it treats the centers as engaged in such speech, the court implicitly recognizes the belief-based status of the centers. The case is a free speech case only because the court treats CPCs as committed to a position opposing abortion that the disclosures potentially weaken, and yet does not identify this position with religion. The court, like the CPCs, cares more about protecting that political position, including protecting it from the charge of offering faith-based care, than with protecting truth in advertising, truth in medical provision, and the knowledge-dependent autonomy of women seeking help with an unplanned pregnancy. The court endorses the displacement of each by traditional morality free from state interference and expanded into the public sphere, precisely embodying the neoliberal vision articulated in the three preceding chapters.

In fact, the majority opinion identifies abortion neither as a right nor as a legally available medical procedure. Rather, it depicts abortion as a subject of ethical controversy about which the state has no right to impose its "viewpoint" or "preferred message"; a topic on which dissenting views ought to be settled in "the marketplace of ideas"; and a product to which the CPCs object and should therefore not be required to "advertise." Together, these convert the disclosures required by the FACT

Act into what the court finds to be "content-based" and "viewpoint-specific" speech. Justice Thomas writes for the majority, "the FACT requirement is content based because it compels individuals to speak a particular message and alters the content of their speech" when "Centers have to provide a government drafted script about availability of state-sponsored services which petitioners are devoted to opposing."[49] However, identifying the availability of such services only alters the content of the centers' speech *because* they are committed to obscuring this availability. The claim that the script *alters the message* of the centers tacitly endorses the CPCs practice of dissimulation and nontransparency, confirming that their "speech" involves omission, deception, and denial that is countered by a "government drafted script." The claim recognizes that the centers are not the health providers they pretend to be, but engaged in a political battle in which pregnant girls and women may be unwitting because insufficiently informed pawns. At the same time, in rejecting the principle that "professional speech" bears any special restrictions under the First Amendment and reducing the speakers at issue to the individuals who staff CPCs, it licenses religiously animated antiabortion advocates to front as unregulated purveyors of professional services.

In this vein, it is significant that the court accords free speech rights to the centers themselves, yet identifies individuals as those whose speech the FACT Act "compels." The required notice about state-provided services, Justice Thomas writes, compels "*individuals* to speak a particular message" as they "provide a government-drafted script about the availability of state-sponsored services," one of which "is abortion."[50] In fact,

CPC personnel need not speak for the centers to comply with the FACT Act, any more than individual workers "speak" the messages contained in required postings about hygiene, safety, or whistleblower protections hanging in their workplaces. Only because center personnel are presumed committed to the duplicity employed by the centers—only because they are part of the staged deception—can the disclosures be considered to compel their speech.

The argument that the disclosures compel speech also tacitly confesses that the mission of CPCs is religious and political, even as they purport to be health care providers. Were CPCs to foreground their religion and politics (which would undermine their tactics), "professional speech" would not be at issue. If they were forthrightly Christian antiabortion organizations offering help to pregnant women seeking such help, discussion of whether professional speech may be regulated would be irrelevant to the case. CPCs' pretense that they are offering professional services to the public, however, requires the court to deal with the question of whether professional speech may be subjected to special restrictions, presumably comporting with the ethics, knowledge, and responsibilities of the profession. The court concludes that professional speech has the same First Amendment protections as any other kind, a conclusion easy to treat as simply animated by an antiregulatory spirit. This is what Justice Breyer does in his dissent. While it unquestionably draws on the majority's impulses in this regard, the argument against restricting professional speech does something far more significant in permitting religiously animated antiabortion advocates to front as unregulated purveyors of professional services.

Here is how this unfolds. Professions, Justice Thomas opines, and hence professional speech, are impossible to define precisely, and any effort to do so involves a nefarious statism, one giving states an "unfettered power to reduce a group's First Amendment rights by simply imposing a licensing requirement."[51] Equally dangerous in the attempt to restrict or regulate professional speech, he adds, is the prospect of distorting the "uninhibited marketplace of ideas in which truth will ultimately prevail."[52] Citing Justice Holmes's famous encomium that "the best test of truth is the power of the thought to get itself accepted in the competition of the market," Justice Thomas ignores the CPCs' strenuous efforts to distort this competition and to prevent their own ideas from being transparent enough to be market tested.[53] If CPCs sought to have their truth prevail in an ideas marketplace, they would forsake their ruses, misinformation, and deceptions. They would not fear signs on the wall informing clients of the facts. That the court endorses their free speech claim in the name of "an uninhibited marketplace of ideas" perhaps says as much about standards for "free" markets today as it does about "speech" today—neither of which would be recognizable as such in previous eras.

There is a second problem related to this one: What relationship is Justice Thomas positing between a putatively free market of ideas where competition yields a winner and the realm of "deeply held beliefs" of those whose speech he claims is wrongly compelled by the required disclosures? Even if one accepts the validity of the "ideas market" for some things, how does it bear on matters of conscience and religious faith? Is religious pluralism in a secular age really supposed to generate winners from a competition? Isn't the realm of faith where markets, competition, and other tests of belief are bracketed, where individuals legitimately hold beliefs unaccountable to others, to reason, or to truth? Isn't this partly why belief and conscience are given protected and private berth in secular democratic orders?

If all this is so, Thomas's invocation of a "free market of ideas" for religious conviction operates as something of a revealing slip in which a liberal principle considered appropriate to the realm of marketing or politics is accidentally transposed into the realm of faith . . . or in which the realm of faith is collapsed into politics and marketing. The slip suggests the same nihilistic symptom that we glimpsed in *Masterpiece Cakeshop* as it casts belief into a marketplace where advertising, branding and targeting populations are all appropriate means of competing and winning. It mobilizes the ostensibly testable claims of political speech for the untestable doctrines of faith, making clear that the abortion battle is fundamentally political and that the CPCs are politically motivated entities, despite obtaining protection for their speech on the basis of conscience. It thus reveals the court as permitting a free speech claim to provide a cloak for religiously animated public agency; at the same time, the court is permitting a religious claim to shield CPCs from accountability to truth in advertising and other forms of regulation. As with *Masterpiece Cakeshop*, the court is permitting the vehicle of free speech to facilitate conservative Christianity's escape from the private sphere to become a force in the commercial and public one and at the same time is protecting it *as religion* ("belief") from laws regulating commerce and public life. This is the real significance of the court's insistence that there is nothing distinctive about "professional speech" in considering the reach of the First Amendment. By simultaneously treating the case as one of the rights of professional speech and as one of compelled speech at the site of deeply held beliefs, the court creates a portal through which misrepresentation and even fraud become protected speech. Truth, transparency, and accountability all take a back seat to religious purposes dressed up as professional services.

The court, however, spies a very different danger in this case. It does not worry about truth, transparency, accountability, professional norms, or potential exploitation of the vulnerable. Rather, the distinctive danger identified in both the majority and concurring opinions is imposing "state speech" on CPCs. The danger is state-mandated disclosures, not Christian evangelists masquerading in the white coats of the medical profession.[54] Both the majority and concurring opinions go so far as to identify the FACT Act with the statism of authoritarian or totalitarian regimes. The state "speaks," Justice Thomas writes, not on behalf of public interest, public health, or democracy, but with the power to "suppress unpopular ideas or information" and advance its own "viewpoint."[55] Finding this typical of governments that have historically "manipulated the content of doctor-patient discourse" to increase state power and suppress minorities, he quotes from legal scholar Paula Berg:

During the Cultural Revolution, Chinese physicians were dispatched to the countryside to convince peasants to use contraception. In the 1930s, the Soviet government expedited completion of a construction project on the Siberian railroad by ordering doctors to . . . reject requests for medical leave from work. . . . In Nazi Germany . . . German physicians were taught that they owed a higher duty to the "health of the Volk" than to the health of individual patients. Recently, Nicolae Ceausescu's strategy to increase the Romanian birth rate included prohibitions against giving advice to patients about the use of birth control devices.[56]

Analogizing the FACT Act with repressive twentieth-century regimes directly manipulating physicians and public health for nefarious state ends may seem hyperbolic. Yet Thomas's hyperbole is mild compared with that of Justice Kennedy. His short, furious concurring opinion, joined by Justices Alito and Gorsuch, lambasting California's effort to regulate CPCs, denounces "the viewpoint discrimination . . . inherent in the design and structure" of the FACT Act through which the state's "preferred message advertising abortions . . . compels individuals to contradict their most deeply held beliefs."[57] Adding that there is a "real possibility that these individuals were targeted *because* of their beliefs"—representing a persecution of minorities for their dissent from the state's position—Kennedy pounces on the statement by the California legislative majority that the act's passage represents California's legacy of "forward thinking."[58] Treating this declaration as the open confession of an ideologically animated state, Kennedy writes:

it is not forward thinking to force individuals to "be an instrument for fostering public adherence to an ideological point of view [they] fin[d] unacceptable." *Wooley v. Maynard*, 430 U.S. 705, 715 (977). It is forward thinking to begin by reading the First Amendment as ratified in 1791; to understand the history of authoritarian government as the Founders then knew it; to confirm that history since then shows how relentless authoritarian regimes are in their attempts to stifle free speech; and to carry those lessons onward. . . . Governments must not be allowed to force persons to express a message contrary to their deepest convictions. Freedom of speech secures freedom of thought and belief. This law imperils those liberties.[59]

As both the majority and concurring opinions identify the FACT Act with statist authoritarianism, they accuse California of forcing individuals to "speak" and "advertise" the state's own "position" in a "controversy." Yet the FACT Act does not stifle speech, and as we have seen, it is a stretch to claim that it compels speech. The mandatory disclosures neither promote nor advertise abortions, but simply correct for the deliberate and systematic deceits of crisis pregnancy centers in pursuing and servicing clients. California aims to ensure that citizens have access to facts the CPCs do not want them to have. It is rightly concerned about political operations pretending to be medical facilities and misinforming the clientele it often lures under false pretenses. The court, conversely, has tied back the hand of the law so that religious evangelical institutions may operate in unrestricted fashion in the sphere of public health. It has done so by demonizing democratic legislation on behalf of the public interest as authoritarianism and by widening the spheres of both unregulated markets and morality.

The point is not the obvious one that the court sided with antiabortion petitioners in *NIFLA*. Rather, it tacitly affirmed and replicated CPC tactics as it accepted *NIFLA*'s framing of the case. It facilitated the CPCs own use of the state—in which they obtain public funds and First Amendment protection to advance traditional morality, without regulation or oversight, in the public domain, under the sign of freedom. At the same time, without mentioning religious liberty, the court licensed religious groups to operate freely in civic, commercial, and public life. This depended on the following moves.

First, the court treated the disclosures required by the FACT Act as speech advertising abortion and promoting the state's viewpoint in an ethical and political "controversy." The designation of abortion as controversial is how the court turns facts into viewpoints and health care information into advertising for those viewpoints.

Second, the decision identifies the speech of CPC personnel as violated by the FACT Act. This identification implicitly acknowledges that CPCs are the instrument of individuals committed to preventing abortions, even as the FACT Act requires the centers, not individuals, to post disclosures. The focus on the compelled speech of individuals, however, has the important effect of eliminating the operations of the centers themselves from consideration in the case: the "deeply held beliefs" of CPC personnel are all that the court is concerned with protecting, while the systematic dissimulations and misrepresentations of the CPC industry, which, again, make no appearance in the court's opinion, is all that the FACT Act is concerned with regulating. This links the *NIFLA* case to those protecting corporate "speech," cases in which corporations are identified as persons or identified with the persons owning them and in which civil rights intended for individuals are used to deregulate professional or commercial conduct. Treating regulations intended to force transparency for CPCs as violations of the free speech of individuals is how the court reduces public interest to the state's "viewpoint" and challenges democracy on behalf of morality in the name of freedom.

Third, by treating the required notices as state speech opposing CPC speech and declaring that the FACT Act "regulates speech as speech," the court converts regulation in the public interest into partisan positioning.[60] Casting everything as speech makes everything into a viewpoint and treats all viewpoints as equivalent. It also makes everything appropriately submitted to the "competition of the market of ideas" where no competitor should be required to advertise for another. Making everything into speech at once obscures and legitimates the deliberate deceptions of the CPCs; it reformats these deceptions as quotidian tactics in the competitive struggle for market share within the marketplace of ideas.[61]

Fourth, "deeply held beliefs," protected as speech, become the basis for rejecting regulation and also link *NIFLA* to *Masterpiece Cakeshop*. While *NIFLA* does not engage the free exercise clause, that clause is lurking in the shadows, just as organized conservative Christian purposes and funding lurk in back rooms of the CPCs, but are rarely in their window fronts or website homepages.

Fifth, "controversy" is mobilized as a designation to limit state regulation in general and demands for factual accountability in particular. It converts state regulation itself into a viewpoint in the controversy and any venue shaped by it, hence any venue where moral traditionalism contests democratic protections against discrimination or unequal treatment. This permits the requirement that reproductive service agencies inform women of adoption options, but not abortion (adoption is formally uncontroversial). "Controversy" foregrounds the claims of free speech and cancels accountability to science, public health, and consumer protection.[62]

Through these five moves, without even mentioning religious freedom, the Supreme Court licenses religious groups to avoid accountability to science or regulation as it unbinds their power to act in civic, commercial, and public life.[63] In addition to what Justice Breyer argued in his dissent, that the majority opinion threatens the "constitutional validity of much, perhaps most government regulation," the opinion also resets the relationship between private moral or religious views and democratic concerns with protecting against distortions, lies, and deceptions in the representation and provision of services to an unwitting public.[64] Like *Masterpiece Cakeshop*, the decision fosters a rollout of traditional morality and a rollback of government regulation that together transform a society organized by democratic principles and decisions into something else. Like *Masterpiece Cakeshop*, the decision both empowers Christian morality in the social sphere and depowers state-secured justice there. This has become a key legal strategy for realizing Hayek's ambition to replace social democracy and social justice with an order organized by markets and traditional morality.

Finally, the decision comports with and abets the nihilism of the age in which values become instrumentalized as they lose their foundations and become political cudgels or commercial brands. The decision affirms this nihilism in its comportment with the tacticalization of religion and dethronement of truth in public life. It makes the U.S. Supreme Court itself and the Constitution it is bound to interpret into weapons in the culture wars. It heralds a world of "fake news" all the way down, one where conservative Christianity, property ownership, and wealth are empowered as freedoms against social and political democracy.

5

No Future for White Men

Nihilism, Fatalism, and Ressentiment

Nihilism and Desublimation

Nihilism begins, Nietzsche argues, with the rise of reason and science as challenges to God and other forms of authority, challenges that reveal all meaning to be constructed and all facts to be without inherent meaning. Max Weber calls it "disenchantment." Tolstoy "descralization"—their different inflections and approaches to the problem converge in agreement that intrinsic value flees the world. However, for Nietzsche, the age of nihilism heralds not the end of values, but a world in which "the highest values devaluate themselves" as they are unmoored from their foundations.[1] These values, which include the Christian virtues along with democracy, equality, truth, reason, and accountability, do not vanish as they lose their foundations, but become fungible and trivial, superficial and easily instrumentalized.[2] This trivialization and instrumentalization, ubiquitous in commercial, political, and even religious life today, further degrade the value of values, which further abets the nihilism . . . an unending spiral shaping political culture and subjectivity.

When a Martin Luther King Jr. speech about public service is used to advertise Dodge trucks during the Super Bowl, when Catholic clergy are revealed to have molested thousands of children while their superiors looked away, when "moral values" politicians are exposed for consorting with prostitutes or making abortion payments for mistresses—these things bring not shock, but a knowing grimace, nihilism's signature.

However, Nietzsche's profound account of nihilism was limited by his preoccupation with God and morality as they were being challenged by science and reason. Charting nihilism in this way leaves out the nihilistic force of other human powers that are uncontrolled and imperiling, an order in which the omniscience and omnipotence of both God and man are toppled. Or as Carl Schmitt teaches in his "Dialogue on Power," almost simultaneous with the recognition that power itself is radically human, that it derives neither from nature nor from God, there is supersession of its containment within and by humans, an end to the dialectic of power/powerlessness. With modernity, Schmitt argues, human power not only loses its human face (kings, barons, militia), but takes novel forms that diffuse and multiply its effects. This diffusion and multiplication means that power comes to be set against everyone, "even the holder of power."[3] It is a multiplying, intensifying force without respect for its creators, exceeding the will to power and any institution or individual.[4] This also becomes the occasion for ressentiment, power's eternal progeny, to diffuse widely, well beyond those who suffer from immediate oppression or deprivation. As power's historically novel forms and unprecedented ubiquity and uncontainability thwart the mighty and well-placed, along with the downtrodden, and as it inadvertently vanquishes familiar privileges and forms of life, ressentiment roams everywhere.

Schmitt's focus was concentrations of power in the nation-state and novel powers of technology such as the atomic bomb: the undirected powers of capital were not on his mind, the unique techniques of administering human life that Foucault called "biopower" were not in his lexicon, and relentless financialization and digitalization had not been born. Together, these powers intensify the problem Schmitt identified and yield one with which he had not reckoned. The paradox of humanly created powers that diminish the human and especially its capacity to shape its world, reaching new intensities just as this capacity is revealed to be all there is—this breeds new quantities and subjects of ressentiment, and a nihilism beyond Nietzsche's vivid dreams. Again, Nietzsche reflected on the nihilism emanating from the accidental human toppling of the divine; he did not explore formations of power that do not merely trivialize, but openly defile and defy moral values.

There is more. The economizing side of neoliberalism added force to the nihilism of the age and also quickened it, first in leaving nothing untouched by entrepreneurialization and monetization and then, with financialization, submitting every aspect of human existence to investor calculations about its future value. As we become human capital all the way down and all the way in, neoliberalism makes selling one's soul quotidian, rather than scandalous. And it reduces the remains of virtue to branding, for capital large and small. But economization, with its effect on values, is not the only problem here. Nihilism also has its way with the moral values project in neoliberalization as it desublimates the will to power in morality.[5] Here is how this goes.

As nihilism devalues values (voiding them of foundation and truth), it lessens the claim and force of conscience both formed and chained by values. More than simply making subjects less conscience bound, there is a cascading set of effects, the most important of which is the desublimation of the will to power. Recall that sublimation of the will to power, demanded by Judeo-Christian morality, includes turning the will against itself. This turning of the will to power inward, unleashing it on the subject, is what Nietzsche (and Freud, though differently) place at the seat of conscience. It is why both thinkers treat conscience as self-cruelty, not just self-containment. Conscience is the formation through which we internally attack and berate ourselves, not only restrain ourselves.

As the nihilistic devaluation of values lightens the force of conscience, it frees us from the restraint, self-blame, and self-abuse that conscience imposes. Desublimation sends the will to power outward again as it releases the subject from the lash and restraint of conscience. Hans Sluga puts it this way: "with nihilism, there is a falling back and collapse of the will to power into its own elementary form . . . even religion and the appeal to religious values become cynical instruments for the unrestrained use of power."[6] Yet more is at stake in this collapse than a will to power unbridled by humility or ethics. Rather, Sluga writes, "what also goes by the way in this unrestrained will to power is any concern for others . . . in particular the compact between generations on which our entire social order has rested so far."[7] If this desublimated force, tinged by the pain of a wound (dethroned white masculinity) courses through traditional values politics today, we could not be further from the voluntary conformity with rules and spontaneous order that the neoliberal intellectuals counted on tradition to provide. It has turned into something else.

Not quite a century after Nietzsche wrote, Herbert Marcuse considered desublimation from a different angle to theorize the nonliberatory release of instinctual energies in postwar capitalism. What Marcuse famously termed "repressive desublimation" occurs within an order of capitalist domination, exploitation, and "false needs" as technology reduces the demands of necessity and as desire is everywhere incorporated into a commodity culture enjoyed by a growing middle class. This order features plenty of pleasure, including that obtained by radically reduced strictures on sexuality (less grueling work requires less sublimation), but does not feature emancipation. Instinctual energies, no longer directly opposed by the mandates of society and economy and thus no longer requiring heavy repression and sublimation, are now co-opted by and for capitalist production and marketing. As pleasure and especially sexuality are everywhere incorporated into capitalist culture, the pleasure principle and the reality principle slip their ancient antagonism.[8] Pleasure, instead of being an insurrectionary challenge to the drudgery and exploitation of labor, becomes capital's tool and generates submission.[9] Far from dangerous or oppositional, no longer sequestered in aesthetics or utopian fantasy, pleasure becomes part of the machinery.

This much is familiar. Marcuse's next turn in developing the implications of repressive desublimation, however, bears most directly on our problem. According to Marcuse, nonliberatory desublimation facilitates "happy consciousness," Hegel's term for resolving the conflict between desire and social requirements by aligning one's consciousness with the regime. Marcuse draws on Freud and Marx to radicalize Hegel's formulation: in ordinary cultures of domination, Marcuse argues, "unhappy consciousness" is the effect of conscience—superegoic condemnation of "evil" urges in both self and society.[10] Conscience is thus at once an element in the superego's arsenal for internal restraint and a source of moral judgment about society. As repressive desublimation offers a reprieve from this strict censorship and gives rise to "happy consciousness" (a less divided self because a less conscientiously repressed one), conscience is the first casualty. Importantly, conscience relaxes not just in relation to the subject's own conduct, but also in relation to social wrongs and ills . . . which are no longer registered as such. In other words, less repression in this context leads to a less demanding superego, which means less conscience, which, in an individualistic, unemancipated society, means less ethical-political concern across the board. In Marcuse's words, "loss of conscience due to the satisfactory liberties granted by an unfree society makes for a *happy consciousness* which facilitates acceptance of the misdeeds of this society." This loss of conscience "is the token of declining autonomy and comprehension."[11]

That desublimation lessens the force of conscience makes intuitive sense, but why does Marcuse associate this with the subject's declining autonomy and intellectual comprehension? His complex point here differs from Freud's argument in *Group Psychology and the Analysis of the Ego* that conscience weakens when the subject effectively transfers it to an idealized leader or authority. For Marcuse, autonomy declines when comprehension declines (this is the cognitivist, if not the rationalist, in him), and comprehension declines when it is not required for survival and when the unemancipated subject is steeped in capitalist commodity pleasures and stimuli. Put the other way around, instinctual repression takes work, including the work of the intellect.[12] Therefore, as late capitalist desublimation relaxes demands against the instincts, but does not free the subject for self-direction, demands for intellection are substantially relaxed.[13] Free, stupid, manipulable, absorbed by if not addicted to trivial stimuli and gratifications, the subject of repressive desublimation in advanced capitalist society is not just libidinally unbound, released to enjoy more pleasure, but released from more general expectations of social conscience and social comprehension. This release is amplified by the neoliberal assault on the social and attack on intellectual knowledge as well as by the depression of conscience fostered by nihilism.

Repressive desublimation, Marcuse argues, is "part and parcel of the society in which it happens, but nowhere its negation."[14] It looks like freedom, but shores up the domination of the status quo. Its expressions, Marcuse says, may be bold or vulgar enough even to appear as maverick or dissident—it may be "wild and obscene, virile and tasty, quite immoral."[15] However, this daring and disinhibition (manifest today in Alt-Right tweets, blogs, trolling, and public conduct) symptomizes or iterates, rather than counters the order's violence and prejudices, as well as its ordinary values.[16] In Marcuse's view, repressive desublimation twins "freedom and oppression," transgression and submission, in a distinctive way, as is apparent in the wild, raging, and even outlaw expressions of patriotism and nationalism frequently erupting from the extreme Right today.[17]

Repressive desublimation also unleashes new levels and perhaps even new forms of violence through opening the spigot of that other well of human instinct, Thanatos. Desublimation of Eros is compatible, Marcuse argues, "with the growth of unsublimated as well as sublimated forms of aggressiveness."[18] Why? Because repressive desublimation doesn't release Eros for freedom *tout court*, but instead involves a compression or concentration of erotic energy at the site of sexuality—this is part of what makes it "controlled" or "repressive" desublimation. Desublimated Eros may therefore bestir, blend with, and even intensify aggression. Thus Marcuse explains growing accommodation or acquiescence to social and political violence—a "degree of normalization where . . . individuals are getting used to the risk of their own dissolution and disintegration."[19] His own reference was to the mid-twentieth-century Cold War nuclear weapons buildup, but the point is easily adapted for accommodation to world-ending climate change and other existential threats. Most importantly for our purposes, his insight is suggestive for understanding the quantity and intensity of aggression spilling from the Right, especially the Alt-Right, amidst its frenzied affirmation of individual freedom, about which more shortly.

Finally, there is Marcuse's account of the role of the market in intensifying the nihilism theorized by Nietzsche. Writing well before the neoliberal revolution, Marcuse argues that the market has become both reality principle and moral truth: "The people are led to find in the productive apparatus"—the market—"the effective agent of thought and action to which their personal thought and action can and must be surrendered," and "in this transfer, the apparatus also assumes the role of a moral agent. Conscience is absolved by reification, by the general necessity of things. In this general necessity, guilt has no place."[20] Already depleted by desublimation yielding a happy consciousness, the weak remains of conscience are taken over by market reason and market requirements. The real is both the rational and the moral. At once reality principle, imperative, and moral order, capitalism becomes necessity, authority, and truth rolled into one; suffusing every sphere and immune from criticism, despite its manifest devastations, incoherencies, and instabilities. There is no alternative.

Bringing Marcuse's version together with Nietzsche's, the historically specific nihilistic depletion of conscience and desublimation of the will to power perhaps explains several things. To begin with, it may animate what is commonly called a resurgence of tribalism, but is better framed as a broken relation to the world demographically outside and temporally after one's own. It may be the decoding key for Melania Trump's infamous "I really don't care, do u?" emblazoned Zara jacket worn on her visit to migrant children separated from their parents at the Texas border. It may explain the routinized mocking, on right-wing websites and in comments sections, of "libtard" concern with human suffering, injustice, or ecological devastation. In *Strangers in Their Own Land*, Arlie Hochschild sympathetically recounts her right-wing interviewees desire to be free "from the strictures of liberal philosophy and its rules of feeling." They felt

they were being asked "to feel compassion for the downtrodden" when "they didn't want to," although they identified as
devout Christians.[21] They spurned environmentalism on similar grounds (and because it involved big government) notwithstanding the devastation of their health and habitat resulting
from polluting industries.[22] Refracting this politics of indifference through the nihilistic disintegration of a social compact
and through lost faith in capacities to control human powers and
arrangements takes us beyond Hochschild's inclination to root
this sentiment in her subjects' experience of social and political
neglect. It explains their attraction to leaders calling for aggressive door-slamming to "outsiders" and a humanly habitable
future, leaders who build this sentiment into an affirmative
political passion animated by a desublimated will to power. It
explains why such policies are celebrated with gleeful, vengeful
rallying cries. The wreckage that nihilism makes of conscience
may also help explain the unprecedented aggression and viciousness emanating from right-wing cable and internet news,
blogs, and tweets. This aggression and viciousness is fed by neoliberal valorization of libertarian freedom, by wounded, angry
white maleness, and by nihilism's radical depression of conscience and social obligation.[23] It is discursively organized by
neoliberal assaults on the social and the political and by neoliberal legitimation of indifference to the predicaments or fate
of other humans, other species, or the planet. However,
attacks on liberals and leftists, feminists, antiracists, and others are also a nihilistic form of action. The passion and pleasure
in trolling and trashing are signs of what Nietzsche called
"wreaking the will" simply to feel its power when world

affirmation or world building are unavailable. Perhaps negation—whether crude or moralistic—is what remains when the powers shaping the world appear uncontrollable and uncontainable, and existential doom appears imminent. Again, however, it is important to register the active quality of this negation: right-wing spurning of ethical or political enjoinders to care for or repair the world is a form of "doing." And, as Nietzsche points out, "there is so much that is festive" in it—especially in the pleasures of provocation and piling on, of humiliating others or making them suffer, of dancing at the bonfires of what one is burning down.[24]

In this consequential turn, where nihilism intersects neoliberalism, freedom is torn out of the habitus in traditional values by which it was to be contained and disciplined in the original neoliberal formation. The combination of neoliberalism's deprecation of the political and the social and a desublimated, wounded white masculinity together generate a disinhibited freedom, one symptomizing ethical destitution even as it often dresses in religious righteousness or conservative melancholy for a phantasmatic past. This freedom is paradoxically expressed as nihilism and against nihilism, attacking and destroying while faulting its objects of derision for the ruin of traditional values and order. It is freedom unbridled and uncultured, freedom to put a stick in the eye of accepted norms, freedom from care of the morrow. This is the freedom remaindered by nihilism, in the making for centuries and intensified by neoliberalism itself. It is the freedom of "I will because I can, because I believe in nothing and I am nothing other than my will to power."[25] This is humanity without a project other than revenge, without restraint by conscience, faith, or value and without belief in either human or divine purposes. One extreme expression of such subject production and orientation may be the so-called "incel" movement, composed of men whose wrath at being spurned or ignored by women is turned against the women themselves through online aggressions such as trolling and Gamergate, but also in the form of terror attacks such as those in Isla Vista and Toronto.[26] Here, desublimation permits what was formerly the material of shame, misery, and self-loathing to be acted out as murderous rage. At the same time, the movement draws on a nihilistic version of moral traditionalism, "before feminism," in which male sexual access to women was a matter of right.

Attention to the desublimated will to power in subjects and morality itself would explain another feature of the present, namely, how the Right, with its values agenda, routinely survives the moral scandals so frequently enveloping its religious and political leaders, indeed, survives them better than the Left. Why were Clinton's blowjobs from an intern more damaging to his presidency than Trump's pussy grabbing, assault allegations from Miss Universe contestants, peeing prostitutes, and affairs with porn actresses and *Playboy* bunnies have been to his—especially given their respective constituencies? How does a right-wing Supreme Court justice nominee survive allegations that would have taken down a Democratic nominee in a heartbeat? One answer is that nihilism depresses the significance of conduct, consistency, and truth: one no longer need be moral, only shout about it. Another is that nihilism makes values politics contractual: Trump's evangelical base does not care who he is or what he does so long as he delivers on Jerusalem, abortion, the trans ban in the military, prayer in school, and the rights of Christian businesses and individuals to discriminate. As we saw in chapter 3, there is plenty of evidence that both sides understand this deal.[27] Evangelical leader Pat Robertson also makes the contractualism explicit. Responding to Saudi Arabia's murder of the journalist Jamal Khashoggi, he wrote, "For those who are screaming blood for the Saudis—look, these people are key allies . . . it'll be a lot of jobs, a lot of money come to our coffers. It's not something you want to blow up willy-nilly."[28]

However, neither the contractualism nor the decreased importance of moral consistency tap the most important feature of nihilism here. Nihilism releases the will to power not only in subjects, but in traditional values themselves, baldly revealing the privilege and entitlement they encode, their raw power purposes and energies. Thus, morality, too, "falls back" to its elementary form, its will to power, as nihilism shatters its foundations and devalues its value. Pussy grabbing, adultery, consorting with prostitutes, scamming contractors and undocumented workers—these are rights of the powerful that traditional values implicitly license as they explicitly prohibit, encode as they disavow.[29] If the power purposes in traditional morality are enormous, they are what remain when nihilism takes its Sermon on the Mount drapery off. More, for constituencies anxious about their ebbing place and privilege, nothing is more reassuring than Trump's crass sexual entitlement to all women, the crude contractualism of his marriage, and for that matter, all of his crude conduct and flaunting of law and the protocols of the presidency . . . none of which a female or nonwhite politician could emit and survive for a nanosecond—which is precisely the point. Trump's boorishness and rule breaking, far from being at odds with traditional values, consecrates the white male supremacism at their heart, whose waning is a crucial spur to his support.

Nihilism and Ressentiment

In addition to nihilism, Nietzsche is the master theorist of another symptom of our age—suffering experienced as wrongful victimization. He posited whole moral systems born from suffering and rage, offering a formulation of ressentiment as the basis of their emergence and unfolding. Again, we will have to revise Nietzsche here, since waning entitlement, aggrieved supremacism, and not merely the frustrations of what he called "weakness" are at the heart of these logics today, but let us reprise his account first.

Judeo-Christian morality, Nietzsche suggests in the first essay of *On the Genealogy of Morals*, was born as the revenge of the weak, those who suffered in a value system affirming strength, power, and action. The weak were resentful not of their own weakness, but of the strong, whom they (mistakenly) blamed for their suffering. And so they invented a new value system in which strength would be reproached as evil and weakness lofted as good.[30] The invention of this new value system, Nietzsche says, occurs when ressentiment stops seething long enough to "become creative and give birth to values."[31] The weak cannot act, only react; this is what their moralizing critique is, and because it is all they have, they will pursue it doggedly until it triumphs. Thus does a Judeo-Christian valorization of meekness, humility, self-abnegation, and asceticism, but also equality and democracy, emanate from the wound of weakness and take down the strong and the powerful, whom this new morality constrains and punishes. Again, the creature of ressentiment, in its incapacity to make the world, reproaches the world it blames for its suffering and humiliation, thereby anesthetizing their sting. This means the moral system it builds has rancor, reproach, negation, and even revenge at its heart.

Ressentiment, rancor, rage, reaction to humiliation and suffering—certainly all of these are at play in right-wing populism and support for authoritarian leadership today. However, this politics of ressentiment emerges from the historically dominant as they feel that dominance ebbing—as whiteness, especially, but also masculinity provides limited protection against the displacements and losses that forty years of neoliberalism have yielded for the working and middle classes. This ressentiment thus varies from Nietzschean logics rooted in the psychic vicissitudes of weakness. Though linked by humiliation, the frustrations of weakness (existential or historical) and of aggrieved power are worlds apart, obvious enough in the radically different responses by working-class whites and working-class blacks to the displacements and demotions delivered by neoliberal economic effects. Only the former is aggrieved by its dethronement.

And yet there is an important aspect of the neoliberalization of everyday life that salts this wound: the deep inequality of access and hierarchies of status organizing every part of commerce and what remains of public life. As works such as Michael J. Sandel's *What Money Can't Buy* argue, today there is hardly a contemporary activity or sphere of life unstriated by tiers or classes of access dependent on wealth: from boarding an airplane to the legroom and food inside it; from access to sports events to access to uncongested highway lanes; from who obtains family leave in a corporation to who obtains an MRI authorized by their health insurance; from how quickly you can renew a passport, get on to the rides at Disney World, or get your offspring into rehab.[32] These stratifications are written so deeply into contemporary culture that they are an essential part of branding: the lousiest motel chains have "premier lounges," and "upgrade" is a ubiquitous term in every industry and service. The more of public life that is privatized—national parks, education, roads, emergency, schools, and other city services—the more this inequality heaps up the have-nots into crowded underserved piles of misery while offering the haves (the top 30 percent, not the top 1 percent) every possible way to buy their way out of crowding, waiting, and suffering.

Wealth-determined stratification of access and provision is hardly new under the sun. But neoliberal privatization and legitimation of inequality make it more intense, more widely disseminated, and more deeply penetrated into everyday life than at any time since feudalism. The tiered pricing of service, access, and treatment for everything everywhere accustoms all to inegalitarianism and makes us more feudal than democratic in subjectivity and ethos. This phenomenon also surely

176

intensifies the anger of the dethroned, when Boarding Group 1 passengers, exuding cosmopolitanism along with the importance conferred by rank, push past the middle-aged white couples from the fly-over states smashed together in Boarding Group 5. Attention to such effects resets the tired Left debate about whether right-wing populism today is born of class or other kinds of resentment, whether it is the rage of the economically left behinds or the rage of dethroned white masculinism. The neoliberalization of everyday life—not merely its inegalitarian effects, but also its relentlessly inegalitarian spirit—richly compounds the two.

What happens when ressentiment is born of dethronement, from lost entitlement, rather than from weakness? I want to offer two speculations.

First possibility: the rancor and rage are not developed into refined moral values, but remain rancor and rage. They are not sublimated into the Christian self-abnegation and love of thy neighbor that Nietzsche treats as the apex (or nadir) of the process he accounts for in *On the Genealogy of Morals*. Suffering and humiliation, ressentiment unsublimated, become a permanent politics of revenge, of attacking those blamed for dethroned white maleness—feminists, multiculturalists, globalists, who both unseat and disdain them. The unstanched wound and unsublimated rage, combined with a nihilism that mocks in advance all values, means that high levels of affect, not developed moral systems, not what Nietzsche called "unprecedented cleverness" building whole systems of critique, animate populations mobilized by them. This is raw ressentiment without the turn toward discipline, creativity, and ultimately, intellectual mastery that Nietzsche tracks as slave morality in building Judeo-Christian civilization. This is ressentiment without diversion into clever critiques and refined moral logics that invert by reproaching domination. This is ressentiment stuck in its trapped rancor, unable to "become creative." It has only revenge, no way out, no futurity.

It is significant that Trump himself identifies revenge as his sole philosophy of life: revenge and nothing else, revenge without end, because there is nothing else.[33] Beyond efforts to destroy anyone who questions or opposes him, revenge saturates his so-called agenda and is also what satisfies the basest part of his base. It animates the drive to overturn every Obama-era achievement, of course, from climate accords to the Iran deal, but also to destroy what those policies aimed at protecting or preserving: the earth and its many species, the rights and protections of the vulnerable (LGBT, women, minorities), and the health of Americans secured through Obamacare.[34]

It is also significant that many Trump supporters, when interviewed about his lies, affairs, flouting of truth or law, say "I don't care. I'm tired of the disrespect his opponents have for him and for me."[35] What kind of defense of your man is this? Insofar as it eschews reasons and values, it, too, expresses nihilism. Insofar as it expresses a wound as the basis of an attachment, it puts into discourse ressentiment toward those they know are the real winners today: those in Boarding Groups 1 and 2. In affirming the propriety of respect for the president, regardless of his conduct, it reiterates the hollowness of "support for the troops" fighting wars no one believes in—loyalty to the shell of what was once filled with value. In confessing that Trump embodies a retort to their pain, it explains why it does not matter what policies he pursues, only that he opposes those they hold responsible for their suffering. In fact, his abuses of power—marital and political—are vital to this desire, not at cross purposes with it. He has power they lack and is nothing but the will to power. His base knows this, needs this, electing him not for moral rectitude, let alone political competence, but for revenge against the wound of nothingness by destroying the imagined agent of that wound. This is ressentiment in a nasty stew with nihilism.

Second possibility: a table of values does in fact emerge from the ressentiment of those suffering the lost entitlements of historically conferred power. If Nietzsche is right that ressentiment of the weak redeems its predicament by naming "evil" what it holds responsible for its pain and naming itself "good," then dethroned entitlement would denounce equality and even merit in order to affirm its supremacy based on nothing more than traditional right. "Make America Great Again," "France for the French," "Pure Poland, White Poland"—all the right-wing slogans express this. In affirming supremacy and entitlement based on past supremacy and entitlement, these formations perform a historic inversion of values to close out three centuries of modern experiments with democracy. Indeed, they attack the very Judeo-Christian morality whose production Nietzsche charted, suggesting a completion of what nihilism began. They stage supremacy now as a raw entitlement claim—a staging that converges powerfully with neoliberalism's assault on equality and democracy, the social and the political.

The white male supremacism in contemporary traditional values politics becomes explicit, then, not only because nihilism pulls the moral drapery off those values and makes them contractual or instrumentalizable, but also because this supremacism has been wounded without being destroyed. Its subject abhors the democracy it holds responsible for its wounds and seeks to pull democracy down as it goes down.

Perhaps we are also witnessing how nihilism goes when futurity itself is in doubt. Perhaps there is a form of nihilism shaped by the waning of a type of social dominance or the waning social dominance of a historical type. As this type finds itself in a world emptied not only of meaning, but of its own place, far from going gently into the night, it turns toward apocalypse. If white men cannot own democracy, there will be no democracy. If white men cannot rule the planet, there will be no planet. Nietzsche was immensely curious about what would come after the two centuries of the intensifying nihilism he expected. But what if there is no "after"? What if supremacy is the rosary held tight as white civilization itself appears finished and takes with it all futurity? What if this is how it ends?

Nihilism for Nietzsche emanates from the death of God. Inaugurating the recognition that humans make their own meanings, values, worlds, we first shift our reverence from God to man and then lose faith in what we have created ourselves as groundless and contingent. Moreover, as he writes in *On the Genealogy of Morals*, we have been made small and miserable, rather than noble and happy through the building of Judeo-Christian civilization and thus have grown weary of man: "together with the fear of man we have also lost our love of him, our reverence for him, our hopes for him, even the will to him." As a result, "what is nihilism today if is not that?—We are weary *of man*."[36]

However, as I discussed at the beginning of this chapter, Nietzsche's account of nihilism, in which first God and then man is toppled as foundational sources of truth and morality, is inadequate to our present. Other things inflect nihilism's contemporary course and manifestations. Today, for example, nihilism intensifies in a world that reflects humanity as having brought the species to unprecedented misery and the planet to the brink of destruction. "Man" has not merely lost value or stable meaning, but is indicted by myriad powers generated, but not controlled by humans, powers that diminish, mock, reproach, and endanger us, not only devalue us. We appear not only without nobility and greatness, but without even the ability to provide for ourselves or clean up after ourselves. A species of giant toddlers, appetitive for power, pleasure, and play, we have yet to become responsible for our creations, our history. The paradox of humanly created powers that diminish the human by revealing our incapacity to direct our fates or even preserve ourselves and our habitat, reaching new heights as these powers are revealed as all that makes the world—this breeds a nihilism beyond Nietzsche's wildest imagination. Charting nihilism as emanating from the desacralization and hence devaluation of values, Nietzsche did not take the measure of the formations and effects of power that trivialize and mock humans themselves, at which point nihilism intersects with fatalism, apocalypticism, or despair. Little wonder that rapture Christianity, with its end-times eschatology, is the religion of the age.[37]

Space

If neoliberalism is conceived only as economic policy and effects, the frame for discontent is limited to economic factors—growing inequality, deindustrialization, loss of union jobs and of the provisions of the social state. The resulting analysis focuses on the "left behind," especially the economic and political neglect of the white working and middle class generated by a rising tide of elites, cosmopolitans, and the beneficiaries of identity politics. If neoliberalism is conceived only as a political rationality featuring the ubiquity of markets and *homo oeconomicus* (my claim in *Undoing the Demos*), we cannot grasp the affective investments in privileges of whiteness and First World existence in the nation and national culture or in traditional morality. We also cannot grasp the ways that the hierarchies and exclusions of "tradition" legitimately challenged democratic equality in the name of both family values and freedom. This means that we cannot grasp the new formations of subjectivity and politics that are, in good part, neoliberal effects. At the same time, we cannot grasp what the forces are that neoliberalism accidentally intersects or instigates and thus what it produces inadvertently and even against its own aims. These are the kinds of genealogical emergences (to use Michel Foucault's language) or conjunctures (to use Stuart Hall's) occluded by historiographies bound to progress, regression, dialectics, or determinism.[38] They may be complex to map and narrate, but without them, we remain lost.

Above all, when neoliberalism is reduced to economic policy or rationality, it blinds us to three tectonic shifts in the organization and consciousness of space that both spur certain political reactions today and organize the theater in which they occur. The first of these shifts is the lost horizon of the nation-state consequent to globalization. From capital flows to immigrant flows, from digital networks to supply chains, the world has invaded the nation, weakening its borders and its sovereignty, redistributing production and consumption, and transforming the existential conditions and prospects of every kind of population—rural, suburban, and urban. If this shift has incited rancor against both new immigrants and the politics and politicians held responsible for allowing them into the West, it is also producing a divide between those accommodating the shift and those furiously rebelling against it.

The second spatial shift involves the neoliberal destruction of the social discussed in chapter 2. As neoliberalism dissolves that sphere into a market order, on the one hand, and a familial one, on the other, the space of civic equality and concern with the common good that democracy requires disappears. At the same time, the rise of the digital generates a novel, radically deterritorialized and dedemocratized sociality. This sociality features no clear protocols of power sharing, enfranchisement, or commitment to negotiating diverse views and needs, inclusion, or plurality. Whatever their merits, digitalized "societies" are detached from the challenge of sharing power equally in order to rule ourselves. They may have other democratizing potentials, but they are not themselves substitutes for democratic practices and the political equality they require.

The third spatial shift pertains to the rise of finance capital and the modality of value that it ushers into the world. Multinational corporations and global assembly lines of post-Fordism already challenged the visibility and tangibility of capital ownership and control. However, the vaporous powers of finance, which rule everything, but live nowhere, are akin to a Copernican revolution for subjectivity in relation to the powers making and governing the world. Indeed, just as the round earth cannot be seen, but can be known only deductively, through its effects, rule by finance involves a transformation of spatial consciousness that paradoxically hinges on the despatialization of power as such, not only the deterritorialization identified with globalization in its early decades.

One popular account of the effects of all three shifts is capsulated by British pundit David Goodhart's notion of "somewheres" and "anywheres."[39] "Somewheres" are people rooted in a specific place or community, rural or suburban, generally have limited education and exposure to the world, and harbor conservative social views. "Anywheres" he depicts as relatively rootless, urban, and urbane; they tend to be more educated, progressive, and open to the future. With this popular demography, Goodhart aims to offer a geopolitical wellspring for contemporary political divides—one that exceeds the conventions of beneficiaries versus victims of globalization, but that also attempts to bypass the conventional framing of the urban/

rural divide in which those who profit from globalization are pitted against those who are devastated by it and those inhabiting multicultural milieus are divided from those who heretofore inhabited homogenous white worlds or long-standing racially hierarchicalized ones. With this map and lexicon, Goodhart seeks to bring into relief the political divide between those who experience profound threats to their demographic rootedness, on the one hand (the somewheres) and those he casts as born into or at least embracing an urban, cosmopolitan, deterritorialized existence, on the other (the anywheres). The different horizons and affects he aims to encode with this division of the world distinguish between those who cling to place and those who have embraced globalization—culturally, socially, economically, and politically.

Goodhart's map is overdrawn and occludes important features. However, like Hochschild's figure of "strangers in their own land," it captures an aspect of subjective white Western reaction to globalization. To develop Goodhart's thesis, Carl Schmitt is again helpful because of his close attention to the ontological implications of space. In *Land and Sea* and *Dialogue on Power and Space* Schmitt throws down this provocation: humans are land mammals and orient themselves through land demarcation and organization.[40] A close relationship to the earth secures both ground and horizon for humans. It orients humanity toward demarcation, possession, and lineage, which are concretely achieved through property, house, marriage, family and inheritance. In contrast, efforts to extend sovereignty through or across the sea and even develop livelihoods from the sea orient people differently: toward boundarylessness, but also toward use and consumption, rather than ownership and culti-vation.[41] Schmitt is thinking here not only about the difference between fishing and farming, extraction and reproduction, but about how and why sea-surrounded England becomes an empire and how all the coastal nations of Europe attempt infinite out-ward expansion, while other European peoples and nations remain oriented toward Europe.[42] By his own acknowledgment, he is responding to Hegel's remark in the *Philosophy of Right* that land "is the condition for the principle of family life," while "for industry the outward enlivening natural element is the sea," and he is openly wrestling with the fusion of industry and coloni-zation that Hegel mirrors from his time.[43] In this discussion, Schmitt's wariness of seafaring people but also of denational-ization is palpable: loss of ground entails loss of boundary and horizon, loss of ties to the local across time, loss of the primacy of family, tradition, religion. Blood and soil indeed.

Schmitt knows this speculative history does not stay con-fined to actual peoples and places and that there is, rather, a transformation of (European) consciousness that comes with discovery of the New World, the Copernican Revolution, and the "spatial revolution" that "involves a change in the concepts of space encompassing all the levels and domains of human existence."[44] "It is no overstatement," he writes, "to claim that all domains of life, all forms of existence, all kinds of human creative force, art, science, and technology partake in the new concept of space."[45] It even becomes the foundation of Occiden-tal rationalism that "advances irresistibly" and destroys "the medieval forms of human community, builds new states, fleets, and armies, invents new machines, subjugates the non-European peoples, and places them before the dilemma of either adopting European civilization or of descending to the status of a mere colonial people."[46]

However problematically, incompletely, and tendentiously, Schmitt anticipates the experience of globalization by Goodhart's "somewheres" for whom attachments to nation, family, property, and whiteness are mobilized as a politically reactionary formation. Missing from both accounts is the toxic mix of nihilism, fatalism, and ressentiment with neoliberal assaults on the social and the political and valorization of markets and morals that this book limns. Frightened by the loss of values and goods heretofore secured by the "*nomos* of the earth," this population rages against secular cosmopolitans oriented toward use in place of ownership and embracing racial indeterminacy, gender fluidity, "families we choose," godlessness, open borders, speculation, virtual sociality, and the rootlessness of everyday life. The somewheres cling to the soil, even if it is planted in suburban lawn devastated by droughts and floods from global warming, littered with the paraphernalia of addictive painkillers, and adjacent to crumbling schools, abandoned factories, terminal futures. Families become shells, ownership and savings vanish, marriages teeter and break, depression, anxiety, and other forms of mental illness are ubiquitous, religion is commercialized and weaponized, and patriotism is reduced to xenophobic support for troops in aimless, endless wars and useless, but spectacular border barricades. Nation, family, property, and the traditions reproducing racial and gender privilege, mortally wounded by deindustrialization, neoliberal reason, globalization, digital technologies, and nihilism, are reduced to affective remains. To date, these remains have been activated mostly by the Right. What kinds of Left political critique and vision might reach and transform them?

Notes

Introduction

Thanks are due to Corey Robin, who sent me the line from *Middlemarch* used in the epigraph.

1. Nativist, racist, homophobic, sexist, anti-Semitic, Islamophobic, but also antisecular Christian sentiments have acquired political footing and legitimacy unimaginable even a decade ago. Opportunistic politicians ride this wave as more principled conservatives aim to dive under it; the political agendas of both often run more toward plutocracy than toward the furious passions of a base demanding criminalization of immigrants, abortion, and homosexuality, preservation of monuments to a slaveholding past, and nations rededicated to whiteness and Christianity.

2. Thomas Frank, *What's the Matter with Kansas* (New York: Metropolitan Books, 2004).

3. Many thoughtful pundits treat the long tail of the 2008 crisis as *the* precipitating cause of the hard-right turn. See, among others, Yanis Varoufakis, "Our New International Movement Will Fight Rising Fascism and Globalists," *The Guardian*, September 13, 2018, https://www.theguardian.com/commentisfree/ng-interactive/2018/sep/13/our-new-international-movement-will-fight-rising-fascism-and-globalists; and David Leonhardt, "We're Measuring the Economy All Wrong: The Official Statistics Say That the Financial Crisis Is Behind Us. It's Not," *New York Times*, September 14, 2018, https://www.nytimes.com/2018/09/14/opinion/columnists/great-recession-economy-gdp.html; Manuel Funke, et al., "The Financial Crisis is Still Empowering Far-Right

Populists: Why the Effects Haven't Faded," *Foreign Affairs*, September 2018, https://www.foreignaffairs.com/articles/2018-09-13/finan cial-crisis-still-empowering-far-right-populists; Philip Stevens, "Populism is the True Legacy of the Global Financial Crisis," *Financial Times*, August 29, 2018, https://www.ft.com/content/687c0184-aaa6 -11e8-94bd-cba20d67390c; Khatya Chhor, "Income Inequality, Financial Crisis, and the Rise of Europe's Far Right," *France 24*, November 20, 2018, https://www.france24.com/en/20181116-income-inequality-fin ancial-crisis-economic-uncertainty-rise-far-right-europe-austerity.

4. David Neiwert, *Alt-America: The Rise of the Radical Right in the Age of Trump* (New York: Verso, 2017).

5. See James Kirchik, *The End of Europe: Dictators, Demagogues, and the Coming Dark Age* (New Haven, CT: Yale University Press, 2017); Douglas Murray, *The Strange Death of Europe* (London: Bloomsbury Continuum, 2017); and Walter Laqueur, *After the Fall: The End of the European Dream and the Decline of a Continent* (New York: Thomas Dunne Books, 2011).

6. Nikhil Singh, *Race and America's Long War* (Oakland: University of California Press, 2017).

7. See, for example, Jonah Goldberg, *Liberal Fascism* (New York: Doubleday, 2007), 361–67.

8. The developments helping to grow and animate what was previously a fringe formation in the United States and Europe include the aftermath of the finance capital meltdown; the rise of a highly sectoralized and siloed media, including social media; various political and economic crises, from the Syrian civil war to gang warfare in Guatemala, generating a surge in refugees and migrants to Europe and north America; ISIS and other sources of Islamic terror; the two-term presidency of an African American in the United States; Left promulgation of multicultural justice and citizenship; decline in public school quality and college access for working and middle-class families; and above all, the development of the internet. Neoliberal globalization is also responsible for much of the rank discontent of the white working and middle classes in the Global North, whose fortunes and futures crashed as manufacturing capital chased cheap labor in the Global South, finance capital turned the human need for shelter and old age provision into a source of megaprofits from speculation, and the idea of taxation to support civilization went the way of the typewriter.

9. Some of the Ordoliberals came close to endorsing fascism, and for none of them was establishing buffers between markets and politics their only aim. See Quinn Slobodian in *Globalists: The Birth of Neoliberalism and the End of Empire* (Cambridge, MA: Harvard University Press, 2018), which offers a compelling account of the world order they sought to build. In addition, while I cite the conventional dating of the origins of neoliberalism, commencing with the 1947 meeting of the Mont Pelerin Society, William Callison makes a compelling argument for tracing its origins to the period between the world wars. See William Callison, "Political Deficits: The Dawn of Neoliberal Rationality and the Eclipse of Critical Theory" (PhD diss., University of California, Berkeley, 2019).

10. See Thomas Biebricher, "The Biopolitics of Ordoliberalism," *Foucault Studies*, no. 12 (October 2011): 171–91; Claus Offe, *Europe Entrapped* (Cambridge: Polity, 2015); Wolfgang Streeck, *Buying Time: The Delayed Crisis of Democratic Capitalism* (New York: Verso, 2014); and Yanis Varoufakis, *And the Weak Suffer What They Must: Europe's Crisis and America's Economic Future* (New York: Nation Books, 2016) for accounts of how and why banks and financial institutions increasingly undermine political autonomy in decision making. Brian Judge is completing "The Financialization of Liberalism," a dissertation in the UC Berkeley Department of Political Science that examines the mechanisms of this undermining in subnational governmental operations.

11. Many scholars of political economy have critically analyzed the economic contradictions and limitations of neoliberal economics. In addition, William Callison, in "Political Deficits," offers a close genealogical and analytical account of neoliberalism's internal blind spots vis-à-vis "the political." Thomas Biebricher has written about its contradictions and aporias vis-à-vis political neutrality and sovereignty in Biebricher, "Sovereignty, Norms, and Exception in Neoliberalism," *Qui Parle* 23, no. 1 (2014): 77–107.

12. See Rahel Jaeggi, *Fortschritt Und Regression* (Berlin: Suhrkamp: 2018).

13. Wendy Brown, *Undoing the Demos: Neoliberalism's Stealth Revolution* (New York: Zone Books, 2015).

14. Wendy Brown, "American Nightmare: Neoliberalism, Neoconservatism and De-Democratization," *Political Theory* 34, no. 6 (December 2006): 690–714.

15. See Philip Mirowski, "Neoliberalism: The Political Movement That Dared Not Speak Its Name," *American Affairs* 2, no. 1 (Spring 2018),

https://americanaffairsjournal.org/2018/02/neoliberalism-movement
-dare-not-speak-name; and Mirowski, "This Is Water (or Is It Neoliberalism?)," Institute for New Economic Thinking, May 25, 2016, https://
www.ineteconomics.org/perspectives/blog/this-is-water-or-is-it-neolib
eralism. Mirowski chose the appellation "Neoliberal Thought Collective" to capture the extent to which the central ideas of neoliberalism
were not those of one person or even one time. Rather, the Mont Pelerin
Society itself comprised modestly diverse and changing personnel and
refined its ideas over time. Those who were outliers at one time became
central at another, and the different schools of which the society was
composed never achieved intellectual unity even as they shared and
advanced a common political, economic, and moral project.

16. In the 1947 "Statement of Aims" of the Mont Pelerin Society, the first
    item listed as requiring further study was "the analysis and exploration
    of the nature of the present crisis so as to bring home to others its essen-
    tial *moral and economic* origins" (emphasis added). The statement also
    identified a "view of history which denies all absolute moral standards"
    as among the dangers to "the central values of civilization" and free-
    dom. Available at http://www.montpelerin.org/statement-of-aims.

17. Melinda Cooper, *Family Values: Between Neoliberalism and the New
    Social Conservatism* (New York: Zone Books, 2017).

18. While these challenges draw on several elements of the United States
    Constitution, none has been more important than the freedoms wrung
    from the First Amendment. This is the subject of chapters 3 and 4.

19. See Wolfgang Streeck, *Buying Time: The Delayed Crisis of Democratic
    Capitalism* (London: Verso, 2014), especially chapters 2 and 3; Claus
    Offe, *Europe Entrapped* (Cambridge: Polity, 2015); and Greta R.
    Krippner, *Capitalizing on Crisis: The Political Origins of the Rise of Finance*
    (Cambridge, MA: Harvard University Press, 2011), as well as Brian
    Judge's critique of Krippner in his dissertation. With financialization,
    not only are states and even supranational institutions subordinated to
    the powers and vicissitudes of financial markets, but subject production
    and subjectivity also change: risk, credit, and speculation, rather than
    disciplined productive or entrepreneurial conduct shape not just eco-
    nomic life, but political life. See Michel Feher, *Rated Agency: Investee
    Politics in a Speculative Age* (New York: Zone Books, 2018).

20. The claim that neoliberalism's unsettled meaning casts doubt on its exis-
    tence is as odd as claiming that the contested meaning of capitalism,

liberalism, or Christianity means that they don't exist. George Monbiot has also noted that denial of its existence is a tremendous boon to its power. See Monbiot, "Neoliberalism: The Ideology at the Root of All Our Problems," *The Guardian*, April 15, 2016, https://www.theguardian .com/books/2016/apr/15/neoliberalism-ideology-problem-george -monbiot. In a similar vein, see Mirowski, "This is Water (or Is It Neoliberalism?)"; and Mirowski, "The Political Movement That Dared Not Speak Its Own Name." See also the introduction to William Callison and Zachary Manfredi, eds., *Mutant Neoliberalism: Market Rule and Political Rupture* (New York: Fordham University Press, 2019).

21. See Juan Gabriel Valdes, *Pinochet's Economists: The Chicago School of Economics in Chile* (Cambridge: Cambridge University Press, 2008).
22. Slobodian, *Globalists*, see especially the introduction and chapter 1.
23. Guido Brera and Edoardo Nesi, *Everything Is Broken Up and Dances: The Crushing of the Middle Class* (New York: Other Press, 2018) is a brilliant, lyrical, and moving account of this process.
24. Michel Foucault, *The Birth of Biopolitics: Lectures at the College de France, 1978–79*, ed. Michel Sennelart, trans. Graham Burchell (New York: Picador, 2004).
25. Examples of this include my own previous work, *Undoing the Demos: Neoliberalism's Stealth Revolution* (New York: Zone Books, 2015); Michel Feher's *Rated Agency: Investee Politics in a Speculative Age* (New York: Zone Books, 2018); and Pierre Dardot and Christian Laval, *The New Way of the World: On Neoliberal Society* (London: Verso, 2014).

1. Society Must Be Dismantled

1. What Ancient Athenians meant by *demos* is disputed by contemporary scholars. See, for example, Josiah Ober, "The Original Meaning of Democracy," https://papers.ssrn.com/sol3/papers.cfm?abstract _id=1024775, and Daniela Cammack's critique of Ober in "The Dêmos in Dêmokratia," https://papers.ssrn.com/sol3/papers.cfm?abstract_id =2881939.
2. Jean-Jacques Rousseau, *The Social Contract*, trans. Maurice Cranston (London: Penguin, 1968), book 2, chapter 11, 96.
3. Alexis de Tocqueville, *Democracy in America*, trans. Harvey C. Mansfield and Delba Winthrop (Chicago: Chicago University Press, 2000), 2–7.

4. Sheldon Wolin, *Fugitive Democracy and Other Essays* (Princeton, NJ: Princeton University Press, 2001).

5. Wolin, "Democracy and the Political," in *Fugitive Democracy*, 247. Wolin takes Marx to mean that the legitimacy of the modern state rests in the claim to govern for the good of the entire society, to deliver the common good, rather than being the instrument of elites. From Hegel, Marx accepts the aspiration or conceit of the modern state to be "universal" and then famously reveals the "revolution in material life" that must occur for the aspiration to be realized.

6. Wolin, "Democracy and the Political," in *Fugitive Democracy*, 247

7. Wolin, "Democracy and the Political," in *Fugitive Democracy*, 247.

8. About our times, Wolin says, "the containment of political democracy is . . . intimately connected with the animus against social democracy." Preface to *Fugitive Democracy*, ix.

9. Wolin, preface to *Fugitive Democracy*, ix.

10. While often reflexive, these efforts at times take shape as the kinds of carefully crafted projects developed by James Buchanan, the Koch brothers, and the Cato Institute, where the deliberate aim is to replace democracy with wealthy white rule and to capture political institutions and political discourse for this end. See Nancy MacLean, *Democracy in Chains: The Deep History of the Radical Right's Stealth Plan for America* (New York: Viking, 2017). Gerrymandering and voter suppression have become overt and direct tactics for the Republican Party in recent years and were vividly on display in the 2018 midterm elections. Sascha Meinrath, "Two Big Problems with American Voting That Have Nothing to Do with Russian Hacking," *The Conversation*, November 6, 2017, http://theconversation.com/two-big-problems-with-american-voting-that-have-nothing-to-do-with-russian-hacking-86889; German Lopez, "Voter Suppression Really May Have Made the Difference for Republicans in Georgia," *Vox*, November 7, 2018, https://www.vox.com/policy-and-politics/2018/11/7/18071438/midterm-election-results-voting-rights-georgia-florida.

11. Wolfgang Streeck calls this de-economizing democracy. See Streeck, *Buying Time: The Delayed Crisis of Democratic Capitalism* (London: Verso, 2014).

12. Trump thus affably explained to his supporters why he put a "rich person in charge of the economy" and populates his cabinet with the

ultrawealthy, making plutocracy into a commonsensical rather than subversive political form.

13. Ashley Parker and Philip Rucker, "Trump Taps Kushner to Lead a SWAT Team to Fix Government with Business Ideas," *Washington Post*, March 26, 2017, https://www.washingtonpost.com/politics/trump-taps -kushner-to-lead-a-swat-team-to-fix-government-with-business -ideas/2017/03/26/9714a8b6-1254-11e7-ada0-1489b735b3a3_story.html ?utm_term=.de72e20479d1.

14. Parker and Rucker, "Trump Taps Kushner to Lead a SWAT Team to Fix Government with Business Ideas."

15. F. A. Hayek, *Law, Legislation, and Liberty, Volume 2: The Mirage of Social Justice* (Chicago: University of Chicago Press, 1973), 69.

16. F. A. Hayek, *The Fatal Conceit: The Errors of Socialism* (Chicago: University of Chicago Press, 1989), 112–13.

17. Hayek, *Law, Legislation, and Liberty, Volume 2*, 66–68.

18. Hayek, *The Fatal Conceit*, 112.

19. Hayek, *Law, Legislation, and Liberty, Volume 2*, 67.

20. Hayek, *Fatal Conceit*, 113.

21. Hayek, *Law, Legislation, and Liberty, Volume 2*, 75–76, and *The Fatal Conceit*, 116.

22. Hayek, *Law, Legislation, and Liberty, Volume 2*, 76–78.

23. Hayek, *The Fatal Conceit*, 113.

24. Hayek attributes each of these beliefs to Marx, which is a misreading of Marx's own theory of social power, history, and even the possibilities of communism.

25. Hayek, *Law, Legislation, and Liberty, Volume 2*, 68.

26. In fact, no moral code can be submitted to rational justification, because it evolves and carries meanings and value that are beyond the reach of intentionality and comprehension. Hayek, *Law, Legislation, and Liberty, Volume 2*, 68–70.

27. Hayek, *Law, Legislation, and Liberty, Volume 2*, 68.

28. Hayek, *Law, Legislation, and Liberty, Volume 2*, 79.

29. Hayek, *Law, Legislation, and Liberty, Volume 2*, 31–36.

30. Hayek, *Law, Legislation, and Liberty, Volume 2*, 63.

31. Hayek, *Law, Legislation, and Liberty, Volume 2*, 74.

32. Disparity between contributions and rewards for them is inevitable and inevitably disappointing, but not unjust. Hayek, *The Fatal Conceit*, 118.

33. Hayek recognizes that the resulting envy and frustration can breed anti-capitalist attitudes, but these attitudes misunderstand both how capitalism works and what justice is. *The Fatal Conceit*, 199.

34. Hayek, *Law, Legislation, and Liberty, Volume 2*, 5, 8.

35. Hayek, *Law, Legislation, and Liberty, Volume 2*, 8.

36. Hayek, *The Fatal Conceit*, 74.

37. Hayek, *The Fatal Conceit*, 74.

38. Hayek, *The Fatal Conceit*, 74, 118.

39. Hayek, *Law, Legislation, and Liberty, Volume 2*, 71.

40. Hayek, *Law, Legislation, and Liberty, Volume 2*, 62–63.

41. "The curious task of economics is to demonstrate to men how little they really know about what they imagine they can design." Hayek, *The Fatal Conceit*, 76.

42. Michael White, "Nick Clegg's 'Politics of Envy': A Brief History," *The Guardian*, August 29, 2012, https://www.theguardian.com/politics/shortcuts/2012/aug/29/nick-clegg-politics-of-envy.

43. Wilhelm Röpke, *The Moral Foundation of Civil Society* (New Brunswick, NJ: Transaction Books, 2002), 32, quoted in Werner Bonefeld, "Human Economy and Social Policy: On Ordo-Liberalism and Political Authority," *History of the Human Sciences* 26, no. 2 (2013): 114.

44. Alexander Rüstow, *Die Religion der Marktwirtschaft* (Berlin: LIT, 2009) 65, and Rüstow, *Freiheit und Herrschaft: Eine Kritik der Zivilisation* (Münster: LIT, 2005), 365, quoted in Bonefeld, "Human Economy and Social Policy," 114. See also Rüstow, "Social Policy or Vitalpolitik," in The Birth of Austerity: German Ordoliberalism and Contemporary Neoliberalism, ed. Thomas Biebricher and Frieder Vogelman (London: Rowman and Littlefield, 2017), 163–75.

45. Bonefeld, "Human Economy and Social Policy," 114.

46. Melinda Cooper calls this the return of British Poor Laws. See *Family Values: Between Neoliberalism and the New Social Conservatism* (New York: Zone Books, 2017), chapter 3.

47. Michel Feher, *Rated Agency* (New York: Zone Books, 2018), pp. 180–81. See also Michel Feher, "Self-Appreciation; or, The Aspirations of Human Capital," *Public Culture* 21. 1 (2009), p. 27–28.

48. Cooper, *Family Values*. See also Janet Halley and Libby Adler, "You Play, You Pay: Feminists and Child Support Enforcement in the U.S.," in *Governance Feminism: Notes from the Field*, ed. Janet Halley, et al. (Minneapolis: University of Minnesota Press, 2019).

49. Apparently part of what qualified Carson for the post of HUD Secretary was his 2015 screed against an Obama-era regulation requiring that a designated portion of federally subsidized housing be built in neighborhoods with access to public transportation and decent jobs and schools. This, too, he decried as "social engineering." "Ben Carson's Warped View of Housing," editorial, *New York Times*, December 19, 2016, https://www.nytimes.com/2016/12/19/opinion/ben-carsons-warped-view-of-housing.html.

50. Christie Blatchford, "Trudeau Government's Needless Obsession with Gender Is Exhausting," *National Post*, March 21, 2018, https://nationalpost.com/news/christie-blatchford-trudeau-governments-needless-obsession-with-gender-is-exhausting.

51. Michael Taube, "No Boys Allowed, and No Girls Either," *Wall Street Journal*, May 30, 2018, https://www.wsj.com/articles/no-boys-allowed-and-no-girls-either-1527717077.

52. Toni Airaksinen, "'Social Justice Warriors' Are Ruining Engineering, Prof Warns," *Campus Reform*, August 4, 2017, https://www.campusreform.org/?ID=9543; George Leef, "Social Justice Has Invaded Engineering," *National Review*, August 2, 2017, https://www.nationalreview.com/corner/social-justice-engineering-higher-education-martin-center-article.

53. Daisuke Wakabayashi, "Contentious Memo Strikes Nerve Inside Google and Out," *New York Times*, August 8, 2017, https://www.nytimes.com/2017/08/08/technology/google-engineer-fired-gender-memo.html, and Paul Lewis, "'I See Things Differently': James Damore on His Autism and the Google Memo," *The Guardian*, November 17, 2017, https://www.theguardian.com/technology/2017/nov/16/james-damore-google-memo-interview-autism-regrets.

54. Kate Conger, "Exclusive: Here's the Full 10-Page Anti-Diversity Screed Circulating Internally at Google," *Gizmodo*, August 5, 2017, https://gizmodo.com/exclusive-heres-the-full-10-page-anti-diversity-screed-1797564320.

55. Aja Romano, "Google's Fired 'Politically Incorrect' Engineer Has Sparked a Broad Ideological Debate," *Vox*, August 9, 2017, https://www.vox.com/culture/2017/8/9/16112050/google-fired-engineer-james-damore-alt-right-free-speech.

56. Bonnie Honig, *Public Things: Democracy in Disrepair* (New York: Fordham University Press, 2017).

1. Society Must Be Dismantled

57. Hannah Arendt, *The Human Condition* (Chicago: University of Chicago Press, 1958), 40–41.

58. Arendt, *The Human Condition*, 40.

59. Arendt, *The Human Condition*, 46.

60. Arendt, *The Human Condition*, 43.

61. Hannah Arendt, *On Revolution* (New York: Viking, 1963), 17.

62. Arendt, *On Revolution*, 60.

63. Arendt, *On Revolution*, 60. See also Seyla Benhabib, "The Personal Is Not the Political," *Boston Review*, October 1, 1999, http://bostonreview .net/books-ideas/seyla-benhabib-personal-not-political.

64. Hanna Pitkin, *The Attack of the Blob: Hannah Arendt's Concept of the Social* (Chicago: University of Chicago Press, 1998), 4.

65. A fascinating paper by Alexander Somek, "The Social Question in a Transnational Context," drew my attention to this argument by Schmitt. LEQS Paper No. 39/2011, June 2011, available at http://eprints.lse.ac.uk /53215/1/LEQSPaper39.pdf. See 47–48.

66. Carl Schmitt, *The Nomos of the Earth in the International Law of the Jus Publicum Europaeum*, trans. G. L. Ulmen (1950; New York: Telos Press 2003), 79.

67. Somek, "The Social Question," 48.

68. We know this from its inverse, in what Baudrillard called the "mirror of production" in Marx's vision for society, where (notwithstanding his passing appreciation of freedom taking shape beyond production) he grounded life and freedom in the giant industrial organization of the laboring masses that populated his own world. See Jean Baudrillard, *The Mirror of Production*, trans. Mark Poster (St. Louis: Telos Press, 1975).

2. Politics Must Be Dethroned

The epigraph is from F. A. Hayek, *Law, Legislation, and Liberty, Volume 3: The Political Order of a Free People* (Chicago: University of Chicago Press, 1979), 149.

1. James Wiley offers an intellectual history of "the political" in *Politics and the Concept of the Political: The Political Imagination* (New York: Routledge, 2016). There (pp. 3–4), he notes that "the 'concept of the political' was coined in 1927 by Carl Schmitt," but that the "concept" is

different from the use of the term "the political," which Wiley traces back to a letter by Max Weber referring to "das Politics" as his old "secret love."

2. "When philosophy paints its grey in grey, then has a shape of life grown old. By philosophy's grey in grey it cannot be rejuvenated but only understood. The owl of Minerva spreads its wings only with the falling of the dusk." G. W. F. Hegel, preface to *Philosophy of Right*, trans. T. M. Knox (London: Oxford University Press, 1967), 13.

3. *Pace* Marx, the political is not a mere effluent of the mode of production, its superstructure, or the stage on which its class conflicts play out. *Pace* Schmitt, it is not reducible to the friend-enemy distinction organizing war and national identity. *Pace* Arendt, the political is neither distinct from violence nor primarily a domain for achieving recognition or immortality through speech and deed. *Pace* Weber, the political is neither defined by its unique recourse to violence nor centered on the state. And *pace* Wolin, the political is not pertinent only to free societies and the project of their well-being, nor is it distinguishable from politics by its rare and episodic appearance.

4. Karl Marx, *The German Ideology*, in *The Marx-Engels Reader*, ed. Robert C. Tucker (New York: Norton, 1978), 160–61.

5. "We are subjected to the production of truth through power and cannot exercise power except through the production of truth. . . . We must produce truth as we produce wealth, indeed we must produce truth in order to produce wealth in the first place." Michel Foucault, "Two Lectures," in *Power/Knowledge* (New York: Vintage, 1980), 93–94.

6. The exercise of democratic power, Sheldon Wolin writes, entails "the fullest possible participation by equals" and is "far from an exercise of crude mass power." Wolin, "Democracy and the Political," in *Fugitive Democracy and Other Essays*, ed. Nicholas Xenos (Princeton, NJ: Princeton University Press, 2016), 249.

7. Increasingly open-handed practices of voter suppression in U.S. elections extend earlier neoliberal practices of limiting enfranchisement and containing the reach of electoral democracy.

8. Quinn Slobodian, *Globalists: The End of Empire and the Birth of Neoliberalism* (Cambridge, MA: Harvard University Press, 2018), 92.

9. Financial, economic, and security crises have added fuel to the fires licking at constitutional democracies, of course, auguring their replacement with novel, twenty-first-century regimes.

10. John Solomon, "Bush, Harvard Business School, and the Makings of a President," *New York Times*, June 18, 2000, http://www.nytimes.com /2000/06/18/business/bush-harvard-business-school-and-the-makings -of-a-president.html.

11. Philip Rucker and Robert Costa, "Bannon Vows a Daily Fight for "Deconstruction of the Administrative State,'" *Washington Post*, February 23, 2017, https://www.washingtonpost.com/politics/top-wh-strategist -vows-a-daily-fight-for-deconstruction-of-the-administrative-state/2017 /02/23/03f6b8da-f9ea-11e6-bf01-d47f8cf9b643_story.html?utm_term= .e3d37a64f9d0; Paul Waldman, "Donald Trump Has Assembled the Worst Cabinet in American History," *Washington Post*, January 19, 2017, https://www.washingtonpost.com/blogs/plum-line/wp/2017/01 /19/donald-trump-has-assembled-the-worst-cabinet-in-american -history/?utm_term=.db6375fb5c58; Jenny Hopkinson, "Trump Hires Campaign Workers Instead of Farm Experts at USDA," *Politico*, September 21, 2017, https://www.politico.com/story/2017/09/21/trump-agri culture-department-usda-campaign-workers-242951; Eugene Robinson, "Surprise: Trump's Newest Cabinet Nominee Has No Relevant Experience," *Washington Post*, March 29, 2018, https://www.washington post.com/opinions/surprise-trumps-newest-cabinet-nominee-has-no -relevant-experience/2018/03/29/07d34886-338e-11e8-8abc-22a366b72f2d _story.html?utm_term=.26f0e351b083.

12. See David Neiwert, *Alt-America: The Rise of the Radical Right in the Age of Trump* (London: Verso, 2017). On "statism" as the leading friend of progressives and foe of freedom, see Mark Levin, *Liberty and Tyranny: A Conservative Manifesto* (New York: Threshold Editions, 2010).

13. See Cornel West, "Goodbye, American Neoliberalism. A New Era is Here," *The Guardian*, November 17, 2016, https://www.theguardian.com /commentisfree/2016/nov/17/american-neoliberalism-cornel-west-2016 -election; Michael A. Peters, "The End of Neoliberal Globalization and the Rise of Authoritarian Populism," *Educational Philosophy and Theory* 50, no. 4 (2018): 323–25; Martin Jacques, "The Death of Neoliberalism and the Crisis in Western Politics," *The Guardian*, August 21, 2016, https://www.theguardian.com/commentisfree/2016/aug/21/death-of -neoliberalism-crisis-in-western-politics.

14. Thomas Biebricher, *The Political Theory of Neoliberalism* (Stanford, CA: Stanford University Press, 2019), is immensely helpful in answering this question, and I draw extensively on this text and on William Callison,

"Political Deficits: The Dawn of Neoliberal Rationality and the Eclipse of Critical Theory" (PhD diss., University of California, Berkeley, 2019), in this chapter.

15. Slobodian, *Globalists*.

16. For neoliberal rationality's approach to science, technique, and the political, see Biebricher, *The Political Theory of Neoliberalism* and Callison, "Political Deficits."

17. Hayek and Friedman are suspicious of all conceits of knowledge and reason that usurp spontaneous order, while the ordos, who put more faith in social science, objected to the inherently unscientific character of these endeavors, the difficulty of binding them to technical expertise and mechanisms.

18. Nancy MacLean, *Democracy in Chains: The Deep History of the Radical Right's Stealth Plan for America* (New York: Viking, 2017), 43–44, 67–70.

19. Enervating democracy was thus a vital part of what Foucault formulated as neoliberalism's radical reprogramming of liberalism, even as Foucault himself gave democracy scant attention. Michel Foucault, *The Birth of Biopolitics: Lectures at the College de France, 1978–79*, ed. Michel Sennelart, trans. Graham Burchell (New York: Picador, 2004), 117–121.

20. The state's focus, as one ordoliberal put it, should be wholly on "the task of guaranteeing that the economy functioned in an orderly manner." See Christian Joerges, "Europe After Ordoliberalism," in *The Birth of Austerity: German Ordoliberalism and Contemporary Neoliberalism*, ed. Thomas Biebricher and Frieder Vogelmann (London: Rowman and Littlefield, 2017), 198. See also Josef Hien and Christian Joerges, eds., *Ordoliberalism, Law, and the Rule of Economics* (London: Bloomsbury, 2017).

21. This form of state, as Thomas Biebricher has argued, required a new form of political theory and practice in which states were legitimated, but not saturated by democracy (now limited to universal suffrage and equality under the law) and in which state action was relentlessly tied to the well-being of the market order.

22. As Callison makes clear, the ordoliberals approached the social question a bit differently—seeking to co-opt, rather than disband it. With their "Third Way" social market economy, they aimed to solve it better than the Left could with socialism or social democracy. See "Political Deficits," chapter on the ordoliberals. See also *The Walter Lippmann Colloquium: The Birth of Neo-Liberalism*, ed. and trans. Jurgen Reinhoudt and Serge Audier (Cham, Switzerland: Palgrave, 2018), where the social

question features prominently. And as Callison and Slobodian argue in their discussion of contemporary German politics, Aufstehen is placing the social question and the "strong social state" at the center of their platform in a way that draws from both ordoliberal and socialist traditions, again a co-optive strategy. See William Callison and Quinn Slobodian, "An Ordosocialism Rises in Germany," forthcoming in *Dissent* (Summer 2019).

23. Milton Friedman, *Capitalism and Freedom* (Chicago: University of Chicago Press, 1962), 8.

24. Friedman, *Capitalism and Freedom*, 8.

25. Friedman, *Capitalism and Freedom*, 8–11.

26. Friedman, *Capitalism and Freedom*, 11.

27. Friedman, *Capitalism and Freedom*, 9.

28. Friedman, *Capitalism and Freedom*, 15.

29. Friedman, *Capitalism and Freedom*. 15.

30. Friedman, *Capitalism and Freedom*, 15.

31. Michael MacDonald and Darrel Paul, "Killing the Goose That Lays the Golden Egg: The Politics of Milton Friedman's Economics," *Politics and Society* 39, no. 4 (2011): 565–588.

32. Hayek, *Law, Legislation, and Liberty, Volume 3*, 108, 110.

33. Hayek, *Law, Legislation, and Liberty, Volume 3*, 109.

34. Hayek, *Law, Legislation, and Liberty, Volume 3*, 111.

35. Hayek believed that the unboundedness of government can be offset to some degree by vigilant separation of powers in which legislative, judicial, and executive functions are assiduously confined to their tasks and kept apart from one another.

36. Hayek, *Law, Legislation, and Liberty, Volume 3*, 3, 40. Again, the role of the legislature in a democracy is solely to formulate rules of conduct equally applicable to all. It cannot make "policy" or empower the state to do things.

37. Hayek, *Law, Legislation, and Liberty, Volume 3*, 32–33.

38. Hayek, *Law, Legislation, and Liberty, Volume 3*, 40.

39. Hayek, *Law, Legislation, and Liberty, Volume 3*, 33. Emphasis added.

40. Hayek, *Law, Legislation, and Liberty, Volume 3*, 33.

41. Hayek, *Law, Legislation, and Liberty, Volume 3*, 33.

42. Hayek, *Law, Legislation, and Liberty, Volume 3*, 33.

43. Of course, there is a theological dimension to Hayek's own ontology of power, which consists in the spontaneous emanation of views and

practices evolved over time. Like Marx's critique of Hegel, and in many ways mirroring it, his is a theological critique of a theological political cosmology.

44. Hayek, *Law, Legislation, and Liberty, Volume 3*, 34.

45. Hayek, *Law, Legislation, and Liberty, Volume 3*, 35.

46. Hayek, *Law, Legislation, and Liberty, Volume 3*, 35.

47. Hayek, *Law, Legislation, and Liberty, Volume 3*, 35.

48. Interestingly, this attack on sovereignty is shared by many on the left, including but, not only, the anarchist Left. See, for example, Giorgio Agamben, *Homo Sacer: Sovereign Power and Bare Life*, trans. Daniel Heller-Roazen (Stanford, CA: Stanford University Press, 1998); and Michael Hardt and Antonio Negri, *Multitude: War and Democracy in the Age of Empire* (New York: Penguin, 2004). See also Thomas Biebricher on the sovereignty problem in neoliberalism, "Sovereignty, Norms, and Exception in Neoliberalism," *Qui Parle* 23, no. 1 (2014): 77–107, https://read.dukeupress.edu/qui-parle/article-abstract/23/1/77/10282 /Sovereignty-Norms-and-Exception-in-Neoliberalism?redirectedFrom =PDF.

49. F. A. Hayek, "Majority Rule," in *The Constitution of Liberty* (Chicago: University of Chicago Press, 1960), 166.

50. Hayek, "Majority Rule," in *The Constitution of Liberty*, 167.

51. Hayek, "Majority Rule," in *The Constitution of Liberty*, 167, 168.

52. Hayek, "Majority Rule," in *The Constitution of Liberty*, 167.

53. Hayek, "Majority Rule," in *The Constitution of Liberty*, 166.

54. Hayek, "Majority Rule," in *The Constitution of Liberty*, 167.

55. Hayek, "Majority Rule," in *The Constitution of Liberty*, 166.

56. Hayek, "Majority Rule," in *The Constitution of Liberty*, 170.

57. Hayek, "Majority Rule," in *The Constitution of Liberty*, 170

58. Hayek, "Majority Rule," in *The Constitution of Liberty*, 171.

59. Slobodian, *Globalists*, 92.

60. Report of the Trilateral Commission, 64, https://archive.org/stream /TheCrisisOfDemocracy-TrilateralCommission-1975/crisis_of_demo cracy_djvu.txt

61. Hayek, "Majority Rule," in *The Constitution of Liberty*, 171. Emphasis added.

62. Given his Burke-inspired organicism, Hayek might wince at the strategy by which the imposition of community norms as individual freedoms has come to pass, where the First Amendment is a hammer for

shattering democratic laws of inclusion, equality, and antidiscrimination and values thus become rights, rather than bonds. Still, he would surely approve the invocation of market freedoms and tradition as the basis of a critique of those laws. He would favor, too, the regrowth and relegitimation of authority claims and structures in family and civil society and perhaps even the roles of the legislature and the courts in securing the rights of individuals and traditional morality over social justice claims and economic "fairness."

63. MacLean, *Democracy in Chains*, chapters 4–6.

64. Hayek's threefold brief for democracy is that it offers a peaceful transition of power, safeguards individual liberty, and provides incentive for an educated citizenry and, hence, talented political officers. See "Majority Rule," 172–74.

65. There are several recent excellent accounts of the complex ordoliberal conceptualization of the political. In *The Political Theory of Neoliberalism*, Thomas Biebricher offers an excellent and in-depth account of the novel ordoliberal conceptualization of politics. In "Political Deficits," Callison also develops an account. See chapter 3.

66. A number of economists working for the EU identify directly or indirectly as ordoliberals.

67. Biebricher, *The Political Theory of Neoliberalism*, 38, 133.

68. Walter Eucken, "Structural Transformations of the State and the Crisis of Capitalism," in Biebricher and Vogelmann, eds., *The Birth of Austerity*, 59.

69. "The transformation of the liberal state into an economic state," Eucken argues, "had great significance for the life of both *state* and *economy*." Eucken, "Structural Transformations of the State and the Crisis of Capitalism," 59. Emphasis in the original.

70. Eucken, "Structural Transformations of the State and the Crisis of Capitalism," 59.

71. Eucken, "Structural Transformations of the State and the Crisis of Capitalism," 60, 70.

72. Eucken, "Structural Transformations of the State and the Crisis of Capitalism," 69.

73. Eucken, "Structural Transformations of the State and the Crisis of Capitalism," 69

74. Franz Böhm, "Economic Ordering as a Problem of Economic Policy and a Problem of the Economic Constitution," in Biebricher and Vogelmann, eds., *The Birth of Austerity*, 118.

75. Böhm, "Economic Ordering as a Problem of Economic Policy and a Problem of the Economic Constitution," 118.

76. Böhm, "Economic Ordering as a Problem of Economic Policy and a Problem of the Economic Constitution," 118.

77. Böhm, "Economic Ordering as a Problem of Economic Policy and a Problem of the Economic Constitution," 119.

78. The two constitutions limit and complement each other. Böhm's telling metaphor for their relation draws on a people at war. The political constitution provides "courage and discipline," while the economic constitution provides "tactical principles and strategic leadership." Both are necessary. Böhm, "Economic Ordering as a Problem of Economic Policy and a Problem of the Economic Constitution," 118.

79. Biebricher, *The Political Theory of Neoliberalism*, 30, 45, and chapter 4.

80. Böhm writes: "the more dynamic economic life becomes, the more stable must its order be. A comparison can be made with a machine: the more complex a machine is, and the more intricately interdependent the movement of its separate parts, the more precise must its construction be." Böhm, "Economic Ordering as a Problem of Economic Policy and a Problem of the Economic Constitution," 116.

81. Eucken, "Structural Transformations of the State and the Crisis of Capitalism," 70.

82. Böhm, "Economic Ordering as a Problem of Economic Policy and a Problem of the Economic Constitution," 117. Emphasis added.

83. Brigitte Young, "Is Germany's and Europe's Crisis Politics Ordoliberal and/or Neoliberal?" in Biebricher and Vogelmann, eds., *The Birth of Austerity*.

84. On the ordoliberal DNA of EU institutions, see the essays in Hien and Joerges, eds., *Ordoliberalism, Law, and the Rule of Economics*.

85. Böhm, "Economic Ordering as a Problem of Economic Policy and a Problem of the Economic Constitution," 117.

86. Johanna Oksala, "Ordoliberalism as Governmentality," in Biebricher and Vogelmann, eds., *The Birth of Austerity*, 187. This, of course, is the neoliberalism that clued Foucault into its radical inversion of the liberal state-economy relationship.

87. Thus, one scholar writes "ordoliberalism brings to the fore a tradition of state-centric neoliberalism, one that says economic freedom is ordered freedom, one that argues that the strong state is the political form of free markets, and one that conceives of competition and enterprise as a

political task." Werner Bonefeld, "Freedom and the Strong State: On German Ordoliberalism," *New Political Economy* 17, no. 5 (2012): 633.

Even certain aspects of Trumpism could be seen as a kind of aspirational ordoliberalism in its constellation of business principles, attack on the "Washington swamp," authoritarianism, and effort to rule by fiat combined with paeans to individual liberty. Clearly, the economic nationalism, currying of favorites, and impetuous and ideological rather than scientific bases for decisions would not please the ordos.

88. William Callison pursues this thesis in detail in "Political Deficits."
89. Joerges, "Europe After Ordoliberalism," 199.
90. Hayek, "Majority Rule," 170.
91. Böhm writes: "decisions which lack a specific substantive ideal and which leave the economic process untroubled by a clear goal and technical order do not amount to an economic constitution." Instead, "what forms the true core of an economic constitution" is "a steering norm, which guides economic happenings in a politically desirable direction." Böhm, "Economic Ordering," 117.
92. Both democracies and plutocracies will introduce distortions into the economic sphere, the one mainly through rent seeking, the other mainly through redistributions.
93. MacLean, *Democracy in Chains*, chapter 10.
94. Contemporary free market conservatives, such as Mark Levin and Jonah Goldberg, recognize something more like an eternal political struggle between Right and Left, or progressives and conservatives, or egalitarians and libertarians.
95. Callison, "Political Deficits."
96. Even those who sounded early warnings about "too much globalization"—Joseph Stiglitz, Emmanuel Saez, Paul Krugman, Dani Rodrick—were generally more focused on the social and economic damages (especially job displacement and growing inequality) than on its damages to democracy. Not until later would they write about the ways neoliberalism generated plutocracy within nations or the rise of an international financial oligarchy vividly illustrated by the Panama and Paradise Papers, which leaked details of the global elites' hidden wealth. Nor did they anticipate what ghastly regimes might take shape from the antidemocratic political cultures and peoples it spawned.
97. Timothy Mitchell, "Fixing the Economy," *Cultural Studies* 12, no. 1 (1998): 82–101, and Mitchell, "The Character of Calculability," chapter 3

in *Rule of Experts: Egypt, Techno-Politics, Modernity* (Berkeley: University of California Press, 2002).

98. Apart from its parallels with Marx, we might regard neoliberalism's attempt to remove the role of political power in ordering society and to eliminate the political from the realm of justice as having certain continuities with Plato. Notwithstanding the severe neoliberal critique of societies by design, neoliberalism shares the Platonic aim to replace political life with (mythical) organic and harmonious orders tended by metaphysicians of state.

99. Peter S. Goodman, "Bottom Line for Davos Elite: Trump Is Good for Business," *New York Times*, January 24, 2018, https://www.nytimes.com /2018/01/24/business/trump-davos-follow-the-money.html.

100. Susan Harding, *The Book of Jerry Falwell: Fundamentalist Language and Politics* (Princeton, NJ: Princeton University Press, 2001). See also Michael Tackett, "White Evangelical Women, Core Supporters of Trump, Begin Tiptoeing Away," *New York Times*, March 11, 2018, https:// www.nytimes.com/2018/03/11/us/politics/white-evangelical-women -trump.html, and Jeremy Peters and Elizabeth Dias, "Shrugging Off Trump Scandals, Evangelicals Look to Rescue GOP," *New York Times*, April 24, 2018, https://www.nytimes.com/2018/04/24/us/politics/trump -evangelicals-midterm-elections.html.

101. Wendy Brown, *Undoing the Demos: Neoliberalism's Stealth Revolution* (New York: Zone Books, 2015).

102. On Silicon Valley "politics," see David Brookman, et al., "The Political Behavior of Wealthy Americans: Evidence From Technology Entrepreneurs," https://www.gsb.stanford.edu/faculty-research/working -papers/political-behavior-wealthy-americans-evidence-technology; Keith Spencer, *A People's History of Silicon Valley: How the Tech Industry Exploits Workers, Erodes Privacy, and Undermines Democracy* (San Francisco: Eyewear Publishing, 2018); L. Gordon Crovitz, "Silicon Valley's 'Suicide Impulse,'" *Wall Street Journal*, January 28, 2013, https://www.wsj.com /articles/SB10001424127887323539804578266290231304934; and Alexis C. Madrigal, "What Should We Call Silicon Valley's Unique Politics?," *The Atlantic*, September 7, 2017, https://www.theatlantic.com/technol ogy/archive/2017/09/what-to-call-silicon-valleys-anti-regulation-pro -redistribution-politics/539043.

103. Zack Beauchamp, "The Wisconsin Power Grab Is Part of a Bigger Republican Attack on Democracy," *Vox*, December 6, 2018, https://

www.vox.com/policy-and-politics/2018/12/6/18127332/wisconsin-state
-republican-power-grab-democracy; Ian Bruff, in "The Rise of Authoritarian Liberalism," *Rethinking Marxism*, October 2013, tells the story
of the rise of authoritarian liberalism and the vulnerability to populism
that it produces, in the European context.

3. The Personal, Protected Sphere Must Be Extended

The epigraph is from F. A. Hayek, "Closing Speech," Mont Pelerin Society, March 3, 1984, available at https://www.margaretthatcher.org
/document/117193.

1. Tocqueville treated the relationship between freedom and religion as a
    constitutive tension of American democracy and, importantly, a source
    of its health. "In the moral world, everything is classified, coordinated,
    foreseen, decided in advance. In the political world, everything is agi-
    tated, contested, uncertain. . . . Far from harming each other, these two
    tendencies, apparently so opposed, advance in accord and seem to lend
    each other a mutual support. Religion sees in civil freedom a noble exer-
    cise of the faculties of man. . . . Freedom sees in religion the compan-
    ion of its struggles and its triumphs, the cradle of its infancy, the divine
    source of its rights. It considers religion as the safeguard of mores; and
    mores as the guarantee of laws and the pledge of its own duration."
    Alexis de Tocqueville, *Democracy in America*, trans. Harvery C. Mans-
    field and Delba Winthrop, (Chicago: Chicago University Press, 2000),
    43–47.
2. Fractures in right-wing governance may also be understood as happen-
    ing along this fault line, leaning toward libertarianism and free trade
    on one side and statist moralism and nationalism on the other.
3. See Irving Kristol, *Two Cheers for Capitalism* (New York: Basic Books,
    1978).
4. Irving Kristol, "The Neoconservative Persuasion," *Weekly Standard*,
    August 11, 2003, https://www.weeklystandard.com/irving-kristol/the
    -neoconservative-persuasion.
5. Kristol, "The Neoconservative Persuasion," 4.
6. Kristol, "The Neoconservative Persuasion," 4–5.
7. Wendy Brown, "American Nightmare," *Political Theory* 34, no. 6 (2006):
    690–714.

8. Brown, "American Nightmare," 692.

9. William Connolly, *Capitalism and Christianity, American Style* (Durham, NC: Duke University Press, 2008), 39–40. Emphasis in the original.

10. Connolly, *Capitalism and Christianity*, 42.

11. Tim Alberta, "Trump and the Religious Right: A Match Made in Heaven," *Politico*, June 13, 2017, https://www.politico.com/magazine /story/2017/06/13/trump-and-the-religious-right-a-match-made-in -heaven-215251.

12. Jeremy Peters and Elizabeth Dias, "Shrugging Off Trump Scandals, Evangelicals Look to Rescue GOP," *New York Times*, April 24, 2018, https://www.nytimes.com/2018/04/24/us/politics/trump-evangelicals -midterm-elections.html.

13. Melinda Cooper, "All in the Family Debt: How Neoliberals and Con- servatives Came Together to Undo the Welfare State," *Boston Review*, May 31, 2017, 2. This article is a précis of Cooper's book, *Family Values: Between Neoliberalism and the New Social Conservatism* (New York: Zone Books, 2017).

14. Melinda Cooper, "All in the Family Debt," 2.

15. Cooper, "All in the Family Debt," 4

16. Cooper makes this argument compellingly in her account of the aim to restore both political and familial authority through privatizing public higher education. See *Family Values*, chapter 6, especially 232–41. See Nancy MacLean's corroborating account, *Democracy in Chains: The Deep History of the Radical Right's Stealth Plan for America* (New York: Viking, 2017), 102–106. Janet Halley and Libby Adler provide a penetrating the- oretical and empirical account of the shift in child support laws, some- times initiated by feminists, arising in the neoliberal era. See Halley and Adler, "You Play, You Pay: Feminists and Child Support Enforce- ment in the U.S.," in *Governance Feminism: Notes from the Field*, ed. Janet Halley, et. al (Minneapolis: University of Minnesota Press, 2019).

17. MacLean, *Democracy in Chains*; Michael Lienesch, *Redeeming America: Piety and Politics in the New Christian Right* (Chapel Hill: University of North Carolina Press, 1993); Susan Harding, *The Book of Jerry Falwell: Fundamentalist Language and Politics* (Princeton, NJ: Princeton Uni- versity Press, 2000); Linda Kintz, *Between Jesus and the Market: The Emotions That Matter in Right-Wing America* (Durham, NC: Duke Uni- versity Press, 1997); Bethany Moreton, *To Serve God and Walmart: The*

Making of Christian Free Enterprise (Cambridge: Harvard University Press, 2010).

18. MacLean, *Democracy in Chains*, xxvi–xxvii. Also see 243n22.

19. MacLean, *Democracy in Chains*, xxvii.

20. Daniel Cox and Robert Jones, "America's Changing Religious Identity," PRRI, September 6, 2017, https://www.prri.org/research/american -religious-landscape-christian-religiously-unaffiliated. Also see Allison Kaplan Somer, "Armageddon? Bring It On: The Evangelical Force Behind Trump's Jerusalem Speech," *Haaretz*, December 11, 2011, https:// www.haaretz.com/israel-news/.premium-1.827591.

21. "Jimmy Carter sat in the pew with us. But he never fought for us. Donald Trump fights. And he fights for us." This is discussed further in chapter 5. Alberta, "Trump and the Religious Right: A Match Made in Heaven."

22. Harriet Sherwood, "'Toxic Christianity': The Evangelicals Creating Champions for Trump," *The Guardian*, October 21, 2018, https://www .theguardian.com/us-news/2018/oct/21/evangelical-christians-trump -liberty-university-jerry-falwell.

23. *The Prince* and *The Discourses on Titus Livy* regularly refer to the prospects of this mutual exploitation. Machiavelli's comedy *Mandragola* features a corrupt priest willing to use to the authority of the church to suspend Christian virtue. Read as political allegory, *Mandragola* is an extraordinary tale of the deals forged to advance political and religious ambition.

24. Richard Fausset and Jess Bidgood, "Five Alabama Voters on Why They Support Roy Moore," *New York Times*, December 8, 2017, https://www .nytimes.com/2017/12/08/us/roy-moore-alabama-supporters.html.

25. Andrew Whitehead, sociologist, quoted in Sarah Bailey, "'A Spiritual Battle': How Roy Moore Tested White Evangelical Allegiance to the Republican Party," *Washington Post*, December 13, 2017, https://www .washingtonpost.com/news/acts-of-faith/wp/2017/12/13/a-spiritual -battle-how-roy-moores-failed-campaign-tested-evangelicals/?utm _term=.954bacb80127. See also Robert Jones, *The End of White Christian America* (New York: Simon and Schuster, 2016).

26. Tara Isabella Burton, "Christopher Maloney, Director of In God We Trump, on Why Evangelicals (Still) Support Donald Trump," *Vox*, October 26, 2018, https://www.vox.com/2018/10/26/17989084/christo pher-maloney-in-god-we-trump-evangelicals-trump, and Sherwood, "'Toxic Christianity.'"

3. The Personal, Protected Sphere Must Be Extended

27. "Freedom refers solely to a relation of men to other men, and the only infringement on it is coercion by men." F. A. Hayek, "Liberty and Liberties," in *The Constitution of Liberty* (Chicago: University of Chicago Press, 1960), 60

28. Hayek, "Liberty and Liberties," *The Constitution of Liberty*, 60–61

29. F. A. Hayek, *The Fatal Conceit: The Errors of Socialism* (Chicago: University of Chicago Press, 1989), 14.

30. Steven Horwitz, "Hayek and Freedom," *Foundation for Economic Education*, May 1, 2006, https://fee.org/articles/hayek-and-freedom, 26.

31. Horwitz, "Hayek and Freedom," 26.

32. Hayek, "Freedom, Reason and Tradition," *The Constitution of Liberty*, 115.

33. Hayek, "Freedom, Reason and Tradition," *The Constitution of Liberty*, 113.

34. Hayek, *The Fatal Conceit*, 14.

35. True liberalism, which Hayek associates with the British empiricist liberal tradition, is built on this understanding of moral agency. By contrast, the French republican tradition, which Hayek places at the origin of "totalitarian democracy," chased the conceit of a rationalist utopian order. Hayek, "Freedom, Reason, Tradition," *The Constitution of Liberty*, 229.

   With Burke, Hayek treats the survival of a tradition as evidence of its value. Unlike Burke, Hayek draws heavily on evolutionary biology for this claim. Hayek does not embrace Social Darwinism, but, rather sees the biological principle of evolution through adaptation and competition as resting at the root of every dimension of human social order. The evolution of cultures or civilizations emanates from dynamics that are both internal to traditions (allowing them to adapt and transform, yet conserve their foundations) and take the form of competition between traditions (allowing the successful traditions to prevail and others to die out). Hayek, *The Fatal Conceit*, 23–27.

36. Hayek, *The Fatal Conceit*, 137.

37. Hayek, "The Creative Powers of a Free Civilization," *Constitution of Liberty*, 78, and Hayek, "Freedom, Reason and Tradition," *Constitution of Liberty*, 120.

38. Hayek, "The Creative Powers of a Free Civilization," *Constitution of Liberty*, 122.

39. Hayek, "The Creative Powers of a Free Civilization," *Constitution of Liberty*, 122.

40. Hayek, "The Creative Powers of a Free Civilization," *Constitution of Liberty*, 123.

211

41. Thus, slavery could be ended or women could be granted suffrage to comport with the evolving appreciation of universal freedom in liberalism. Hayek, "The Creative Powers of a Free Civilization," *Constitution of Liberty*, 124.

42. Hayek, *The Fatal Conceit*, 135–36. There is, of course, a confession here that tradition is a heavier clamp on behavior and entails more dislike and resistance than the notion of "voluntary conformity" would suggest.

43. Hayek, *The Fatal Conceit*, 136–37.

44. Hayek, *The Fatal Conceit*, 140.

45. Hayek, *The Fatal Conceit*, 137.

46. Hayek, *Law, Legislation, and Liberty, Volume 3: The Political Order of a Free People* (Chicago: University of Chicago Press, 1979), 33.

47. Displacement of public truths with the authority of traditional and religious belief is exactly the formula that permits the Supreme Court to permit what it deems "controversial" issues such as abortion and homosexuality to become matters of protected "speech" and to push back equality law. Chapter 4 explores this phenomenon in detail.

48. That the state should not legislate morality becomes a serious problem when social democracy has divested traditional morality of its organicism. How, exactly, is this morality to be "regrown" for a Hayekian order without the help of the state? It is also a problem for the ordoliberals and neocons, for whom capitalism ravages the ground of morality even without the intervention of the social state.

49. Hayek, "Coercion and the State," *The Constitution of Liberty*, 206–7.

50. Hayek, "Coercion and the State," *The Constitution of Liberty*, 207.

51. Hayek, "Coercion and the State," *The Constitution of Liberty*, 207.

52. Hayek, "Coercion and the State," *The Constitution of Liberty*, 207.

53. Hayek, *Law, Legislation, and Liberty, Volume 2: The Mirage of Social Justice* (Chicago: University of Chicago Press, 1973), 67.

54. Hayek, "Coercion and the State," *The Constitution of Liberty*, 207.

55. Hayek, "Freedom, Reason, Tradition," *The Constitution of Liberty*, 123.

56. Hayek, "Freedom, Reason, Tradition," *The Constitution of Liberty*, 127.

57. Hayek, "Freedom, Reason, Tradition," *The Constitution of Liberty*, 127.

58. Hayek, "Freedom, Reason, Tradition," *The Constitution of Liberty*, 127.

59. Hayek, "Freedom, Reason, Tradition," *The Constitution of Liberty*, 123.

60. See, for example, Edward Feser's use of Hayek's formulation of tradition to explain the importance of taboos on homosexuality and sex

outside of marriage. Edward Feser, "Hayek on Tradition," *Journal of Libertarian Studies*, 17, no. 1 (2003), available at http://citeseerx.ist.psu .edu/viewdoc/download?doi=10.1.1.163.3432&rep=rep1&type=pdf.

61. Hayek, "Freedom, Reason, Tradition," *The Constitution of Liberty*, 123.

62. John Stuart Mill, *On Liberty*, ed. Stefan Collini (Cambridge: Cambridge University Press, 1989), chapter 1.

63. Hayek writes, "Coercion may sometimes be avoidable only because a high degree of voluntary conformity exists, which means that voluntary conformity may be a condition of a beneficial working of freedom." "Freedom, Reason, Tradition," *The Constitution of Liberty*, 123.

64. Cooper, *Family Values*, chapters 3, 4, and 6.

65. Valerie Strauss, "There Is a Movement to Privatize Public Education in America: Here's How Far It Has Gotten," *Washington Post*, June 23, 2018, https://www.washingtonpost.com/news/answer-sheet/wp/2018/06 /23/there-is-a-movement-to-privatize-public-education-in-america -heres-how-far-it-is-has-gotten.

66. Tim Wu, "The First Amendment as Loser's Revenge," available at https://www.law.berkeley.edu/wp-content/uploads/2018/11/The-First -Amendment-as-Losers-Revenge_Tim-Wu.pdf.

67. Emma Green, "Trump Wants to Make Churches the New Super PACs," *The Atlantic*, August 2, 2016, https://www.theatlantic.com/pol itics/archive/2016/08/how-trump-is-trying-to-put-more-money-in -politics/493823.

68. John Daniel Davidson, "It's Time to Repeal The Johnson Amendment and Let Pastors Talk Politics," *Federalist*, December 1, 2017, http://the federalist.com/2017/12/01/time-repeal-johnson-amendment-let -pastors-talk-politics.

69. See ADF International, "Advocacy," https://adfinternational.org/advo cacy, and Alliance Defending Freedom, " ADF Intl Defends Right to Life of Unborn Before European Court," April 30, 2015, http://www .adfmedia.org/News/PRDetail/9627.

70. See ADF International, "Advocacy.". In principle, the ADF supports all forms of religious freedom. In fact, it has taken up very few non- Christian cases and it has strongly supported both of President Trump's "Muslim bans."

71. See Alliance Defending Freedom, https://www.adflegal.org. Also see Sarah Posner, "The Christian Legal Army Behind 'Masterpiece

Cakeshop,'" *Nation*, November 28, 2017, https://www.thenation.com
/article/the-christian-legal-army-behind-masterpiece-cakeshop.
72. Posner, "The Christian Legal Army Behind 'Masterpiece Cakeshop.'"
73. Alliance Defending Freedom, "Religious Freedom: Our First Freedom," https://adflegal.org/issues/religious-freedom.
74. Alliance Defending Freedom, "Religious Freedom: Living Your Faith
in the Public Square," https://adflegal.org/issues/religious-freedom/pub
lic-square.
75. Alliance Defending Freedom, "Religious Freedom: Our First Freedom," https://adflegal.org/issues/religious-freedom.
76. Posner, "The Christian Legal Army Behind 'Masterpiece Cakeshop.'"
77. Alliance Defending Freedom, "Statement of Faith: Alliance Defending Freedom," http://www.adflegal.org/about-us/careers/statement-of
-faith.
78. Posner, "The Christian Legal Army Behind 'Masterpiece Cakeshop.'"
79. U.S. Department of Justice, "Attorney General Sessions Delivers
Remarks at the Department of Justice's Religious Liberty Summit,"
July 30, 2018, available at https://www.justice.gov/opa/speech/attorney
-general-sessions-delivers-remarks-department-justice-s-religious
-liberty-summit.
80. See the Mont Pelerin Society, "Statement of Aims," https://www
.montpelerin.org/statement-of-aims, and Mary Ann Glendon, *Rights
Talk: The Impoverishment of Political Discourse* (New York: Free Press,
1991). Glendon writes: "The strident rights rhetoric that currently dom-
inates American political discourse poorly serves the strong tradition
of protection for individual freedom for which the United States is justly
renowned. . . . It contributes to the erosion of the habits, practices and
attitudes of respect for others that are the ultimate and surest guaran-
tors of human rights." In addition, "it is turning American political discourse into a parody of itself and challenging the very notion that politics can be conducted through reasoned discussion and compromise. For
the new rhetoric of rights is less about human dignity and freedom than
about insistent, unending desires" (171).
81. This is the subject of my previous book on neoliberalism and democracy, *Undoing the Demos: Neoliberalism's Stealth Revolution* (New York:
Zone Books, 2015).
82. Melinda Cooper, *Family Values.*

83. Kevin Johnson, "Trump's 'Big Beautiful Door' Is a Big, Beautiful Step in the Right Direction," *Time*, October 29, 2015, http://time.com/4092571/republican-debate-immigration.

84. "Full Transcripts: Trump's Speech on Immigration and the Democratic Response," https://www.nytimes.com/2019/01/08/us/politics/trump-speech-transcript.html.

85. Lauren Collins, "Letter from France: Can the Center Hold? Notes from a Free-for-All Election?," *New Yorker*, May 8, 2017, 26.

86. Collins, "Letter from France: Can the Center Hold?," 24.

87. There is some irony in this as the sequel to the "nanny state" loathed by neoliberals.

88. The force of tradition, Hayek reminds us, depends on "undesigned rules and conventions whose significance and importance we largely do not understand," based upon "reverence for the traditional." Hayek, "Freedom, Reason, and Tradition," *The Constitution of Liberty*, 236.

89. Max Weber, *Economy and Society, Volume 2*, ed. Guenther Roth and Claus Wittich, (Los Angeles: University of California Press, 1978), 1116–17.

90. Fyodor Dostoyevsky, *The Brothers Karamazov*, trans. Richard Pevear and Larissa Volokhonsky (New York: Farrar, Straus and Giroux, 2002).

91. William Callison, "Political Deficits: The Dawn of Neoliberal Rationality and the Eclipse of Critical Theory" (PhD diss., University of California, Berkeley, 2019).

92. Friedrich A. Hayek, "Why I Am Not a Conservative," *The Constitution of Liberty*, 523.

93. Hayek, "Law Commands and Order," *The Constitution of Liberty*, 228–29.

94. The right-wing backlash against "gender ideology" around the world underscores the way that tradition justifies gender hierarchy today. On the other hand, the #MeToo movement reveals routine sexual entitlement to women by men as "traditional" from Hollywood to Wall Street, Washington, DC, to Silicon Valley. Trump's dismissal of his infamous "pussy grabbing" as "locker-room talk" tapped a discourse about what traditional men do and traditional women accept.

95. At the extreme, these values are adduced for a politics of ethnic purity for which controlling women is essential. See David Niewert, *Alt-America: The Rise of the Radical Right in the Age of Trump* (London: Verso, 2017).

4. Speaking Wedding Cakes and Praying Crisis Pregnancy Centers: Religious Liberty and Free Speech in Neoliberal Jurisprudence

The epigraph is from the Mont Pelerin Society, "Statement of Aims," available at https://www.montpelerin.org/statement-of-aims.

1. National Institute of Family Life Advocates v. Becerra, 138 S. Ct. 2361 (2018), 2380.

2. See Adam Liptak, "How Conservatives Weaponized the First Amendment," *New York Times*, June 30, 2018, https://www.nytimes.com/2018/06/30/us/politics/first-amendment-conservatives-supreme-court.html; Tim Wu, "The Right to Evade Regulation," *New Republic*, June 2, 2013, https://newrepublic.com/article/113294/how-corporations-hijacked-first-amendment-evade-regulation; Tim Wu, "Is the First Amendment Obsolete?," Knight First Amendment Institute, September 2017, https://knightcolumbia.org/content/tim-wu-first-amendment-obsolete; John Coates IV, "Corporate Speech and the First Amendment: History, Data, and Implications," SSRN, February 2015, https://papers.ssrn.com/sol3/papers.cfm?abstract_id=2566785; Tamara Piety, *Brandishing the First Amendment* (Ann Arbor: University of Michigan Press, 2012); Adam Winkler, *We the Corporations* (New York: Liveright, 2018); Nelson Tebbe, *Religious Freedom in an Egalitarian Age* (Cambridge, MA: Harvard University Press, 2017); and Jim Sleeper, "First Amendment's Slippery Slope: Why Are Civil Liberties Advocates Joining Forces with the Right?," *Salon*, August 3, 2018, https://www.salon.com/2018/08/03/free-speech-on-a-slippery-slope-why-are-civil-liberties-advocates-joining-forces-with-the-right.

3. For some, the mobilization of religious liberty and free speech to enthrone Christianity is pure historical irony—or regression. For others, it is proof of what Western secularism was all along—a way of securing while disavowing Christian hegemony. See Saba Mahmood, *Politics of Piety: The Islamic Revival and the Feminist Subject* (Princeton, NJ: Princeton University Press, 2011); Talal Asad, *Formations of Secularism: Christianity, Islam, Modernity* (Stanford, CA: Stanford University Press, 2003); Winnifred Fallers Sullivan, et al., eds., *Politics of Religious Freedom* (Chicago: University of Chicago Press, 2015); Charles Taylor, *A Secular Age* (Cambridge, MA: Harvard University Press, 2007);

Michael Warner, Jonathan VanAntwerpen, and Craig Calhoun, eds., *Varieties of Secularism in a Secular Age* (Cambridge, MA: Harvard University Press, 2013); and Talal Asad, et al., *Is Critique Secular? Blasphemy, Injury, and Free Speech* (New York: Fordham University Press, 2013).

4. I have written previously about the bid for victimized status when corporations and Christians make these bids. See the discussion of the court's depiction of corporations as victimized by prohibitions on their participation in electoral speech in *Undoing the Demos: Neoliberalism's Stealth Revolution* (New York: Zone Books, 2015), chapter 5, and the discussion of the jurisprudence of aggrieved power as it relates to Christian business ownership in "When Persons Become Firms and Firms Become Persons: Neoliberal Jurisprudence and Evangelical Christianity in *Burwell v. Hobby Lobby Stores, Inc.*," in *Looking for Law in All the Wrong Places: Justice beyond and Between*, ed. Marianne Constable, Leti Volpp, and Bryan Wagner (New York: Fordham University Press, 2018).

5. Mark David Hall, "A Missed Opportunity: *Masterpiece Cakeshop v. Colorado Civil Rights Commission*," *Law and Liberty*, June 6, 2018, http://www.libertylawsite.org/2018/06/06/masterpiece-cakeshop-v-colorado-civil-rights-commission, and German Lopez, "Why You Shouldn't Freak Out about the Masterpiece Cakeshop Ruling," *Vox*, June 4, 2018, https://www.vox.com/identities/2018/6/4/17425294/supreme-court-masterpiece-cakeshop-gay-wedding-cake-baker-ruling.

6. Lawrence G. Sager and Nelson Tebbe, in a terrific comment on the case, resist the reading of *Masterpiece* as narrow, especially in Justice Kennedy's allusion "to the possibility that Colorado's practice of protecting gay couples, but not those who reject marriage equality, violates the government's obligation of neutrality toward religion." See Sager and Tebbe, "The Reality Principle," forthcoming in *Constitutional Commentary* 34 (2019), and a shorter version, "The Supreme Court's Upside-Down Decision in *Masterpiece*," available at *Balkinization*, https://balkin.blogspot.com/2018/06/the-supreme-courts-upside-down-decision.html.

7. Masterpiece Cakeshop v. Colorado Civil Rights Commission, 138 S. Ct. 1719 (2018), 1729. This is an extraordinary distortion of the commissioners' comments and also misunderstands the meaning of "rhetoric."

8. Masterpiece Cakeshop v. Colorado Civil Rights Commission, 138 S. Ct. 1719 (2018), 1724.

9. See Bethany Moreton's *To Serve God and Wal-Mart: The Making of Christian Free Enterprise* (Cambridge, MA: Harvard University Press, 2009).

10. Lawrence Glickman notes that ownership is kept in the background, but that this also keeps the workers at Phillips's bakery backgrounded. See Glickman, "Don't Let Them Eat Cake," *Boston Review*, June 7, 2018, http://bostonreview.net/law-justice/lawrence-glickman-masterpiece -cakeshop.

11. Masterpiece Cakeshop v. Colorado Civil Rights Commission, 138 S. Ct. 1719 (2018), 1724.

12. See the Masterpiece Cakeshop website at http://masterpiececakes.com.

13. Between Phillips's status as an owner and practice as an artist, the beliefs and practices of his employees are nowhere to be heard or seen. Thus, as Lawrence Glickman has argued, this already conflates "Phillips, the baker, and his business, the bakery." Glickman adds, "by insisting that the key issues in the case are Phillips's artistic expression and his religious liberty, the Court was silent on the question of how a company can possess these rights. It did so by assuming not only that corporations are people, but that the cakes made by Masterpiece Cakeshop are produced by Phillips alone, when in fact we know that the bakery has other workers." Glickman, "Don't Let Them Eat Cake."

14. Apparently, Phillips also considers Halloween to be sinful or sacrilegious, but it is not clear whether he simply refuses to use his artistry to make Halloween-themed baked goods or whether he refuses to sell any goods for Halloween parties.

15. Masterpiece Cakeshop v. Colorado Civil Rights Commission, 138 S. Ct. 1719 (2018), 1724.

16. Masterpiece Cakeshop v. Colorado Civil Rights Commission, 138 S. Ct. 1719 (2018), 1726.

17. Masterpiece Cakeshop v. Colorado Civil Rights Commission, 138 S. Ct. 1719 (2018), 1743.

18. Masterpiece Cakeshop v. Colorado Civil Rights Commission, 138 S. Ct. 1719 (2018), 1739.

19. Masterpiece Cakeshop v. Colorado Civil Rights Commission, 138 S. Ct. 1719 (2018), 1744.

20. Masterpiece Cakeshop v. Colorado Civil Rights Commission, 138 S. Ct. 1719 (2018), 1724.

21. Masterpiece Cakeshop v. Colorado Civil Rights Commission, 138 S. Ct. 1719 (2018), 1743.

22. Masterpiece Cakeshop v. Colorado Civil Rights Commission, 138 S. Ct. 1719 (2018), 1721. The opinion of the court cites one commissioner as stating that Phillips can believe "what he wants to believe," but cannot act on his religious beliefs "if he decides to do business in the state." Masterpiece Cakeshop v. Colorado Civil Rights Commission, 138 S. Ct. 1719 (2018), 1729.

23. See Douglas NeJaime and Reva Siegel, "Conscience Wars: Complicity-Based Conscience Claims in Religion and Politics," *Yale Law Journal* 124 (2015): 2516–91.

24. Hosanna-Tabor Evangelical Lutheran Church & School v. Equal Employment Opportunity Commission, 565 U.S. 171 (2012), in granting an exemption requiring equal opportunity in employment at religious institutions, stands out in this regard.

25. The personal and private character of religion normally protected by the First Amendment is partly what makes the *Hobby Lobby* decision so radical.

26. Citizens United v. Federal Election Commission, 558 U.S. 310. See my discussion in chapter 5 of *Undoing the Demos*.

27. Masterpiece Cakeshop v. Colorado Civil Rights Commission, 138 S. Ct. 1719 (2018), 1720.

28. The effect is to make credible the maligned Colorado civil rights commissioner's outburst about "situations where freedom of religion has been used to justify discrimination" "to hurt others." Masterpiece Cakeshop v. Colorado Civil Rights Commission, 138 S. Ct. 1719 (2018), 1729.

29. Alliance Defending Freedom, "Brush & Nib Studio v. City of Phoenix," https://www.adflegal.org/detailspages/case-details/brush-nib-studio -v.-city-of-phoenix.

30. Alliance Defending Freedom, "Brush & Nib Studio v. City of Phoenix."

31. Of course, another plank of neoliberalism paved this road: many businesses now brand themselves through their political and ethical commitments. As Justice Thomas notes in his concurring opinion and as opinions in *Hobby Lobby* also noted (craftily using examples from the Left), this increasingly common practice undermines the argument that profit alone does or should motivate business owners. There is an irony here, of course, given neoliberal founding father Milton Friedman's

infamous screed against "social responsibility" in business practices. See Friedman, "The Social Responsibility of Business is to Increase its Profits," *New York Times*, September 13, 1970, https://www.nytimes.com /1970/09/13/archives/article-15-no-title.html.

32. National Institute of Family Life Advocates v. Becerra, 138 S. Ct. 2361 (2018), 2367.

33. CPCs outnumber abortion providers by as much as fifteen to one in some parts of the country.

34. From the NARAL report on CPCs: "With over 1,300 CPC affiliates, the National Institute of Family and Life Advocates states plainly on its website that it is 'on the front line' of the "cultural battle" over abortion. The organization's vision is to 'provide [CPCs] with legal resources and counsel, with the aim of developing a network of life-affirming ministries in every community across the nation in order to achieve an abortion-free America.' 'I left so confused and feeling awful. I can't stop thinking about how that would have been a terrible way to find out you're pregnant.' Heartbeat International, formerly called Alternatives to Abortion International, runs a network of 1,800 CPCs in the United States and globally. Like NIFLA, Heartbeat is direct about its mission and ideology on its website: 'Heartbeat's life-saving vision is to make abortion unwanted today and unthinkable for future generations.' Care Net has a network of more than 1,100 affiliate CPCs across North America. Its website states: 'Care Net works to end abortion, not primarily through political action but by building a culture where every woman receives all the support she needs to welcome her child and create her own success story.' Likewise, the Family Research Council is blunt about the true purpose of CPCs: 'There are sharply rising numbers of women coming to [CPCs] who are not 'at risk' for abortion. These women have decided to carry their children to term and come in for material assistance or other services. . . . These trends could threaten the primary mission of the centers—to reach women at risk for abortion.'" Available at https://www.prochoiceamerica.org/wp-content/uploads /2017/04/cpc-report-2015.pdf.

35. Jor-El Godsey, "4 'Abortion-Minded' Myths," Heartbeat International, https://www.heartbeatservices.org/4-abortion-minded-myths (account and sign-in required), and Sydna Massé, *Effective Ministry to the Abortion Vulnerable*, available at https://ramahinternational.org/product /effective-ministry-to-the-abortion-vulnerable-training-manual.

36. Madeleine Schmidt, "Billboards in Denver Warn Pregnant Women of 'Fake Health Centers' in Their Neighborhoods," *Colorado Times Recorder*, April 17, 2018, http://coloradotimesrecorder.com/2018/04/bill boards-denver-warn-pregnant-women-fake-health-centers-neighbor hoods/8658.

37. Some even claim to be the most unbiased source of information about abortion *because* they do not provide them as part of their services. NARAL, "Pregnancy Centers Lie: An Insidious Threat to Reproductive Freedom," 5, available at https://www.prochoiceamerica.org/wp -content/uploads/2017/04/cpc-report-2015.pdf. See also https://www .valleypregnancycenter.com and http://www.rupregnant.org.

38. Claris Health: "Get the Care You're Looking For: Take Simple Steps for Your Sexual Health," https://www.clarishealth.org/get-care.

39. Nicole Knight, "Abortion Clinic Closures Leave Openings for Crisis Pregnancy Centers to 'Prey' on Women," *Rewire*, November 30, 2015, https://rewire.news/article/2015/11/30/abortion-clinic-closures-leave -opening-crisis-pregnancy-centers-prey-women.

40. Care Net and Heartbeat International spend more than eighteen thousand dollars per month on pay-per-click advertising campaigns that target women searching for abortion providers and bring them to their websites and "Option Line" call center. Care Net and Heartbeat International place bids on more than one hundred keywords, including "abortion," "morning-after pill," and "women's health clinics." NARAL, "Crisis Pregnancy Centers Lie," 4.

41. The San Francisco Women's Clinic (similar in name to several abortion-providing clinics in the city) has developed particularly clever ways of camouflaging its purposes on its website. Advertising itself as offering both abortion counseling and "post-abortive counseling", the website presents a great deal of information about abortion, none of it overtly hysterical, and yet much of it slyly inaccurate. For example, it slips the statement, "no anesthesia is used during a medical abortion" into a paragraph offering a vague and misleading account of medical abortion, itself under the heading, "Abortion Pill." It also twists the fact that Plan B is a prescription drug into evidence of its danger: to the question "Can I get the abortion pill over the counter?" the website states, "No, the abortion pill must be prescribed by a physician. In fact, the FDA warns against abortion-inducing drugs that have not been prescribed. *This puts the patient at risk of taking a drug that has not been approved by the FDA.*"

4. Wedding Cakes and Pregnancy Centers

The website includes a phone number and a chat line but no address for the clinic, https://sanfranciscowomens.clinic. "Support Circle" is another network of antiabortion clinics in my region whose website emerges at the top of a Google search for "I need an abortion now," https://supportcircle.org.

42. Nicole Knight, "Crisis Pregnancy Centers Are Pretty Bad at Dissuading People Seeking Abortion," *Rewire*, May 10, 2016, https://rewire .news/article/2016/05/10/crisis-pregnancy-centers-pretty-bad-dissuad ing-people-seeking-abortion.

43. Guttmacher Institute, "Crisis Pregnancy Centers Offer Misleading Information on Abortion Risks," July 18, 2006, https://www.guttmacher .org/article/2006/07/crisis-pregnancy-centers-offer-misleading-infor mation-abortion-risks.

44. Laura Bassett, "What Are 'Crisis Pregnancy Centers? and Why Does The Supreme Court Care About Them?," *Huffington Post*, November 13, 2017, https://www.huffingtonpost.com/entry/crisis-pregacy-centers -supreme-court_us_5a09f40ae4b0bc648a0d13a2.

45. Kristen Dold, "The Truth About Crisis Pregnancy Centers," *Women's Health*, January 23, 2018, https://www.womenshealthmag.com/health /a19994621/crisis-pregnancy-centers.

46. Erwin Chemerinsky writes, "The California statute was enacted so that women would receive accurate information about the existence of state healthcare programs. It mandates only that the notice be made available to patients. The words can be printed out and handed to patients or clients, or the notice can be posted on a wall. No one is required to say anything. Nor is there any requirement to provide additional information; for instance, specifics about contraception or a referral to a clinic that performs abortions. "If It Wasn't Related to Abortion, California's FACT Act Would Easily Be Upheld by the Supreme Court," *Los Angeles Times*, March 20, 2018, http://www.latimes.com/opinion/op-ed/la-oe -chemerinsky-fact-act-oral-arguments-20180320-story.html.

47. National Institute of Family Life Advocates v. Becerra, 138 S. Ct. 2361 (2018), 2380, 2379.

48. Of course, were the case to rest on or even invoke the right to the free exercise of religion, regulation of a pregnancy center purporting to provide health information and health care might have been more challenging to overturn.

49. National Institute of Family Life Advocates v. Becerra, 138 S. Ct. 2361 (2018), 2365.

50. National Institute of Family Life Advocates v. Becerra, 138 S. Ct. 2361 (2018), 2371. Emphasis added.

51. National Institute of Family Life Advocates v. Becerra, 138 S. Ct. 2361 (2018), 2375.

52. National Institute of Family Life Advocates v. Becerra, 138 S. Ct. 2361 (2018), 2366 citing McMullen v. Coakley 134 S. Ct. 2518.

53. National Institute of Family Life Advocates v. Becerra, 138 S. Ct. 2361 (2018), 2375 citing Abrams v. United States 250 U.S. 616.

54. On the one hand, unlicensed centers with no medical professionals or other experts on staff may hide that fact from potential clientele while continuing to pose as pseudomedical facilities. On the other hand, "professional speech" is protected, need not be factual, and may indulge any "philosophical, ethical or religious beliefs (the opinion states 'precepts' instead of 'beliefs')" in its utterances. Since the centers do not provide or refer for abortions, and abortions are controversial, the *Zauderer* requirement of "factual and uncontroversial information about the terms under which services will be available" is held not to apply to CPCs—abortions are not available, and they are also controversial. Above all, the majority opinion, along with the Kennedy concurrence (with Roberts, Alito, and Gorsuch joining) cast the state's effort to require disclosure into a matter of "partisanship" and worse, totalitarian overreach. National Institute of Family Life Advocates v. Becerra, 138 S. Ct. 2361 (2018), 2379.

55. National Institute of Family Life Advocates v. Becerra, 138 S. Ct. 2361 (2018), 2382.

56. National Institute of Family Life Advocates v. Becerra, 138 S. Ct. 2361 (2018), 2374. See Paula Berg, "Toward a First Amendment Theory of Doctor-Patient Disclosure and the Right to Receive Unbiased Medical Advice," *Boston University Law Review* 74 (1994): 201–266.

57. National Institute of Family Life Advocates v. Becerra, 138 S. Ct. 2361 (2018), 2379.

58. National Institute of Family Life Advocates v. Becerra, 138 S. Ct. 2361 (2018), 2379.

59. National Institute of Family Life Advocates v. Becerra, 138 S. Ct. 2361 (2018), 2379.

4. Wedding Cakes and Pregnancy Centers

60. National Institute of Family Life Advocates v. Becerra, 138 S. Ct. 2361 (2018), 2374.

61. They are not competing for truth, but for clientele, and the less the clients know, the better.

62. See Piety, *Brandishing the First Amendment*, chapters 5 and 6. This use of "controversy" is also what links the *NIFLA* case to the larger right-wing strategy of bracketing concern with scholarly evidence in arguing for the rights of "unpopular positions" or "balance" in classrooms and textbooks. It legitimates the call for including materials on Creationism in science classes, Holocaust denial in history classes, and the putative genetic basis of racial socioeconomic inequality in social studies.

63. One might well argue that if CPCs are antiabortion groups, they should declare this openly and be protected by the First Amendment. If, on the other hand, they are women's clinics providing pregnancy services, they should be regulated.

64. National Institute of Family Life Advocates v. Becerra, 138 S. Ct. 2361 (2018), 2380.

5. No Future for White Men: Nihilism, Fatalism and Ressentiment

1. Hans Sluga called my attention to this aspect of Nietzsche's nihilism and the importance of its desublimation of the will to power in "Donald Trump: Between Populist Rhetoric and Plutocratic Rule," a splendid paper presented at the UC Berkeley Critical Theory Symposium on the election, February 2017. Sluga's paper is part of his larger work in progress on nihilism. I rely heavily on his reading of Nietzsche on nihilism in the following paragraphs.

2. Sluga, "Donald Trump," 16. Nietzsche's nihilism, Sluga writes "is not one in which there are no values at all; nihilism is not a condition of anomie; it is rather a state in which the values we possess have become unanchored. This will show itself in a multiplication of values, in the production of ever new values, but also in their ever-continuing devaluation, in their constantly being discarded and replaced. Values themselves have thus lost their value; and there are, consequence, no higher or lower values; all values are equal; they have become fashions that come and go all equally trivial. In this condition, no greatness is

224

possible anymore; triviality itself becomes one of our values. One sign of this form of nihilism is the dissolution of the distinction between true and false, the moment when we can no longer discriminate between real and fake news."

3. Carl Schmitt, *Dialogues on Power* (Cambridge: Polity, 2015), 47.
4. Max Weber's parallel diagnosis focused more narrowly on the phenomenon of the rationalization process set loose by the ascendance of instrumental over value rationality. Marxism gave us the fantasy of recontainment at the site of production, ignoring all the other power forms not comprised by that recontainment.
5. Sluga again called this to my attention. "Donald Trump," 17.
6. Sluga, "Donald Trump," 17.
7. Sluga, "Donald Trump," 17.
8. Herbert Marcuse, *One-Dimensional Man* (Boston: Beacon Press, 1964), 76.
9. "Deprived of the claims which are irreconcilable with the established society, pleasure, thus adjusted, generates submission." Marcuse, *One-Dimensional Man*, 76.
10. Marcuse, *One-Dimensional Man*, 76.
11. Marcuse, *One-Dimensional Man*, 76. Emphasis in the original.
12. Repression of instincts takes work, even as saying a strong "no" to them or sublimating their energies into socially acceptable forms is supported and organized by prevailing social morality and theology and takes place at a largely unconscious level.
13. Marcuse describes an "atrophy of the mental organs for grasping the contradictions and the alternatives" and famously claims that for the happy consciousness, "the real is rational" and "the established system, in spite of everything, delivers the goods." Marcuse, *One-Dimensional Man*, 79.
14. Marcuse, *One-Dimensional Man*, 77.
15. Marcuse, *One-Dimensional Man*, 77.
16. Marcuse, *One-Dimensional Man*, 79.
17. Marcuse, *One-Dimensional Man*, 78.
18. Marcuse, *One-Dimensional Man*, 78. Marcuse is departing here from Freud, who in his later years understood aggression to be weakened by a greater outlet for libidinal energies. For Marcuse, however, repressive desublimation involves what he calls a "compression" or concentration of erotic energy.

19. Marcuse, *One-Dimensional Man*, 78.

20. Marcuse, *One-Dimensional Man*, 79.

21. Arlie Hochschild, *Strangers in Their Own Land: Anger and Mourning on the American Right* (New York: New Press, 2016), 219, 128.

22. Hochschild, *Strangers in Their Own Land*, 176–79.

23. I have argued elsewhere that neoliberalism is itself an expression of nihilism in its explicit abandonment of God or human deliberation as the basis of value, order, and right conduct. See Wendy Brown, *Undoing the Demos: Neoliberalism's Stealth Revolution* (New York: Zone Books, 2015), chapter 7. I would add here that neoliberalism probably could not take hold until an advanced stage of nihilism already was reached. Notwithstanding its concern with securing traditional morality, neoliberalism is a nihilistic social theory and practice built on and advancing desacralization.

24. "To see others suffer does one good, to make others suffer even more. . . . Without cruelty there is no festival . . . and in punishment there is so much that is festive!" Friedrich Nietzsche, *On the Genealogy of Morals*, trans. Walter Kaufmann (New York: Vintage, 1967), 67. Manifest in the immediate aftermath of Trump's election and Brexit, this glee is ubiquitous in right-wing blogs and comment sections where trolls compete for the most vulgar, insulting, and even terrorizing attacks on the opposition.

25. There are countless variations on this Trump voter's account of her support for him: "It doesn't seem like it makes any difference which party gets in there. Whatever they say they'll do when they get in there, they can't really do it. . . . I just want him to annoy the hell out of everybody, and he's done that." Steven Rosenfeld, "Trump's Support Falling Among Swing-State Voters Who Elected Him, Recent Polls Find," *Salon*, July 23, 2017, http://www.salon.com/2017/07/23/trumps-support-falling-among-swing-state-voters-who-elected-him-recent-polls-find_partner.

26. Jessica Valenti, "When Misogynists Become Terrorists," *New York Times*, April 26, 2018, https://www.nytimes.com/2018/04/26/opinion/when-misogynists-become-terrorists.html.

27. Ralph Reed, chairman of the Faith and Freedom Coalition: "Jimmy Carter sat in the pew with us. But he never fought for us. Donald Trump fights. And he fights for us." Quoted in Tim Alberta, "Trump and the Religious Right: A Match Made in Heaven," Politico, June 13, 2017,

https://www.politico.com/magazine/story/2017/06/13/trump-and-the
-religious-right-a-match-made-in-heaven-215251.

28. See Tara Isabella Burton, "Prominent Evangelical Leader on Khashoggi
Crisis: Let's Not Risk '$100 Billion Worth of Arms Sales,'" *Vox*, October
17, 2018, https://www.vox.com/2018/10/17/17990268/pat-robertson-khash
oggi-saudi-arabia-trump-crisis, and Tara Isabella Burton, "The Biblical
Story the Christian Right Uses to Defend Trump," *Vox*, March 5, 2018,
https://www.vox.com/identities/2018/3/5/16796892/trump-cyrus-christ
ian-right-bible-cbn-evangelical-propaganda.

29. Karl Marx, Clara Zetkin, and Alexandra Kollontai were not alone in
depicting prostitution as the handmaiden of bourgeois morality.

30. Nietzsche, *On the Genealogy of Morals*, 33–39.

31. Nietzsche, *On the Genealogy of Morals*, 36.

32. Michael J. Sandel, *What Money Can't Buy: The Moral Limits of Markets*
(London: Allen Lane, 2012), chapter. 1.

33. Chauncey Devega, "Pulitzer-Prize Winning Reporter David Cay
Johnston: 'The Evidence Suggests Trump Is a Traitor,'" *Salon*, April 23,
2018, https://www.salon.com/2018/04/23/pulitzer-winning-reporter
-david-cay-johnston-the-evidence-suggests-trump-is-a-traitor.

34. Trump ordered Obamacare weakened as one of his first executive orders,
an order that has been carried out through strategies to sow chaos in
the insurance markets, reduce enrollment periods and staff, enhance
terms for junk policies that escape the insurance exchanges, and more.
The sole aim in all of this is to make Obamacare fail. Tami Luhby, "8
Ways Trump Hurt Obamacare in His First Year," CNN, January 20, 2018,
https://money.cnn.com/2018/01/20/news/economy/obamacare-trump
-year-one/index.html; and Politico Staff, "Trump Administration Freezes
Billions in Obamacare Payments, Outraging Advocates," *Politico*, July 8,
2018, https://www.politico.com/story/2018/07/08/insurance-obamacare
-adjustment-payments-701907.

35. James Hohmann, "The Daily 202: Trump Voters Stay Loyal Because
They Feel Disrespected," *Washington Post*, May 14, 2018, https://www
.washingtonpost.com/news/powerpost/paloma/daily-202/2018/05/14
/daily-202-trump-voters-stay-loyal-because-they-feel-disrespected
/5af8aac530fb0425887994cc/?utm_term=.8da76c532097. "Trump voters
complain that there is no respect for President Trump or for people like
them who voted for him. One older white working-class woman from
Macomb recalled when she first started voting 'there was so much

respect for the president. And I don't care what he did, or what he said, there was always respect. It was always "Mr. President." And now, it disgusts me.'" Democracy Corps, "Macomb and America's New Political Moment: Learning from Obama-Trump Working Class Voters in Macomb and Democratic Base Groups in Greater Detroit," May 7, 2018, https://static1.squarespace.com/static/582e1a36e58c62cc076cdc81/t /5af05743f950b7ef0550767f/1525700420093/Macomb%20%26%20 America%27s%20New%20Political%20Moment_Democracy%20Corps _May%202018.pdf.

36. Nietzsche, *On the Genealogy of Morals*, 44. Emphasis in the original.

37. William Connolly saw this early. See *Capitalism and Christianity, American Style* (Durham, NC: Duke University Press, 2008), especially chapter 3.

38. For Foucault's theorization of "emergence" as genealogy's prize, see Michel Foucault, "Nietzsche, Genealogy, History," in *Language, Counter-Memory, Practice: Selected Essays and Interviews*, ed. Donald. F. Bouchard, trans. Donald F. Bouchard and Sherry Simon (Ithaca, NY: Cornell University Press, 1977). "Conjuncture" is Stuart Hall's signature enrichment of Marxist analysis, inflected heavily by Gramsci. For one example among scores of its usefulness, see Stuart Hall, "The Great Moving Right Show," in Hall, *Selected Political Writings: The Great Moving Right Show and Other Essays* (Durham, NC: Duke University Press, 2017).

39. David Goodhart, *The Road to Somewhere: The Populist Revolt and the Future of Politics* (London: Hurst, 2017). See also Jonathan Freedland, "The Road to Somewhere by David Goodhart—A Liberal's Right-Wing Turn on Immigration," *The Guardian*, March 22, 2017, https:// www.theguardian.com/books/2017/mar/22/the-road-to-somewhere -david-goodhart-populist-revolt-future-politics.

40. Carl Schmitt, *Land and Sea* (Candor, NY: Telos Press, 2015), 5–9; Schmitt, "Dialogue on New Space," in *Dialogues on Power and Space*, ed. Andreas Kalyvas and Federico Finchelstein, trans. Samuel Garrett Zeitlin (Cambridge: Polity, 2015), 73–74.

41. Schmitt, "Dialogue on New Space," 73.

42. The text, this formulation in particular, is overtly anti-Semitic.

43. Schmitt, *Land and Sea*, 95.

44. Schmitt, *Land and Sea*, 57.

45. Schmitt, *Land and Sea*, 59.

46. Schmitt, *Land and Sea*, 58.

Index

ADF. *See* Alliance Defending
    Freedom
administrative statism, Hayek and
    Arendt's rejection of, 50
affirmative action, criticism of, as
    diversion, 4
Alberta, Tim, 92, 94
Alger, Horatio, 34
Alito, Samuel, 135, 155
Alliance Defending Freedom
    (ADF): activism by, 110–14;
    Blackstone Legal Fellowship
    Program, 112–13; and Brush &
    Nib, 142; international branch
    of, 110; and *Masterpiece Cakeshop
    v. Colorado CRC*, 142
"American Nightmare"
    (Brown), 11
American Revolution, Arendt on,
    47–48
antidemocratic politics, rise of, 15
anti-Islamicism, 1
anti-Semitism, 1
Arendt, Hannah, 46–50; on French
    vs. American Revolution, 47–49;

On Revolution, 47–49; on society
    as concept, 46–47
artistic expression, First
    Amendment rights for: as issue
    in ADF lawsuit against state of
    Arizona, 142; as issue in
    *Masterpiece Cakeshop v. Colorado
    CRC*, 131, 132–34, 135–36, 140–41;
    public accommodation laws and,
    142
Athens, ancient, three pillars of
    democracy in, 24
authoritarianism: Friedman's
    endorsement of, 66–67; Hayek on
    liberalism's compatibility with,
    72–73, 119; ordoliberals and, 81

Bannon, Steve, 28, 59, 94
Baudrillard, Jean, 197n68
Berg, Paula, 154–55
Biebricher, Thomas, 201n21
Böhm, Franz, 79, 80, 205n80,
    206n91
border wall, analogy of country to
    private home and, 116–18

Index

Breyer, Stephen, 124, 151, 159
British political tradition, Hayek's
    preference for, 68, 211n35
Brush & Nib, 142
Buchanan, James, 62, 194n10
Burke, Edmund, 97, 98, 208n1
Bush, George W., 58
businesses: branding through
    political and ethical
    commitments, 219–20n31;
    neoliberal extension of speech
    rights to, 126, 132, 133–34,
    139–42, 149, 150–51, 157–58,
    218n13; as neoliberal model of
    government, 58–59, 116; and
    social responsibility, Friedman
    on, 219–20n31

Callison, William, 84–85, 120,
    191n9, 201n22
capitalism: and democracy, 25–26;
    neoliberalism's rescue of, 39; and
    repressive desublimation,
    165–68; and "the social
    question," 26–27
Capitalism and Freedom (Friedman),
    65
capitalist democracies: limited
    political equality in, 24; as
    oxymoron, 25–26
capitalist economies, ordoliberals
    on need for economic
    constitution for, 79–80
Care Net, 144, 220n34, 221n40
Carson, Ben, 39–40, 197n49
Cato Institute, opposition to racial
    equality legislation, 76, 194n10
charter schools, 109

Chemerinsky, Erwin, 222n46
"Chicago Boys," 18
Chile, and neoliberalism, 18
Christianity: and family values, 4;
    and nationalism, 8; neoliberal
    jurisprudence's efforts to
    re-Christianize public life,
    110–15, 123–24, 129, 137–38,
    153–54, 214n80; Nietzsche on,
    174–75. *See also* evangelical
    Christians; religious Right
churches, and prohibition
    on political participation,
    109–10
civilization, Hayek on evolution of,
    35–36
Claris Health, 144
class stratification, 176–77
Clinton, William J. "Bill," 13, 172
coercive state power, Hayek on:
    efforts to enlarge, 104–5;
    personal protected sphere as best
    defense against, 104
Colloque Walter Lippmann
    (1938), 17
Colorado Anti-Discrimination Act,
    128
Connolly, William, 91
conscience, loss of, in
    desublimation, 164–65, 166–67;
    and resurgence of tribalism, 169;
    and right-wing leaders' ability to
    survive moral scandals, 172–73;
    and right-wing loss of
    compassion, 169–72
conservatism, Hayek on, 120
Continental political tradition,
    Hayek's critique of, 68–69

Index

Cooper, Melinda, 11–12, 92, 108–9
courts, restrictions on, in neoliberal
    government, 82, 85–86
crisis pregnancy centers (CPCs):
    deceptive practices of, 144–48,
    150, 154, 221–22n41, 223n54;
    extension of free speech rights
    to, 149; federal and state
    funding for, 145; mission of,
    220n34; NARAL report on,
    220n34, 221n37; religious
    organizations supporting, 144,
    148, 220n34; tactics used to
    discourage abortions, 146–47.
    See also *National Institute of
    Family and Life Advocates v.
    Becerra* (2018)

Damore, James, 43–44
dedemocratization,
    neoconservatism's support for, 91
demassification, 37–39
democracy: attacks from both Left
    and Right on, 86–87; capitalism
    as incompatible with, 25–26;
    direct, impossibility in large
    states, 27; and dwindling
    legitimacy of political power,
    87; excesses of, neoliberals on,
    73–74; freedom in neoliberal
    discourse as basis for limiting
    of, 64; Friedman on, 65, 66–67;
    necessity of the political for, 57;
    and neoliberal government,
    incompatibility of, 63, 82–83;
    ordoliberals on damage to
    states and markets by, 77–78;
    political equality as foundation

of, 23–24, 27; public's increasing
    confusion about value of, 87; as
    rule by the people, 23; state
    actions to advance political
    equality in, 26; state's
    obligation to maintain political
    equality in, 24–25. *See also*
    Hayek, on democracy
democracy, neoliberal attacks on:
    as anti-corruption strategy, 83;
    consistency through three major
    schools, 81; effect of, 8; efforts to
    constrain inevitable excesses of,
    61–64; as force of division with
    states, 63; markets-and-morals
    project and, 11, 21; and popular
    confusion about value of
    democracy, 58; and resultant
    antidemocratic political culture,
    86–87; and rise of oligarchies,
    206n96
democracy, role of society in: and
    linked fate across differences, 27;
    and redress of inequalities,
    27–28, 40–41, 42; and social
    power, 52–53; where political
    equality is made, 27
democratic imaginary, society as
    protector of, 51–53
democratic norms, personal
    protected sphere as protection
    from, 105
democratic socialism, Friedman
    on, 65
desublimation, 163–68; and
    aggressiveness of extreme Right,
    167–68; as consequence of
    nihilism, 163–64; increased

231

Index

desublimation (*cont.*)
  aggression in, 164–65, 168; and
  release of Thanatos, 168;
  repressive, Marcuse on, 165–68.
  See also conscience, loss of, in
  desublimation
DeVos, Betsy, 113
Dialogue on Power and Space
  (Schmitt), 185
digitalization: and concentrations
  of power, 163; deterritorialized
  and dedemocratized sociality
  resulting from, 183–84
Dostoyevsky, Fyodor, 119

economic constitution, ordoliberals
  on, 77, 79–80, 205n78
egalitarians and planners,
  protection of state from, as goal
  of neoliberalism, 82, 83, 96,
  105–6, 107–8, 120
election of 2018, Republican voter
  suppression in, 194n10
electoral corruption, as neoliberal
  technique to blunt demands of
  poor and working class, 64
entrepreneurialization, as neoliberal
  policy, 38–39
equality, political: capitalist
  democracies' limited
  implementation of, 24; as
  foundation of democracy, 23–24,
  27; making of, in society, 41;
  neoliberal attacks on, 7, 8, 44–45,
  76, 110–14; social justice policies
  as effort to maintain, 27–28; state
  actions to advance, 26; state's
  obligation to ensure, 24–25

equality and inclusion: imposition
  of traditional values as attack
  on, 115–16; and metaphor of
  country as private home and,
  116–18; neoliberal attacks on, as
  contrary to neoliberal principles,
  114–15, 214n80; neoliberals'
  dismissal of concerns about, 36
Eucken, Walter, 78
European Union, as ordoliberal
  polity, 81
evangelical Christians: and
  neoliberalism, 91–92, 93–95; and
  politicization of religious values,
  95; support for Trump, motives
  for, 92, 94, 220n21, 226n27

Fair Housing Act of 1968, 39–40
Falwell, Jerry, 93–94
Falwell, Jerry, Jr., 94–95
family, traditional: importance in
  neoliberal thought, 11–12; and
  marriage equality campaign, 13;
  neoliberalism's rescue of, 39;
  neoliberals' and social
  conservatives' shared support
  for, 92–93; privatization of
  public sphere through
  familialization, 115–18; substitute
  for social state functions in
  neoliberal thought, 12. *See also*
  personal protected sphere
Family Values (Cooper), 11–12
far-right: agglomeration of
  contradictory elements in, 2;
  aggressiveness of, 2; campaign
  slogans of, 5, 179; differences
  from fascisms of old, 7, 10;

Index

Foucault, Michel (*cont.*)
neoliberalism, 19–20; on
neoliberalism as reprogramming
of liberalism, 8, 19–20, 201n19;
on neoliberal responsibilization,
38; on power, 56, 199n5
Fox News, 4
freedom: compatibility with
traditional values, 75–76;
Friedman on, 65–66; in
liberalism, 68; and social
democracy tradition, 68; and
whiteness and masculinity, 64.
See also Hayek, on freedom
freedom, far-right formulation of:
characterization of social reform
as assault on, 12, 13, 43–44; and
expressions of supremacism as
expressions of liberty, 45–46; and
Left's social justice agenda, 10;
mobilization in support of white
male Christian hegemony, 10;
neoliberal foundations of, 10
freedom, in neoliberalism: and
attacks on American
universities, 42–43; as
deregulation, 41; as freedom
from social restraint, 42, 44–46;
as limiting democratic voice of
the people, 64; maximization of,
as goal, 11; and opposition to
government programs, 37; the
political as danger to, 61;
sacrifice to political and familial
authority, 120; use of, to
reestablish traditional values,
110–15, 123–24, 129, 137–38,
153–54, 214n80

freedom of conscience (free exercise
of religion): extension to
businesses, in *Masterpiece
Cakeshop v. Colorado CRC*, 132;
neoliberal conversion from
private right to public liberty,
114; as private right limited by
public interests, 138–39; to
reestablish Christian values in
public sphere, 110–15, 214n80.
See also freedom of speech
combining with freedom of
conscience, in neoliberal
jurisprudence
freedom of speech: and freedom to
deceive, 151–52, 154, 157–58; as
source of power in democracies,
139–40; subordination of
third-party concerns in, 139; and
verbal attacks on others, 46
freedom of speech, extension to
businesses: in *Masterpiece
Cakeshop v. Colorado CRC*, 132,
133–34, 139–42; as neoliberal
goal, 126; in *NIFLA v. Becerra*,
149, 150–51, 157–58
freedom of speech combining with
freedom of conscience, in
neoliberal jurisprudence: in
*Masterpiece Cakeshop v. Colorado
CRC*, 129–30, 137–38; in *NIFLA
v. Becerra*, 159; and politicization
of religious claims, 141; as
strategy to re-Christianize
public sphere, 125, 137–38,
140–41, 159–60, 216n3; as
strategy to undermine
regulation, 124, 125, 159–60

Index

free exercise clause. *See* freedom of
   conscience
free markets, as check on
   government power, in
   Friedman, 65–66
Freiburg School, 37
French Revolution, Arendt on,
   47–48
Freud, Sigmund, 164, 166–67,
   225n18
Friedman, Milton: and
   authoritarianism, 66–67; on
   democracy, 65, 66–67; on
   freedom, 64, 65–66; on free
   markets, as check on
   government power, 65–66; on
   the political, as dangerous
   self-expanding domain, 60;
   political philosophy of, 65–67;
   on political power as threat,
   65–66; on separation of
   economic and political power,
   66; on socialism and democracy,
   65; on social responsibility in
   business, 219–20n31

gerrymandering, as neoliberal
   technique, 64
Glendon, Mary Ann, 114–15, 214n80
Glickman, Lawrence, 132, 218n13
Globalists (Slobodian), 18–19
globalization: rural and suburban
   whites' rage against, 187–88; and
   Schmitt, 186–87; weakening of
   nation-states by, polarization of
   opinion on, 183
Goodhart, David, 184–85, 187
Google, firing of Damore, 43–44

Gorsuch, Neil: and *Masterpiece
   Cakeshop v. Colorado CRC*, 127,
   129, 135; and *NIFLA v. Becerra*,
   155
government: business as neoliberal
   model of, 58–59, 116; far-right
   demonization of, 4; free markets
   as check on power of, 65–66;
   neoliberal, incompatibility of
   democracy with, 63, 82–83.
   See also democracy; Hayek, on
   government; ordoliberals, on
   government
government programs: neoliberal
   privatization and, 37–39; reasons
   for neoliberal opposition to, 37

happy consciousness, nonliberatory
   desublimation and, 166
Harding, Susan, 93
Hayek, Friedrich: Burke and, 97,
   98, 208n1; on conservatism, 120;
   The Constitution of Liberty, 72,
   104; on instinct, tradition, and
   reason, 33; on legislatures,
   abuses by, 55, 69; on
   legislatures, needed restrictions
   on, 104; on liberalism's
   compatibility with
   authoritarianism, 72–73, 119; on
   liberalism vs. democracy, 72;
   likely views on contemporary
   traditional values politics,
   203–4n62; on moral systems,
   34–35; on nature of justice,
   33–35, 69; on personal protected
   sphere, 12, 104–5; on planned
   social systems, 105–6, 107–8;

Index

Index

Index

futures, 197n68; on social power, 40; on state responsibility to create political equality, 25, 194n5

Marxist regimes: distortion of theoretical principles in, 83–84; failure to theorize the political, 85–86

masculinity, political appeals to, 64

Masterpiece Cakeshop v. Colorado Civil Rights Commission (2018), 127–43; and antidiscrimination law, challenge to, 127; and artistic expression as unprotected form of speech, 140–41; and cake as speech, 135–37; and cakes as artistic expression, 131, 132–34, 135–36; concurring opinions of Gorsuch, Thomas and Alito in, 127, 129, 131, 135, 136, 219–20n31; and distinction between act-based and person-based discrimination, 134; facts of case, 127–28; issues unresolved in, 129; as narrow ruling on bias of Colorado Civil Rights Commission, 127, 128–29, 137, 138, 217n6; strategic presentations of baker Phillips's identity in, 130–31; and transfer of First Amendment rights to businesses, 132, 133–34, 139–42, 218n13; and use of First Amendment to move Christian values into public square, 129–30, 137–38, 140–41

media consumption, siloization of, 6, 190n8

middle class, neoliberalism's lowering of standard of living, 19

Mill, John Stuart, 34, 106–7

Mirowski, Phillip, 11, 191–92n15

Monbiot, George, 192n–93n20

Mont Pelerin Society: diversity of opinion in, 192n15; founding of, 8; and origin of neoliberalism, 191n9; "Statement of Aims" (1947), 114, 123, 192n16; on traditional morality, 11

morality, right-wing: as contractual, 86, 95. 115, 120, 172–73, 180; nihilism's hollowing-out of, 172–73, 178–79, 187

morality, traditional. *See* values, traditional

Moreton, Bethany, 93

National Institute of Family and Life Advocates, mission of, 220n34

National Institute of Family and Life Advocates v. Becerra (2018), 143–60; attribution of speech rights to both businesses and individuals, 149, 150–51, 157–58; Breyer dissent in, 124; characterization of abortion as controversial practice in, 149–50, 157, 159; critique of ruling in, 156–60; facts of case, 143; and freedom of speech vs. freedom to deceive, 151–52, 154, 157–58; and nihilism, 153; on

239

Index

Index

religion: marketplace of ideas and, 152–53; Tocqueville on, 208n1. *See also* Christianity

religion, Hayek on: as securer and transmitter of tradition, 100–103; and sovereignty, 101–3

Religious Freedom Restoration Act of 1993, 76, 109, 138

religious liberty. *See* freedom of conscience (free exercise of religion)

religious Right, use of individual freedom claims to reestablish Christian values in public sphere, 110–15, 123–24, 129, 137–38, 153–54, 214n80

repressed, return of, in neoliberalism, 16. *See also* desublimation

Reproductive FACT Act of 2015 (California): as issue in *NIFLA v. Becerra*, 143; posted statements required by, 143, 148, 222n46; reasons for enacting, 144–48, 222n46; Supreme Court ruling against, 143–44, 149–52, 154–56

Republican Party, voter suppression and gerrymandering by, 194n10

responsibilization, as neoliberal policy, 38–39

ressentiment: forms of continuation, 177–82; new forms of, 163; Nietzsche on, 174–75; and white male nativist dethronement, 175–77; and white male urge to destroy world it cannot rule, 180–82; wide diffusion of, 162–63

Robertson, Pat, 173

Röpke, Wilhelm, 37–38

Rousseau, Jean-Jacques, 24; Hayek's critique of, 67–68

Rüstow, Alexander, 38

Sager, Lawrence G., 217n6

Sandel, Michael J., 175

Saudi Arabia, murder of Jamal Khashoggi, 84, 173

Schmitt, Carl: "Dialogue on Power," 162; *Dialogue on Power and Space*, 185; on differing orientations of land- and sea-based cultures, 185–86; *Land and Sea*, 51, 52, 185; *Nomos of the Earth*, 51; on ordering of space, 51–52; ordoliberals and, 61, 82; on power, 162, 163; on sovereignty, 70; on spatial orders and eschatological views, 52

school voucher systems, 109

Sessions, Jeff, 113–14

Siegel, Riva, 138

Singh, Nikhil, 7

Slobodian, Quinn, 18–19, 60, 202n22

Sluga, Hans, 164, 224–25nn1–2

Social Contract, The (Rousseau), 67–68

social democracy: Friedman on, 65; moderating effects of, 15

social justice policies: as antidote to inequalities of capitalist orders, 27–28; far-right conception of freedom and, 10; neoliberal characterization as tyrannical political correctness, 41, 45; neoliberal commitment to markets-and-morals project and, 7, 13, 21; neoliberal opposition of traditional values to, 37; neoliberal rejection of, 39–40. *See also* Hayek, on social justice policies

social justice warriors (SJWs), 28

social power, 52–53

social programs: declining investment in, 39; free, responsibilized individuals as neoliberal alternative to, 29; neoliberal efforts to dismantle, 28, 37–39; Trump administration efforts to dismantle, 29–30

"the social question": capitalism and, 26–27; neoliberal worry about, 63; ordoliberals on, 201–2n22

social state: as excess of democracy, 73–74; ordoliberals on, 77; replacement of moral law with social justice, 74; takeover of family functions by, 74

society: and democratic imaginary, 51–53; eschatological importance of, 52–53; as essential site of justice and democracy, 50; personal protected sphere as protection from norms of, 105; as place for recognition and redress of inequalities, 27–28, 40–41, 42; as place to engage social power, 52–53; as place to experience linked fate across differences, 27; as place where political equality is made, 41; reproduction of histories and hierarchies in, 41, 42. *See also* democracy, role of

society in; Hayek, on society; neoliberal dismantling of society

Somek, Alexander, 52

somewheres vs. anywheres, Goodhart on, 184–85, 187

sovereignty: Hayek's critique of concept, 70–71, 101–3; Left's attacks on, 203n48; ordoliberals on, 77. *See also* popular sovereignty, Hayek on

Soviet Bloc, breakup of, and spread of neoliberalism, 18

space, ordering of: neoliberal revisions, effects of, 183–85; as ordering of meaning in human affairs, 51–52

state: liberal vs. neoliberal, 63; weakening through globalization, 183

state power: neoliberal concern with, 11, 59; neoliberal effort to limit and sharpen focus of, 63; role in securing conditions necessary for freedom, in Hayek, 102–3

Strangers in Their Own Land (Hochschild), 169–70

structural discrimination, neoliberal denial of, 27, 40–41, 42, 44, 45

Supreme Court: and ADF, 114; neoliberal weaponization of, 160; support for neoliberal markets-and-morals project, 13, 125. See also *Masterpiece Cakeshop v. Colorado Civil Rights Commission* (2018); *National Institute of Family and Life Advocates v. Becerra* (2018)

Index

Talmon, Jacob, 68

Tebbe, Nelson, 217n6

terrorism, focus on, as diversion from failed neoliberal policies, 4, 5

Thatcher, Margaret, on society, as nonexistent, 28, 115

Thatcher-Reagan neoliberal revolution: basic principles of, 18; and dismantling of social state, 28; and government, 58; neoliberal markets-and-morals project in, 11

Thomas, Clarence: and *Masterpiece Cakeshop v. Colorado CRC*, 127, 129, 131, 135, 136, 219–20n31; and *NIFLA v. Becerra*, 143–44, 150, 152–53, 154–55

TINA (there is no alternative) view, 64

Tocqueville, Alexis de, 24, 25, 50, 208n1

Tolstoy, Leo, 161

tradition: indemnification from criticism in neoliberalism, 14; and protection from democratic norms, 105. *See also* values, traditional

tradition, Hayek on, 96–108; as bearer of markets and morals, 12, 96; capacity for evolution, 97–98, 99–100; and competition between cultures, 98, 208n1; as context for freedom, 75, 97–99; efforts to impose planning in place of, 98–99; family, property, and freedom as strongest pillars of, 98–99; market-like

characteristics of, 100, 106–7; markets as form of, 97–98, 100, 106–7; religion as securer and transmitter of, 100–103; as spontaneous source of order, 97–98; state's role in securing, 102–3; and voluntary conformity, high degree of, 99–100, 106–7, 213n63; and withdrawal of accountability from politics, 102

traditional hierarchies, neoliberal protection of, 12, 13–14, 74, 106, 121–22

tribalisms: neoliberal preparation of ground for, 8; resurgence of, 169

Trilateral Commission Report (1975), on excesses of democracy, 73–74

Trudeau, Justin, 39–40

Trump, Donald: and analogy of nation as private home, 116–17; appeals to white and male supremacy, 173–74; attacks on Obama's legacy, 178, 227n34; evangelical Christians' support for, 92, 94, 220n21, 226n27; on government as business, 116; and Johnson Amendment repeal, 109–10; mutual exploitation of Christian evangelicals, 93–95; opponents' disrespect of, 178–79, 227n35; and revenge, 178; will to power in, 173, 179

Trump, Melania, 169

Trump administration: and ADF, 113; and Muslim ban, 111; and neoliberal model of government, 58–59, 116; and ordoliberalism,

Previously Published Wellek Library Lectures